The Legal Guide for Practicing Psychotherapy in Colorado

2022-23 Academic Year

Denis K. Lane, Jr., M.A., J.D.

Continuing Legal Education in Colorado, Inc.
The nonprofit educational arm of the Colorado and Denver Bar Associations

2022-23

THE LEGAL GUIDE FOR PRACTICING PSYCHOTHERAPY IN COLORADO

2022-23 ACADEMIC YEAR

Published by:

CONTINUING LEGAL EDUCATION IN COLORADO, INC.
(d/b/a Colorado Bar Association CLE)
1290 Broadway, Suite 1700
Denver, CO 80203
E-mail: clebooks@cba-cle.org

Phone: (303) 860-0608
Toll-free: (888) 860-2531
Fax: (303) 860-0624
Website: www.cle.cobar.org

Ellen Buckley, Esq.
Legal Editor
Colorado Bar Association CLE

Kristin Huotari, J.D.
Director of Publications
Colorado Bar Association CLE

ISBN: 978-1-949831-53-5
Library of Congress: 2022942501

CBA · CLE
BOOKS + FORMS

Publisher's Note

The impact of mental health issues on Colorado's courts cannot be understated, whether the case involved relates to family law, guardianship, criminal law, or any other matter. Colorado Bar Association CLE (CBA-CLE) is therefore pleased to offer this comprehensive resource, *The Legal Guide for Practicing Psychotherapy in Colorado,* to mental health practitioners as they navigate the complex judicial system.

The Legal Guide for Practicing Psychotherapy in Colorado walks the practitioner through the relevant state court systems, confidentiality, testifying as an expert, professional liability, licensing considerations, and much more.

We are extremely grateful to Denis K. Lane for the countless hours he has spent to make this Guide the excellent resource that it is. Mr. Lane has a unique and impressive combination of experience with the relevant legal and mental health issues that allows him to write for mental health professionals in an accessible way about the legal system in which they may find themselves participating. It has been a pleasure working with Mr. Lane, and we look forward to many more years of collaboration with him.

Ellen Buckley, Esq.
Legal Editor
Colorado Bar Association CLE

Kristin Huotari, J.D.
Publications Director
Colorado Bar Association CLE

CLE in Colorado, Inc.

CLE in Colorado, Inc. (d/b/a Colorado Bar Association CLE (CBA-CLE)) is a nonprofit educational organization created by the Colorado and Denver Bar Associations. We strive to produce high-quality CLE programs and legal publications at competitive prices, with substantial member discounts. However, we are also financially independent from the Bar Associations and self-supporting. We receive *no membership dues* or other unearned revenue from the CBA or DBA. Nearly all of our income derives from program registration fees and from sales of books, homestudy courses, and course manuals. Every year, hundreds of Colorado lawyers and judges volunteer their time and expertise to help us produce these educational resources for our members. Without this generous contribution of talent, CBA-CLE could not fulfill its mission.

Author's Note

Louie Larimer first conceived of the need for this resource for mental health professionals, and labored over the first volume of the Legal Guide to the Practice of Psychotherapy in Colorado. Since its initial publication in 1992, this book has been a standard for psychotherapists to use in identifying ethical issues and complying with the legal standards established by the Colorado General Assembly for the practice of psychotherapy.

Louie Larimer's contributions to psychotherapists and to the mental health profession itself are enormous. He has advocated the adoption and application of laws that reflect standard ethical practices in the field. Where he perceived a lack of clarity in the law and a need for interpretation of legal guidelines, he sought changes and clarity from the legislature and from the mental health boards. I appreciate the training provided to me by Louie Larimer, his mentoring, and the challenge to carry on his legacy.

Thanks to all of the mental health professionals who continue to submit questions and seek consultation on the difficult issues in the day-to-day practice of psychotherapy, and who inspire a great deal of the discussion and analysis of the ethical issues contained in this work.

This book is dedicated to Toni Zimmerman, Ph.D, LMFT, and all the professors, educators, and supervisors who teach graduate students and clinicians the legal and ethical standards of their profession. It is also dedicated to Colleen Hughes Shea, LPC, to Deb Kinnan, LPC, and all the therapists who provide grief counseling to family members who have lost loved ones, helping them in their time of need. And the book is also dedicated to the Mental Health Professionals who work to strengthen family relationships, save the lives of those who despair, make us all stronger, and help us function! Theirs is truly a labor of love!

Acknowledgment

Production of *The Legal Guide For Practicing Psychotherapy In Colorado*, 2022-23 Academic Year, required the editors to Shepardize® the citations used in the book. This research was made possible by a generous contribution from the Colorado CLE's technology partner, LEXIS-NEXIS®.

How to Cite This Book

As the first full citation, you may cite this book as:

Denis K. Lane, Jr., *The Legal Guide for Practicing Psychotherapy in Colorado*, 2022-2023 Academic Year (CLE in Colo., Inc. 2022).

After the first full citation, you may cite this book as:

The Legal Guide for Practicing Psychotherapy in Colorado, *supra* n.___, at ___.

About the Author

Denis K. Lane, Jr., M.A., J.D.
Attorney at Law
1912 W. Colorado Ave.
Colorado Springs, CO 80904
(719) 636-1017
lanedenis@yahoo.com

Denis K. Lane, Jr., is an attorney who has been practicing mental health law and civil litigation in the District of Columbia and the State of Colorado, beginning in 1978. Mr. Lane received an M.A. in counseling from the University of Oklahoma, prior to attending law school at O.U. While working as an attorney for the District of Columbia, he represented St. Elizabeth's Hospital in landmark litigation involving the rights of adolescents, and also handled mental health commitments, special education litigation, and defense of malpractice litigation on behalf of the District and the Metropolitan Police Department in federal court. Mr. Lane has been practicing in Colorado since 1982, when he served as a Deputy District Attorney for the 4th Judicial District, prosecuting cases involving child abuse, neglect, and other crimes, and also handling mental health certifications. From 1986 to 1995, Mr. Lane was a litigator at Hall & Evans, LLP, where he served on the Management Committee for three years, and represented the State of Colorado, municipalities, county governments, state agencies, and public officials in litigation involving civil rights, governmental immunity, defense of malpractice claims, and mental health issues.

He has been a frequent lecturer and author on legal and ethical standards for mental health professionals. Mr. Lane is author of the *Legal Guide for Practicing Psychotherapy in Colorado* and the *Legal and Ethical Guide for Mental Health Professionals.*

Contents

PART III: PRACTICE POINTERS

Chapter 1:
Colorado Judicial System

1.01 Judicial Districts

The State of Colorado is divided into 22 judicial districts. Each judicial district encompasses at least one county and in some cases two or more counties. For example, the Fourth Judicial District provides judicial services for Teller and El Paso Counties, while the Second Judicial District services only the City and County of Denver.

Within each judicial district there is a County Court and a District Court. These two courts are responsible for deciding cases that arise under appropriate federal and state law.

1.02 County Courts

The County Court is a court with limited jurisdiction. It may only hear and decide certain types of cases. Specifically, the County Court is limited to the following types of cases:

1. Civil actions in which the debt, damage, or value of the personal property claimed does not exceed $25,000;
2. Criminal actions that constitute misdemeanors or petty offenses;
3. Change of name proceedings;
4. Domestic abuse proceedings under Article 4 of Title 14, C.R.S.; and
5. Actions for the issuance of restraining orders to prevent assaults and threatened bodily harm.

1.03 Small Claims

In order to provide public access to the courts, the Colorado General Assembly has established a Small Claims Division within the County Court. Like the County Court, the Small Claims Court is a court of limited jurisdiction.

To qualify for Small Claims treatment, the following conditions must be met:

1. The controversy must be a civil matter (as opposed to a criminal matter); and
2. The monetary amount involved cannot exceed $7,500.

1.04 District Courts

There is a District Court within each judicial district. This court is a court of general jurisdiction; it is not limited as to the types of cases it may hear. Although a District Court may hear and decide cases in which the County Court has jurisdiction, it will be reluctant to do so, since the County Court was established so that the District Court could concentrate on actions of a more serious nature, *e.g.*, criminal actions that are felonies, juvenile cases, probate, mental health, divorce, and civil cases in which the amount in controversy exceeds $15,000.

The District Courts generally have an Office of Dispute Resolution that conducts alternative dispute resolution (ADR) of civil cases, domestic litigation, and dependency and neglect actions. This Office provides dispute resolution at a reasonable cost for litigants, who may otherwise be embroiled in lengthy, expensive litigation. ADR enables parties to resolve both domestic conflicts and civil suits in an efficient, cost-effective process.

1.05 Colorado Court of Appeals

The County and District Courts are trial courts. Evidence is introduced and witnesses testify in a trial setting. There may or may not be a jury, depending on the type of case and the desires of the litigants.

A decision of the County Court may be appealed to the District Court, which will determine whether the County Court Judge erred in his or her application of the law. This review will be made by a single District Court Judge. If it is determined that an error of law was made, the case may be returned to the County Court for retrial or it may simply be decided by the District Court Judge based upon the evidence presented at the trial.

A litigant may appeal the decision of a District Court to the Colorado Court of Appeals. This appeal is a matter of right and cannot be denied. The Court of Appeals is comprised of judges appointed by the governor for an initial term of eight years. Thereafter, each Judge of the Court of Appeals is periodically placed before the public for retention.

1.06 Colorado Supreme Court

The Colorado Supreme Court is the highest court in the State and it is the court of last resort for most litigants. Unless the appeal involves some interpretation of a federal statute or a constitutional issue, there is no other appellate remedy.

Except for a few narrow circumstances, there is no automatic mandatory right of appeal to the Colorado Supreme Court. The Colorado Supreme Court exercises its discretion as to which cases it will review. A litigant seeking to appeal a Court of Appeals decision files for a writ of certiorari. If the Colorado Supreme Court decides that the legal issues are of statewide importance, or if the case would help to clarify the law in Colorado, it may elect to hear the case and grant the request for a writ of certiorari. The writ is an instruction to the Colorado Court of Appeals to forward the case to the Colorado Supreme Court. If the court elects to refrain from hearing the case, the writ is denied and the appeal is over.

Like the Colorado Court of Appeals, the Colorado Supreme Court reviews the trial court record of proceedings, reviews the legal briefs prepared by the attorneys, and listens to oral arguments. There is no direct taking of evidence. Once a decision is reached, a written opinion is prepared and published. The decisions of the Colorado Supreme Court become law and are binding upon the appellate and trial courts in the State.

1.07 Municipal Courts

Municipal Courts are established by various city charters and ordinances. Because municipal entities (cities) promulgate laws known as ordinances, there must be a court in which disputes involving such ordinances can be heard. Accordingly, cities and towns have established local municipal or city courts.

These courts are limited to hearing petty offenses, such as building and zoning violations, minor traffic offenses, minor neighborhood domestic disputes, and dog-at-large cases. These are offenses against the municipality and do not usually involve mental health issues. Hence, the testimony of a psychotherapist is typically not required.

1.08 Federal Courts

The laws of the United States of America require a judicial forum for cases involving federal issues. Accordingly, a federal court system has been established for the purpose of resolving certain civil and criminal cases arising under the statutes and the Constitution of the United States.

The federal court system is organized into various federal districts, which roughly correspond to the geographical boundaries of the 50 states and the territories of the United States. Each District has one Federal District Court. This court is a trial court having specific jurisdiction over cases involving the United States Constitution, federal statutes, rules and regulations, and certain civil cases between citizens of different states, provided the amount in controversy is in excess of $75,000.

Appeals of the decisions of the Federal District Courts and the specialty courts are handled by United States Circuit Courts of Appeals. The Circuit Courts of Appeals operate in a manner similar to the Colorado Court of Appeals.

The United States Supreme Court is the highest court in the United States. There are nine United States Supreme Court Justices. The Court operates in a manner similar to the Colorado Supreme Court, except it interprets and construes federal statutory law and constitutional issues as opposed to state law issues.

1.09 Players and Roles

The smooth and efficient operation of the Colorado judicial system depends upon a variety of people to perform specific duties and fulfill carefully defined obligations.

In order to meaningfully contribute to the judicial system, a psychotherapist must have a clear understanding of who these people are and what roles are expected of them. Although most people have a vague idea of the key players in the judicial system, many do not fully comprehend the specific functions of each. Frequently, this lack of knowledge results in a breakdown in communication, unnecessary frustration, and an inability to effectively serve the psychotherapist's client.

The following paragraphs outline the roles of the key players in the judicial system.

Arbitrator. An arbitrator is a person selected by the parties to a dispute to hear the positions and arguments of both sides and then render a decision that is binding upon both parties. Both parties typically share the arbitrator's fee. Arbitration is a voluntary alternative to a judicial resolution of a controversy. It is generally less expensive and less time-consuming than litigation.

Attorney. An attorney is a person trained in the law to act as an advocate for his or her client.

Attorney General. The Attorney General is a statewide elected official who is responsible for representing the State of Colorado in its various legal matters. Most of the day-to-day legal representation is performed by Assistant Attorney Generals who are appointed by the Attorney General.

CASA Volunteer. "CASA" refers to "court-appointed special advocates." CASA volunteers advocate for the best interests of children in domestic cases. CASA volunteers are appointed by a judge or magistrate whenever, in the opinion of the court, a child who may be affected by such action requires services that a CASA volunteer can provide.

A CASA volunteer's duties include the following:

1. To conduct an independent investigation regarding the best interests of the child, which will provide factual information to the court regarding the child and the child's family;
2. To determine an appropriate treatment plan, designed to render the respondent in a dependency and neglect action fit to provide adequate parenting to the child, considering the child's needs; and if an appropriate treatment plan has been created, to determine whether appropriate services are being provided to the child and family according to the plan;
3. To make recommendations consistent with the best interests of the child regarding placement, visitation, and appropriate services for the child and family, unless otherwise ordered by the court; and
4. To prepare a written report addressing the recommendations made in the best interests of the child.

A CASA volunteer must maintain the confidentiality of information relating to any case to which the CASA volunteer has access, and shall not disclose such information to any person other than the court and parties to the action.

Child and Family Investigator. The District Court Judges who handle domestic relations cases have been appointing both therapists and attorneys as special advocates pursuant to the provisions of C.R.S. § 14-10-116. The name "special advocate" was changed to "child and family investigator" in 2005 by the General Assembly, but the investigator's duties remain the same, as described in C.R.S. § 14-10-116.5. Although the courts have been appointing therapists in this role because of their ability to resolve conflicts and to work in stressful situations, an individual who is appointed a special advocate is not engaged in the practice of psychotherapy. According to C.R.S. § 14-10-116.5, an investigator "shall investigate, report, and make recommendations [regarding]... the best interests" of a child whose parents are involved in domestic litigation. These professionals, therefore, conduct investigations by interviewing family members, parents, children, family friends, and associated professionals in order to make recommendations to the court concerning the allocation of parental responsibilities or regarding parenting time. This provides an invaluable service to the court, helping judges to resolve factual disputes and to make the difficult decisions involved in domestic cases. Guidelines have been published that discuss the scope of a child and family investigator's duties. The investigation conducted must include, at a minimum, the following:

1. A meeting with each parent and the children;
2. Observing the interaction between the children and the parent;
3. Evaluating the home itself;
4. Meeting with and observing the children;
5. Interviewing the children, if they are old enough;
6. Reviewing court files and relevant reports, records, school records, and other documents;
7. Interviewing the parents; and
8. Interviewing teachers and other associated professionals.

Child and family investigators recommend to the court, when needed, psychological evaluations of the parents or children.

This is a new field, and the role of the investigator varies from one judicial district to another. If a therapist is interested in this work, he or she should identify the district judges or magistrates in his or her locality who handle domestic cases, and provide the following: a professional resume; a letter to the judge, expressing interest in having his or her name added to the appointment list maintained by the court; and a brief summary of his or her qualifications. If the local judicial district has a Judicial Administrator, that is the individual whom the therapist should contact to express interest in accepting appointments as an investigator. Fees should be charged on a sliding scale, depending upon the family income.

Collateral. A collateral is a person who is not a counseling client but who may attend a counseling session with the client's consent or who, with client consent, may confer with a therapist in order to provide information regarding the client. In addition, a collateral may receive information with consent of the client in order to better understand the client's condition and how to help that individual. A collateral may be the spouse, significant other, or family member of a client who is receiving individual counseling; or the parent of a child client who is receiving counseling services. The confidentiality or therapist-client privilege relating to information provided to a therapist by a collateral belongs to the client, not the collateral. A Collateral Disclosure form is included in Appendix A as Form 8.

Conservator. A conservator is a person appointed by the court to take charge of and manage another person's financial affairs. There must be a finding by the court that the person to be protected by a conservator no longer has the capacity to handle his or her own financial affairs. A conservator's powers are limited to financial matters and do not encompass other aspects of a protected person's life. Matters such as consent to medical treatment, residency, etc., are handled by a guardian. A conservator's authority is evidenced by the court's issuance of a document known as "Letters of Conservatorship," which should be presented if a question arises as to a conservator's authority. A psychotherapist should never discuss a client's case with a conservator unless a copy of the Letters of Conservatorship is obtained.

Decision-Maker. A decision-maker is either a legal or mental health professional, appointed by the court in a domestic case to resolve parenting issues or to implement a parenting plan.

District Attorney. Each judicial district in the state has an elected official known as the District Attorney. This person is responsible for prosecuting criminal cases on behalf of the State. The District Attorney performs this function by appointing Deputy District Attorneys. Deputy District Attorneys are the individuals most psychotherapists will encounter in criminal proceedings.

Expert Witness. An expert witness is a person found by the court to have special knowledge, skills, education, experience, or training in a particular field. An expert witness is allowed to render opinion testimony. An expert witness receives compensation for his or her testimony from the party calling the expert at trial. Usually a psychotherapist called to testify in court is testifying as an expert witness.

Guardian. A guardian is appointed by the court to take responsibility for the non-financial affairs of a person who has been found by the court to be incapable of making life decisions for himself or herself. The guardian makes decisions that are binding upon the incapacitated person. A guardian may or may not also be given the powers of a conservator. A guardian is generally a family relative or close personal friend of the incapacitated person. The appointment as guardian is evidenced by the court's issuance of a document known as "Letters of Guardianship," which should be presented if a question arises as to a guardian's authority. A psychotherapist should never discuss a client's case with a guardian without first obtaining a copy of the Letters of Guardianship.

Guardian *ad litem*. A guardian *ad litem* or G.A.L. is usually an attorney who has been appointed by the court to represent the interests of a minor or an incapacitated person during a legal proceeding. A guardian *ad litem* is typically appointed in cases involving custody or visitation issues. The guardian *ad litem* conducts an independent investigation and makes a recommendation to the court regarding the appropriateness of the request before the court. The guardian *ad litem* has no power or authority over the minor or protected person. A guardian *ad litem's* appointment is evidenced by a written court order. A psychotherapist should never discuss a client's condition with a guardian *ad litem* unless a copy of the court order appointing the guardian *ad litem* for the client is obtained or the therapist has been authorized by the client to release information to the guardian *ad litem*. A psychotherapist should not hesitate to request a copy of the order. A guardian *ad litem* does not have the authority to authorize the release of therapy records.

C.R.S. § 19-3-203(2) states: "The guardian *ad litem* shall be provided with all reports relevant to a case submitted to or made by any agency or person pursuant to [the Children's Code]." The duties of a guardian *ad litem* are set forth in C.R.S. § 19-3-203(3).

Judge. A judge presides over a legal proceeding by ensuring that the Rules of Procedure, Rules of Evidence, and substantive law are applied to a case. A judge will determine the outcome of a proceeding when there is no jury.

Jury. A jury is comprised of citizens drawn from the judicial district. The jury determines guilt or innocence in a criminal case, and whether a person is liable in a civil case.

Lay Witness. A lay witness has personal firsthand knowledge about an event and is called to relate that knowledge at trial.

Legal Aid. A legal aid office is an organization that provides free legal representation to indigent individuals in civil matters.

Magistrate. A magistrate is a lawyer who is appointed by the chief judge of a judicial district to exercise limited judicial authority over routine legal matters, such as temporary orders in a divorce, juvenile matters, and probate. Magistrates work under the supervision of a District Court Judge. Prior to 1991, they were referred to as Referees or Commissioners.

Mediator. A mediator is a third party selected by the parties to a dispute who is asked to meet with the parties and assist them in reaching an agreement. The mediator has no power to force an agreement upon the parties. He or she simply acts as a facilitator of communication and suggests possible alternatives to the controversy. Mediation is now required as a condition precedent to obtaining a court date in selected judicial districts. Additionally, some divorce litigants are now using trained psychotherapists as mediators to assist them in the resolution of custody and visitation issues.

Parenting Coordinator. A qualified professional may be appointed by the court in a domestic case as a parenting coordinator to assist the court in resolving disputes involving parenting or to assist the parties in learning appropriate parenting skills.

Parole Officer. A parole officer supervises and monitors a person's fulfillment of those conditions under which an early release from prison was allowed.

Probation Officer. A probation officer supervises and monitors a person's fulfillment of those conditions imposed as an alternative to jail or confinement in criminal cases.

Public Defender. A public defender is hired by the State to provide free legal representation to indigent people who are charged with crimes.

Chapter 2: Confidentiality

This chapter outlines Colorado law pertaining to the duty of confidentiality. Specifically, it sets forth the circumstances under which communications between client and therapist are considered confidential, and therefore not subject to disclosure to third parties by a psychotherapist. Conversely, it also describes those instances where a communication is not privileged and disclosure by a psychotherapist to a third party is required.

PART I: DUTY OF CONFIDENTIALITY

2.01 Sources of Confidentiality

Most psychotherapists know that they have a duty to maintain client confidentiality. They know that they have an obligation not to disclose to third parties things that are discussed in therapy or other aspects of the therapeutic process such as diagnosis, prognosis, recommendations, or test results. Few, however, are able identify the sources from which the duty arises.

There are three primary sources of the duty of confidentiality: statutes, common law, and ethical codes.

In Colorado, the legislature has created a specific statutory duty of confidentiality that applies to psychotherapists, C.R.S. § 12-245-220. There are also federal statutes that apply in certain situations where federal money is involved. These are discussed in section 2.05 of this book.

Prior to the enactment of the statutes referred to above, the duty of confidentiality arose from the common law or case law. Most notably, the personal right of privacy created the obligation for psychotherapists to maintain confidentiality. This common law duty still exists.

Professional associations have developed detailed codes of conduct or ethical duties that contain specific confidentiality mandates. Compliance with the codes is not required as a matter of state law. However, the codes reflect the professional standard of care for therapists and therefore, as a practical matter, must be followed in order to avoid a negligence or malpractice action. Psychotherapists should obtain a current copy of the applicable code of conduct from their respective professional association and become familiar with its requirements.

The current addresses for the professional associations for Licensed Professional Counselors (LPCs), Licensed Marriage and Family Therapists (LMFTs), Licensed Clinical Social Workers (LCSWs), Licensed Psychologists, and other mental health professionals are as follows:

Psychologists
Colorado Psychological Association
2851 S. Parker Rd., #1210
Aurora, CO 80014
www.coloradopsych.org
(303) 692-9303

Social Workers
National Association of Social Workers (NASW)
750 First St. NE, Ste. 800
Washington, DC 20002
www.socialworkers.org
(800) 742-4089

Colorado Society for Clinical Social Work
CSCSW
1776 S. Jackson St., Ste. 700
Denver, CO 80210
www.coclinicalsocialwork.org

American Association for Marriage and Family Therapy
112 S. Alfred St.
Alexandria, VA 22314-3061
www.aamft.org
(703) 838-9808

Professional Counselors
American Mental Health Counselors Association (AMHCA)
107 S. West St., Ste. 779
Alexandria, VA 22314
www.AMHCA.org
(800) 326-2642 or (703) 548-6002

Psychiatrists/Physicians
Colorado Medical Society
7351 E. Lowry Blvd., Ste. 110
Denver, CO 80230
www.cms.org

(720) 859-1001

Nurses
Colorado Nurses Association
2851 S. Parker Rd., Ste. 1210
Aurora, CO 80014
www.nurses-co.org
(720) 457-1194

American Association of Christian Counselors
P. O. Box 739
Forest, VA 24551
www.aacc.net
(434) 525-9470
(800) 526-8673

2.02 Colorado Confidentiality Statute

C.R.S. § 12-245-220(1) provides that licensed psychologists, clinical social workers, marriage and family therapists, licensed professional counselors, certified school psychologists, addiction counselors, and registered psychotherapists shall not disclose, without the consent of the client, any confidential communications made by the client, or any advice given, in the course of professional employment; nor shall such persons' employees or associates, whether clerical or professional, disclose any knowledge of confidential communications acquired in such capacity; nor shall any person who has participated in any therapy conducted under the supervision of such persons, including group therapy sessions, disclose any knowledge gained during the course of therapy without the consent of the person to whom the knowledge relates.

The duty of non-disclosure and confidentiality applies to the following:

1. Certified school psychologists who practice psychotherapy and who are licensed in Colorado;
2. Licensed clinical social workers, psychologists, professional counselors, and marriage and family therapists, all of whom are licensed pursuant to Title 12, Article 245 of the Colorado Revised Statutes (hereinafter referred to as "licensed psychotherapists" or "licensees");
3. Registered psychotherapists;
4. Employees and associates of certified school psychologists or psychotherapists; and

5. Those who have participated in any therapy, including group therapy, conducted under the supervision of any licensed or registered psychotherapist.

Mental health professionals must undertake specific steps to inform employees, associates (*e.g.*, secretaries, receptionists, or billing clerks), and group members of the duty of confidentiality. The author strongly recommends that a signed statement be obtained from each of the foregoing classes of people acknowledging that the duty of confidentiality has been explained and will be followed.

Collaterals

A collateral is identified in section 1.09 of this book as a person who is not a client but who may be allowed to attend a treatment session with the client if the client consents, or who may be allowed to confer with a therapist with client consent in order to receive information or to provide information concerning a client's presenting problems. Any information provided to the therapist by the collateral is confidential. It is part of the client's confidential treatment record. If a therapist needs to disclose information provided by a collateral, it is the client who could authorize that disclosure. The confidentiality or therapist-client privilege relating to information provided to a therapist by a collateral belongs to the client, not the collateral. This privilege can and should be explained to the collateral so there is no misunderstanding. The therapist can use the Collateral Disclosure form, contained in Appendix A as Form 8.

On occasion, therapists may meet with a collateral in order to determine if that individual is appropriate to participate in family therapy, couples counseling, or other treatment process. Therapists should disclose to the collateral before any meeting or conference is held that they are not a counseling client and are not receiving treatment. The Collateral Disclosure form, Form 8 in Appendix A, is designed for use by therapists to clarify the therapist's role towards the collateral in order to avoid any misunderstanding.

It is important to stress to collaterals that any information they receive from the therapist or client is confidential treatment information and cannot be disclosed to any third party.

When a therapist is meeting with a collateral with client consent in order to obtain or share information with the individual, the therapist may bill for the time invested in meeting with a collateral using the appropriate Code of Procedural Terminology (such as CPT Code 90801, *etc.*), since meetings with collaterals can be an important part of the psychotherapy process.

Exceptions to Confidentiality

C.R.S. § 12-245-220(2) provides that the duty of non-disclosure and confidentiality does not apply when:

1. A lawsuit or complaint has been filed against a licensee, registered psychotherapist, certified school psychologist, or licensed psychotherapist by a client in connection with the client's care and treatment.
2. A licensee, licensed or certified school psychologist, registrant, or registered psychotherapist was in consultation with a physician, registered professional nurse, licensee, licensed or certified school psychologist, registrant, or registered psychotherapist against whom a suit or complaint is filed, based on the case out of which said suit or complaint arises.
3. A review of services of a psychologist is conducted by any one of the following: (a) the duly authorized Board of Registered Psychotherapists;

(b) the governing board of a licensed hospital; or (c) a professional review committee established pursuant to C.R.S. § 12-245-204(11), if the client has signed a release authorizing such review.

4. The Colorado General Assembly created an exception to confidentiality in 2017 by passing a bill that amended § 12-245-220(2) and states that the duty of confidentiality does not apply when a client, regardless of age, makes an articulable and significant threat against a school or the occupants of the school; or exhibits behaviors that, in the reasonable judgment of a therapist, create an articulable and significant threat to the health or safety of students, teachers, administrators, or other school personnel. When such a threat has been made, or when the behaviors of a client create an articulable and significant threat to the health or safety of students or school personnel, the therapist may disclose the potential threat posed by the client to appropriate school or school district personnel and to law enforcement agencies. School or school district personnel to whom the information is disclosed shall maintain confidentiality of the disclosed information, but may disclose information, if necessary, to protect the health or safety of students or other persons. The therapist whose client poses the potential threat to the health or safety of students or school personnel shall limit the disclosure to appropriate school or school district personnel and law enforcement agencies.

An immunity provision contained in this exception to confidentiality states that a therapist who "discloses or fails to disclose a confidential communication with a client" who poses an "articulable and significant threat" to students or other school personnel is not liable in any civil action for disclosing or not disclosing the communication of the threat.

This exception to confidentiality does not affect or eliminate the statutory duty to warn and protect contained in C.R.S. § 13-21-117, and it does not eliminate any potential liability for failure to comply with the duty to warn and protect established in C.R.S. § 13-21-117.

The definitions of terms applicable to this special exception to confidentiality are as follows:

- "Articulable and significant threat" means a threat to the health or safety of a person that, based on the totality of the circumstances, can be explained or articulated and that constitutes a threat of substantial bodily harm to a person.
- "School" means a public or private preschool, elementary, middle, junior high, or high school, and includes community colleges, colleges, and universities.

C.R.S. § 12-245-220(4) provides that the duty of non-disclosure and confidentiality for licensed psychologists does not apply to delinquency cases or to criminal proceedings, where issues have been raised in a criminal case concerning the defendant's sanity, competency, or impaired mental condition.

C.R.S. § 12-245-220(5) provides that nothing shall be deemed to prohibit any other disclosure required by law. This means that other required disclosures, such as those described in Part II of this chapter, "Exceptions to Confidentiality," will be honored.

One of the most frequent grievances filed against psychotherapists is breach of confidentiality. In many cases, the psychotherapist has simply forgotten or inadvertently disclosed information to third parties. Unfortunately, memory lapses and inadvertent mistakes are not defenses. Psychotherapists must refrain from casual discussions concerning clients with colleagues, family members, friends, and other persons, particularly attorneys.

It is important to note that the duty of confidentiality does not cease upon the death of a client. Psychotherapists must refrain from releasing information about a deceased client, unless disclosure is authorized by the representative of the client's estate or is ordered by the court. This problem is a difficult one, particularly when family members and the personal representative of the deceased are demanding information. If this should occur, the psychotherapist should retain an attorney so that he or she can be advised of the most current law on this matter.

2.03 Common Law

In addition to the duty of non-disclosure found in C.R.S. § 12-245-220, a psychotherapist has a common law duty to refrain from disclosing private facts or private information about a client acquired in the course of treatment. This duty exists under a legal theory known as "Invasion of Privacy." Under this theory, the common law allows a client to recover damages from a psychotherapist who discloses confidential information pertaining to a client, if such disclosure is found to be objectionable. In today's litigious environment, virtually any unauthorized disclosure would be found to violate a client's expectation of privacy.

The common law also imposes a duty of non-disclosure and confidentiality under a legal theory known as "Outrageous Conduct" or "Intentional Infliction of Emotional Distress." Under this theory, a disclosure of a private fact or private information by a psychotherapist to a third party would subject the psychotherapist to a claim for money damages if such disclosure was found by a judge or jury to be shocking to the sensibilities of the community. It is not difficult to imagine that a jury or judge would feel particularly outraged by such a breach of confidentiality.

Court decisions, which constitute the common law applicable to psychotherapists, establish precedents whereby treatment information is recognized as confidential or is ruled to be privileged. *In Jaffee v. Redmond*, 518 U.S. 1 (1996), the U.S. Supreme Court ruled for the first time that federal courts must recognize the psychotherapist-client privilege. Federal courts had long recognized the doctor-patient, psychiatrist-patient, or psychologist-client privilege, as well as the attorney-client privilege. However, until the Supreme Court's decision in *Jaffee*, federal courts had generally rejected a psychotherapist-client privilege. In practical terms, this meant that before 1996 a psychotherapist could be compelled to testify concerning information gained during treatment.

In deciding that federal courts must recognize the psychotherapist-client privilege, the Supreme Court ruled that this privilege serves important public interests, because mental health therapists' ability to help their clients depends upon the clients' "willingness and ability to talk freely." The Court noted that it is difficult, if not impossible, for therapists to function without being able to assure clients that information provided in treatment will be confidential. In extending this "evidentiary privilege" to clients of psychotherapists, the Supreme Court recognized that confidentiality is necessary in order to establish the rapport between therapist and client needed to promote effective therapy. This in turn promotes the improvement of mental health on a national scale.

In discussing its rationale for this ruling, the Supreme Court recognized that clinical social workers and other psychotherapists "provide a significant amount of mental health treatment" to clients who "could not afford the assistance of a psychiatrist." *Id.* at 16-17. Thus, the Court recognized what many mental health professionals already knew: that they provide the bulk of the day-to-day counseling services to the people in this country.

The Supreme Court's decision in *Jaffee* did note that exceptions to this privilege would exist. These exceptions are discussed in Part II of this chapter.

The State of Colorado had already adopted a law prior to this decision recognizing a licensed psychotherapist-client privilege. In 1998, the Colorado General Assembly enacted House Bill 98-1072, which amended the privilege statute in Colorado, C.R.S. § 13-90-107, to include a privilege between registered psychotherapists and clients. In so doing, the Colorado General Assembly recognized that registered psychotherapists in this state provide significant mental health services to their clients, and thereby promote the improvement of mental health within this state.

2.04 Ethical Duties

Most professional associations and credentialing authorities have adopted specific guidelines or standards that require confidentiality and impose a duty of non-disclosure of information acquired in the course of treatment of a client. These ethical standards should be consulted and followed by any psychotherapist who is a member of an association having developed such codes.

For example, the American Association for Marriage and Family Therapists (AAMFT) has issued a code of ethics on topics such as advertising, professional competence, responsibility to clients, and confidentiality. The AAMFT Code of Ethics Principle II, concerning confidentiality, states, "Marriage and family therapists have unique confidentiality concerns because the client in a therapeutic relationship may be more than one person. Therapists respect and guard the confidences of each individual client."

The AAMFT Code of Ethics (2015) discusses the problem that confronts a therapist providing counseling services to a family, when one member of the family wants to release confidential information concerning that therapy. Section 2.2 of the AAMFT Code requires:

> Marriage and family therapists do not disclose client confidences except by written authorization or waiver, or where mandated or permitted by law. Verbal authorization will not be sufficient except in emergency situations, unless prohibited by law. When providing

couple, family, or group treatment, the therapist does not disclose information outside the treatment context without a written authorization from each individual competent to execute a waiver. In the context of couple, family, or group treatment, the therapist may not reveal any individual's confidences to others in the client unit without the prior written permission of that individual.

The American Mental Health Counselors Association, the American Counseling Association, the American Psychological Association, and the National Association of Social Workers have all adopted provisions safeguarding confidentiality that are similar to those of the AAMFT.

2.05 Federal Privacy Statutes

There are various federal privacy statutes that impose detailed duties of confidentiality and non-disclosure upon certain classes of people and agencies that are involved in programs funded by the federal government. These acts include the following:

1. Privacy Act of 1974, which applies to governmental entities.
2. Family Educational Rights and Privacy Act (Public Law 90-247), which applies to all educational agencies or institutions to which funds are made available under any federal program for which the U.S. Commissioner of Education has administrative responsibility.
3. The Health Insurance Portability and Accountability Act of 1996 (HIPAA), Public Law 104-191.

If a psychotherapist works in an agency where these statutes apply, copies of the statutes should be obtained and studied in detail.

2.06 Statutory Privilege

There is much confusion in the psychotherapy community with respect to the concept of "privilege" or "privileged communication." It is important to distinguish and understand the difference between "privilege" and the "duty of confidentiality." The two concepts are distinct, and the differences must be understood in order to adequately protect clients.

A good starting point is to note that the duty of confidentiality is imposed upon those persons set forth in the statute, C.R.S. § 12-245-220: psychotherapists, employees, associates, and those participating in group therapy.

When a lawsuit occurs, the therapist's duty of confidentiality often conflicts with a party's constitutional due process rights to confront witnesses and present evidence. In order to resolve this dilemma and balance the rights of all parties, the legislature enacted a statute, C.R.S. § 13-90-107, to reflect its view that there are particular relationships in which it is the policy of the law to encourage confidence and to preserve it inviolate. C.R.S. § 13-90-107 recognizes that certain relationships are confidential in nature and people in these relationships may not be forced to disclose confidential communications made to them.

C.R.S. § 13-90-107 sets forth the special privileges recognized by the legislature.

1. Spousal (husband-wife) privilege and Civil Union Partner privilege;
2. Attorney-Client privilege;
3. Clergy Member/Minister/Priest/Rabbi-Penitent privilege;
4. Physician/Surgeon/Registered Professional Nurse-Patient privilege;
5. Public Officer privilege;
6. Certified Public Accountant-Client privilege;
7. Psychotherapist (Psychologist, Professional Counselor, Social Worker, Marriage and Family Therapist, Unlicensed Psychotherapist, and Licensed Addiction Counselor)-Client privilege;
8. Qualified Interpreter;
9. Confidential Intermediary;
10. Environmental Audit report;
11. Victim's Advocate-Victim of domestic abuse or sexual assault privilege;
12. A law enforcement or firefighter peer support team member regarding communications made in peer support;
13. A privilege exists which protects statements made by a child to an attorney, to a physician, or to a mental health professional in the presence of the child's parent, and a privilege also applies when a child makes a statement in the presence of the child's parent to a clergy member, minister, priest, or rabbi who has a confidential relationship with the minor child; and
14. An emergency medical service provider or rescue unit peer support team member shall not be examined without the consent of the person to whom peer support services have been provided as to any communication made by the person to the peer support team member.

2.07 Physician-Patient Privilege

The physician-patient privilege is set forth in C.R.S. § 13-90-107(1)(d). It provides that a physician, surgeon, or registered professional nurse shall not be examined without the consent of the patient as to any information acquired in attending to the patient that was necessary to prescribe or act for the patient.

Although psychiatrists are not specifically mentioned in the statute, they are licensed physicians under the Colorado Medical Practices Act, and are therefore within the definition of the privilege. *Bond v. District Court of County of Denver*, 682 P.2d 33 (Colo. 1984). Although no cases are on record, it would appear that a licensed psychiatric nurse would fall under the protective provisions of this statute.

The statute sets forth numerous exceptions in which the privilege does not apply. Most of these exceptions involve a professional malpractice claim against a physician or cases where there is a medical review board or committee examining a physician's conduct. In such cases, client communications can be disclosed to the parties outlined in the exception.

C.R.S. § 13-90-107(3) states that the physician-patient privilege does not apply to a physician eligible to testify concerning a criminal defendant's mental condition pursuant to C.R.S. § 16-8-103.6, which provides for an express waiver of the privilege when a defendant places his or her mental condition at issue by pleading not guilty by reason of insanity or impaired mental condition. This statutory waiver includes any claim of confidentiality arising from communications made by the defendant to a physician in the course of any examination or treatment for such mental condition for the purpose of any trial or hearing on the issue of such mental condition.

C.R.S. § 13-90-107(1)(d)(VI) states that the physician-patient privilege does not apply to civil actions against a physician as a result of his or her consultation for medical care or genetic counseling or screening pursuant to C.R.S. § 13-64-502.

There are several other exceptions to the physician-patient privilege. They are described in Part II of this chapter, entitled "Exceptions to Confidentiality."

2.08 Therapist-Client Privilege

C.R.S. § 13-90-107(1)(g) describes the privilege that applies to psychotherapists:

> A licensed psychologist, professional counselor, marriage and family therapist, social worker, or addiction counselor, a registered psycho-therapist, a certified addiction counselor, a psychologist candidate registered pursuant to section 12-245-304 (3), a marriage and family therapist candidate registered pursuant to section 12-245-504 (4), a licensed professional counselor candidate registered pursuant to section 12-245-604 (4), or a person described in section 12-245-217 shall not be examined without the consent of the

> licensee's, certificate holder's, registrant's, candidate's, or person's client as to any communication made by the client to the licensee, certificate holder, registrant, candidate, or person or the licensee's, certificate holder's, registrant's, candidate's, or person's advice given in the course of professional employment; nor shall any secretary, stenographer, or clerk employed by a licensed psychologist, professional counselor, marriage and family therapist, social worker, or addiction counselor, a registered psychotherapist, a certified addiction counselor, a psychologist candidate registered pursuant to section 12-245-304 (3), a marriage and family therapist candidate registered pursuant to section 12-245-504 (4), a licensed professional counselor candidate registered pursuant to 12-245-604 (4), or a person described in section 12-245-217 be examined without the consent of the employer of the secretary, stenographer, or clerk concerning any fact, the knowledge of which the employee has acquired in such capacity; nor shall any person who has participated in any psychotherapy, conducted under the supervision of a person authorized by law to conduct such therapy, including group therapy sessions, be examined concerning any knowledge gained during the course of such therapy without the consent of the person to whom the testimony sought relates.

This statute is much broader than the physician-patient privilege for psychiatrists. For example, not only are communications made by a client to a psychotherapist considered privileged, but the privilege also extends to the following classes of people:

1. The psychotherapist's secretary, stenographer, or clerk; and
2. Those persons who participated in the psychotherapy under the supervision of a person authorized by law to conduct such therapy, *e.g.*, group therapy clients, psychological assistants, interns, or supervisees.

Like the physician-patient privilege, C.R.S. § 13-90-107(3) states that the psychotherapist-client privilege does not apply to a psychotherapist eligible to testify concerning a criminal defendant's mental condition pursuant to C.R.S. § 16-8-103.6, which provides for an express waiver of the privilege when a defendant places his or her mental condition at issue by pleading not guilty by reason of insanity or impaired mental condition. This statutory waiver includes any claim of confidentiality arising from communications made by the defendant to a psychotherapist in the course of an examination or treatment for such mental condition for the purpose of any trial or hearing on the issue of such mental condition.

There are several other exceptions to the licensed psychotherapist privilege. They are described in Part II of this chapter, "Exceptions to Confidentiality."

2.09 HIV/AIDS Reporting

A little-known Colorado statute requires HIV reporting in specific circumstances. C.R.S. § 25-4-405, provides that when a person has tested positive for HIV or a sexually transmitted infection or has received a diagnosis of HIV or a sexually transmitted infection, then a report must be made to the State Department of Public Health and Environment by: (1) any health care provider in the state; (2) persons who test, diagnose, or treat sexually transmitted infections; or (3) a laboratory or a person performing a test for a sexually transmitted infection. That report must include the name, date of birth, sex at birth, gender identity, address, and phone number of the individual with the sexually transmitted infection, and the name, address, and phone number of the person making the report.

The term "health care provider" means a person whose profession is related to the maintenance of individuals' health. This definition would include mental health professionals, in the author's interpretation of this statute. Immunity is conferred by statute on any person who, in good faith, complies with the reporting and treatment requirements of this law, so that any such person is immune from civil and criminal liability for such actions.

PART II: EXCEPTIONS TO CONFIDENTIALITY

2.10 Mandatory Reporting of Child Abuse or Neglect

C.R.S. § 19-3-304(1)(a) provides that any mandated reporter of child abuse who has reasonable cause to know or suspect that a child has been subjected to abuse or neglect or who has observed the child being subjected to circumstances or conditions that would reasonably result in abuse or neglect shall immediately report or cause a report to be made concerning the suspected abuse to the county department of human services or local law enforcement agency; however, this reporting requirement shall not apply if the person who is required to report does not learn of the suspected abuse or neglect until after the alleged victim of the suspected abuse or neglect is 18 years of age or older, unless the perpetrator of the suspected abuse or neglect: (1) has subjected another child currently under 18 years of age to abuse or neglect; or (2) is currently in a position of trust as defined in C.R.S. § 18-3-401(3.5) with regard to any child currently under 18 years of age.

This statute addresses the previously unanswered question concerning whether therapists were required to report suspected abuse or neglect of persons who are now adults. Now, in answering the question, "Am I required to report suspected abuse or neglect, previously unreported, of a victim who is now over the age of 18," the answer is that the therapist is not required to report the situation unless the perpetrator has committed suspected abuse or neglect of another child currently under 18 years of age or is currently in a position of trust over a child currently under 18 years of age.

Those persons who are required by C.R.S. § 19-3-304(2) to report child abuse or neglect are:

1. Physicians or surgeons;
2. Child health associates;
3. Medical examiners or coroners;
4. Dentists;
5. Osteopaths;
6. Optometrists;
7. Chiropractors;
8. Chiropodists or podiatrists;
9. Registered or licensed practical nurses;
10. Hospital personnel;
11. Christian Science practitioners;
12. Public or private school officials or employees;
13. Social workers and workers in any facility licensed or certified pursuant to C.R.S. §§ 26-6-101, *et seq.* (including child care centers, child care providers, family child care homes, foster care homes, and others listed in C.R.S. § 26-6-102);
14 Mental health professionals, defined in C.R.S. § 19-1-103(77) as a person licensed to practice medicine or psychology in the State of Colorado, or any person on the staff of a facility designated by the executive director of the Department of Human Services for 72-hour treatment and evaluation who has been authorized by the facility to do mental health pre-screenings and who is under the supervision of a person licensed to practice medicine or psychology in Colorado;
15. Dental hygienists;
16. Psychologists;

17. Physical therapists;
18. Veterinarians;
19. Peace officers;
20. Pharmacists;
21. Commercial film and photographic print processors;
22. Firefighters;
23. Victim's advocates, defined in C.R.S. § 13-90-107(1)(k)(II) as "a person at a battered women's shelter or rape crisis organization or a comparable community-based advocacy program for victims of domestic violence or sexual assault." This does not include an advocate employed by any law enforcement agency;
24. Licensed professional counselors;
25. Licensed marriage and family therapists;
26. Unlicensed psychotherapists;
27. Clergy members;
28. Registered dietitians who hold certificates through the commission on dietetic registration and who are otherwise prohibited by 7 C.F.R. § 246.26 from making a report absent a state law requiring the release of this information;
29. Workers in the state department of human services;
30. Juvenile parole and probation officers;
31. Child and family investigators, as described in C.R.S. § 14-10-116.5;
32. Officers and agents of the state bureau of animal protection, and animal control officers;
33. A child protection ombudsman;
34. An educator providing services through the federal WIC program;
35. A director, coach, assistant coach, or athletic program personnel employed by a private sports organization;
36. A person who is registered as a psychologist candidate, marriage and family therapist candidate, or licensed professional counselor candidate, or a person described in C.R.S. § 12-245-217;
37. Emergency medical service providers;
38. Officials or employees of county departments of health, human services, or social services; and

39. Naturopathic doctors registered under article 250, title 12.

According to the provisions of C.R.S. § 19-3-304(3), a person not on the above list may make a report of child abuse or neglect, and such a person is entitled to immunity from any civil liability pursuant to the provisions of C.R.S. § 19-3-309, as are all of the individuals on the above list who comply with their duty to report suspected child abuse or neglect, assuming that the report is made in good faith. This means that the person making the report has information, either based on firsthand observations or secondhand information received from other persons, that forms the basis for a suspicion that child abuse or neglect has occurred.

When confronted with a potential child abuse or neglect reporting problem, a psychotherapist must be aware of the following definition of child abuse or neglect, which appears at C.R.S. § 19-1-103(1)(a).

Child abuse or neglect means an act or omission in one of the following categories, which threatens the health or welfare of a child:

1. "Any case in which a child exhibits evidence of skin bruising, bleeding, malnutrition, failure to thrive, burns, fracture of any bone, subdural hematoma, soft tissue swelling, or death and either: Such condition or death is not justifiably explained; the history given concerning such condition is at variance with the degree or type of such condition or death; or the circumstances indicate that such condition may not be the product of an accidental occurrence."
2. Any case in which a child is subjected to sexual assault, molestation, sexual exploitation, prostitution, incest, "unlawful sexual behavior," human trafficking of a minor for sexual servitude, internet luring of a child, or internet sexual exploitation of a child, as defined in C.R.S. § 16-22-102(9).
3. "Any case in which a child is in need of services because the child's parents, legal guardian, or custodian fails to take the same actions to provide adequate food, clothing, shelter, medical care, or supervision that a prudent parent would take." The requirement of this subparagraph shall be subject to the provisions of C.R.S. § 19-3-103 regarding treatment through a recognized method of religious healing.
4. Any case in which a child is subjected to emotional abuse. Emotional abuse means an identifiable and substantial impairment of the child's intellectual or psychological functioning or development or a substantial risk of impairment to the child's intellectual or psychological functioning or development.

5. Any act or omission described in C.R.S. § 19-3-102(1)(a), C.R.S. § 19-3-102(1)(b), or C.R.S. § 19-3-102(1)(c), which includes the abandonment of a child, allowing another person to mistreat or abuse a child, the lack of proper parental care for the child, or a child's environment that is injurious to his or her welfare.
6. Any case in which, in the presence of a child, or on the premises where a child is found or where a child resides, a controlled substance such as methamphetamine is manufactured or attempted to be manufactured.
7. Any case in which a child tests positive at birth for either a Schedule I or Schedule II controlled substance, such as methamphetamine, cocaine, or heroin, unless the child tests positive for a Schedule II controlled substance as a result of the mother's lawful intake of such substance, as prescribed.
8. Any case in which a child is subjected to human trafficking of a minor for involuntary servitude or sexual servitude.

C.R.S. § 19-3-103 provides that no child who, in lieu of medical treatment, is under treatment solely by spiritual means through prayer in accordance with a recognized method of religious belief shall, for that reason alone, be considered to have been neglected. However, the statute goes on to provide that the religious beliefs of the parent, guardian, or legal custodian shall not limit the medical access of a child in a life-threatening situation or when the condition will result in a serious handicap or disability. When confronted with such a situation, a psychotherapist should file a report rather than refrain from doing so.

As noted above, C.R.S. § 19-3-309 grants immunity to those persons who have made a report of child abuse or neglect, thereby protecting the reporting person from civil and criminal liability as well as termination of employment that otherwise might result from making a report. Such immunity is not extended to the perpetrator, complicitor, co-conspirator, or accessory. Additionally, immunity does not apply if a court of competent jurisdiction determines that a reporting person's behavior was willful, wanton, and malicious. *Montoya v. Bebensee*, 761 P.2d 285 (Colo. App. 1988).

C.R.S. § 19-3-304(4) provides that any person who willfully fails to report child abuse or neglect, or who knowingly makes a false report, shall be civilly liable for damages and commits a class 2 misdemeanor criminal offense.

C.R.S. § 19-3-305 provides that any person who is required to make a report of child abuse or neglect, or who has reasonable cause to suspect that a child died as a result of child abuse or neglect, must immediately report such fact to the police and to the medical examiner.

When making a child abuse or neglect report, an issue arises as to what should be disclosed to the authorities. C.R.S. § 19-3-307 states that such report shall include the following:

1. The name, address, sex, age, and race of the child;
2. The name and address of the person responsible for the suspected child abuse or neglect;
3. The nature of the child's injuries and any evidence of any previous cases of abuse involving the child or the child's siblings;
4. The name and address of any person responsible for the suspected abuse or neglect;
5. The family composition;
6. The source of the report and the name, address, and occupation of the person making the report;
7. Any action taken by the reporting source;
8. Any other information the reporting source believes may be helpful in the investigation; and
9. The military affiliation of the individual who has custody or control of the child.

The statute requires that any oral report be followed by a written report. The statute also provides that the written report may be admitted as evidence in any proceeding relating to child abuse or neglect.

As a practice guide, it is recommended that psychotherapists limit their disclosures to the foregoing items and refrain from other disclosures of client communications.

C.R.S. § 19-3-311 constitutes an exception to the statutory privileges of C.R.S. § 13-90-107, *i.e.,* physician-patient and psychotherapist-client. It does so by providing that these privileges are not grounds for excluding from evidence any client communications that are the basis for the report, or any discussion of future misconduct, or any past misconduct that could be the basis for any report. C.R.S. § 19-3-311 similarly abrogates the duty of non-disclosure and confidentiality set forth in C.R.S. § 12-245-220, which applies to psychotherapists and their clients.

It is important to recognize that C.R.S. § 19-3-311 is not a total denial of these privileges, since it appears that only those communications relating to the basis of the report are admissible in court. Therefore, communications unrelated to child abuse or neglect are still privileged. A psychotherapist should be cautious of what he or she reports and should not allow other communications unrelated to child abuse or neglect to be disclosed without a court order.

Emotional Abuse

Under the Colorado Children's Code, emotional abuse is defined in C.R.S. § 19-1-103(1)(a)(IV) as abuse that causes "an identifiable and substantial impairment of the child's intellectual or psychological functioning or development or a substantial risk of impairment to the child's intellectual or psychological functioning or development." This is a difficult standard to prove, which is why DHS caseworkers are reluctant to take a report of emotional abuse, and why it is rare to see a case prosecuted that involves emotional abuse. While lack of self-esteem is a significant loss in a child's personality development, does it constitute a "substantial impairment" of a child's intellectual or psychological functioning? If a child withdraws socially and is isolated because of low self-esteem, does this demonstrate that a child's intellectual or psychological functioning or development has been substantially impaired? What signs and symptoms or diagnostic criteria demonstrate that a child has been subjected to a substantial impairment of intellectual or psychological functioning or development, resulting from emotional abuse? Therapists should discuss these questions in consultation with one another, so that they have a good understanding of situations in which they would be required to report emotional abuse.

Obviously, just because a parent has yelled at a child and has hurt the child's feelings does not mean that you must report a case of emotional abuse. However, in those cases where your professional judgment causes you to suspect that the statutory standard for emotional abuse has been met, it must be reported. As in all other reports of suspected abuse or neglect to Child Protective Services or to law enforcement, make certain that you document your chart carefully, and follow up by providing a written report concerning the suspected abuse to the person who took the report. This is required by the Colorado Children's Code whenever you make a report of suspected child abuse or neglect.

Colorado Criminal Statutes Regarding Sexual Assaults on Children

C.R.S. § 18-3-405 prohibits sexual assault on a child and provides, in part: "Any actor who knowingly subjects another not his or her spouse to any sexual contact commits sexual assault on a child if the victim is less than fifteen years of age and the actor is at least four years older than the victim." Applying this statute, a child who is 14 years of age could consent to relations with a 17-year-old, but not with an 18-year-old, who is at least four years older than the 14-year-old.

C.R.S. § 18-3-402 also defines sexual assault to include a situation where "the victim is at least fifteen years of age but less than seventeen years of age and the actor is at least ten years older than the victim and is not the spouse of the victim." Applying this statute, a 16-year-old can consent to relations with a 25-year-old, but it is a crime when the victim is 16 years old and the actor is 26 years old.

Sexual Exploitation of Children: Reporting Those Who Possess or Use Child Pornography

The possession or viewing of child pornography is a crime in Colorado, in violation of C.R.S. § 18-6-403, which prohibits sexual exploitation of a child. This statute states in part:

> The mere possession or control of any sexually exploitative material results in continuing victimization of our children by the fact that such material is a permanent record of an act or acts of sexual abuse of a child; that each time such material is shown or viewed, the child is harmed; that such material is used to break down the will and resistance of other children to encourage them to participate in similar acts of sexual abuse.

Accordingly, it is the public policy of the State of Colorado to ban the possession of any child pornography. A violation of this statute is a felony offense. Therapists are mandated to report such an offense to law enforcement when they suspect that an individual possesses or is viewing child pornography.

Sandy Hook Elementary School

As we reflect on another mass shooting, we find tragically that in most of the mass killings, which go back to the Oklahoma City Federal Building, children have been injured, killed, or endangered. Therefore, when we consider client threats to "kill a lot of people" or to shoot people at the client's former school, we need to consider such threats as potential child abuse or child endangerment. The Colorado Children's Code, C.R.S. § 19-3-304, requires therapists to report suspected child abuse or neglect. Keep in mind that child abuse consists not only of injury to children, but also includes situations that pose a risk of injury or harm to children. Therefore, when a client makes a threat that involves a risk of harm to children in a school, in a mall, in a movie theatre, or in any other public setting, you should consider whether you suspect that child endangerment may occur, and then report the threat if potential child endangerment is suspected.

Specific threats of harm also give rise to the *Tarasoff* duty to warn and protect, when the threat is imminent. In complying with the *Tarasoff* duty in Colorado, mental health professionals have immunity after they have hospitalized the client who has made imminent threats, and after law enforcement officials have been notified of the threat.

Keep in mind that Colorado law requires the initiation of a 72-hour hold for individuals who are imminently dangerous to self or others due to a mental disorder.

These are thoughts and considerations that may assist professionals in situations where they may need to report suspected child abuse resulting from a client's threats. As always, if any question exists concerning whether a report needs to be made regarding a client's threat of violence, consultation with colleagues, supervisors, or attorneys may be indicated.

2.11 Criminal Prosecutions for Child Abuse

C.R.S. § 18-6-401(4) provides that no person who reports child abuse will be subjected to criminal or civil liability.

In criminal prosecutions for child abuse, C.R.S. § 18-6-401(3) provides that the statutory privilege between a patient and physician shall not be available for excluding or refusing testimony. Thus, a physician or psychiatrist who is treating a person accused of child abuse may be forced to testify regarding the communications made by the patient in the course of the treatment. Inexplicably, C.R.S. § 18-6-401(3) does not appear to limit the psychotherapist-client privilege, which appears to be intact in this instance.

C.R.S. § 18-6-401(3) provides that the statutory privilege between the victim of child abuse and his or her physician shall not be available for excluding or refusing testimony in any prosecution for an act of child abuse. Hence, a psychiatrist who is treating a victim of child abuse may be forced to testify as to communications made by the victim in the course of treatment. Here again, C.R.S. § 18-6-401(3) inexplicably does not limit the statutory privilege existing between the victim and a treating licensed professional.

2.12 Duty to Warn and Protect

C.R.S. § 13-21-117 sets forth those circumstances in which a physician, social worker, psychiatric nurse, psychologist, mental health professional, mental health hospital, or community mental health facility has an affirmative duty to warn a third party of a mental health patient's violent behavior, including those identifiable by their association with a specific location or entity.

This statute specifically provides that such persons will not be held civilly liable for the failure to warn or protect a third party unless a patient has communicated a serious threat of imminent physical violence against a specific person or persons.

When there is a duty to warn and protect under the statute, the duty can be discharged by:

1. Making reasonable and timely efforts to notify any person or persons specifically threatened or the person or persons responsible for a specific location or entity that is specifically threatened, as well as notifying an appropriate law enforcement agency; and
2. Taking other appropriate action, including, but not limited to, hospitalizing the patient.

The statute does not define what constitutes reasonable and timely notice. It is likely that this will be construed by the Colorado courts to mean notice that is reasonable under the specific circumstances.

The statute also fails to describe what constitutes "other appropriate action," other than hospitalizing the patient. This would include, for example, testifying in court in an action by the potential victim to obtain a restraining order against the patient who made the threat.

The statute does provide for immunity when a therapist has discharged the duty to warn and protect. Thus, an appropriate warning and other action to protect against imminent violence shall not be grounds for the imposition of civil damages or professional discipline. Hence, in those cases falling under the statute, a mental health worker cannot rely upon any privilege or duty of non-disclosure to remain silent. Some affirmative action is required.

Mental health therapists who know they have a duty to initiate a 72-hour hold evaluation for a client who is dangerous to self or others as the result of a mental disorder have a duty to warn of any serious threat of imminent physical violence made against another person or against a specific location or entity.

Therapists must record in the client's records all information concerning the threat made by the client, all action taken by the therapist to comply with the duty to warn, and all information communicated to the potential victim and to law enforcement.

See section 4.04 of this book for further information on C.R.S. § 13-21-117.

Practical Problems:

Scenario 1. You have an adult female client who is depressed and extremely anxious. During the process of counseling her for marital difficulties, you learn that she is in an abusive relationship and has been the victim of a long history of domestic violence.

Your client sees you after a particularly brutal battering has occurred. She tells you, "I am going to get a gun, and if my husband ever gets drunk and starts to beat me like that again, I am going to shoot him."

Are you required, under the "duty to warn and protect" statute, to warn the husband of her intent? After reading the statute, several thoughts occur to you. Has your client confided to you a serious threat of imminent physical violence against a specific person? If you do warn him, is he likely to become enraged and retaliate against your client? Is the threat of violence made by your client sufficiently "imminent" so that you are required to report it to law enforcement authorities and also to your client's husband?

Most people would not sympathize with your client's husband. However, sympathy is not a factor to be considered in weighing whether you have a duty to warn pursuant to the statute. Judges, attorneys, therapists, and law enforcement officers would probably differ in their interpretation of this statute and in their answers to the questions raised by this problem. Always seek competent legal advice in such situations or consult with a supervisor concerning any question regarding whether a duty to warn exists.

Scenario 2. You have an adult male client who is having problems coping with marital difficulties. His wife is having an affair with the manager of a convenience store. In a fit of rage, your client confides to you that his wife's paramour raises show dogs and has a sports car that is his pride and joy. Your client is enraged at the thought of his wife riding around in the passenger seat of that sports car. Your client thinks that it would be therapeutic for him to express his feelings by taking a baseball bat to the sports car, and perhaps to the boyfriend's show dogs.

Are you required to warn and protect? Has your client made a threat of imminent physical violence against a specified person, including one who is identifiable by association with a specific location or entity? Is it likely that after demolishing the sports car with a baseball bat, your client will go after its owner? Is it likely that while attacking the sports car, its owner will hear the commotion, go outside to investigate, and confront your enraged client? Although a volatile situation, this scenario does not meet the statutory criteria that give rise to a duty to warn. The actual threats of violence made by the client involve an automobile and animals. Because the threat does not concern imminent physical violence against a person or specific location, it does not give rise to the statutory duty to warn imposed by C.R.S. § 13-21-117.

This is where a therapist's professional judgment is of paramount importance, and a consultation with other colleagues, a supervisor, or legal counsel may be required. If it is foreseeable to a therapist that imminent physical violence may arise as a result of a client's threat to smash up a sports car or to harm show dogs, then the therapist will need to carry out the duty to warn and protect, by warning the wife's paramour of an imminent threat, by reporting the threat to law enforcement, and by initiating a 72-hour hospital hold of the client.

So that it is clear, the duty to warn and protect applies when a client has made an imminent threat of serious bodily injury against a specific person or persons or against a specific location or entity.

Scenario 3. Your client tells you he is HIV positive and has no intention of telling his sexual partner of his condition and intends to engage in unprotected sex. Do you have a duty to warn and protect the unknowing partner? The inquiry must focus on whether the client made an imminent threat of serious physical violence. If you are confronted with such a dilemma, consult your attorney or a clinical supervisor for specific guidance.

These problems illustrate the difficulty of applying the statute. An easy solution to the dilemma is to provide advance notice to your client of your obligation to warn and protect prior to engaging in therapy, and to obtain your client's written acknowledgment and waiver of confidentiality to these types of disclosures.

2.13 Duty to Report a Crime

C.R.S. § 18-8-115, provides as follows:

> It is the duty of every corporation or person who has reasonable grounds to believe that a crime has been committed to report promptly the suspected crime to law enforcement authorities. Notwithstanding any other provision of the law to the contrary, a corporation or person may disclose information concerning a suspected crime to other persons or corporations for the purpose of giving notice of the possibility that other such criminal conduct may be attempted which may affect the persons or corporations notified. When acting in good faith, such corporation or person shall be immune from any civil liability for such reporting or disclosure. This duty shall exist notwithstanding any other provision of the law to the contrary; except that this section shall not require disclosure of any communication privileged by law.

Applying this statute, licensed mental health professionals and registered psychotherapists have no duty to report a crime that occurred in the past or one that is imminent, unless (1) it involves child abuse or neglect; (2) it falls under the physical violence exception of the "duty to warn and protect" statute; (3) a therapist has a duty to initiate a 72-hour hold evaluation because a client is a danger to self or others as a result of a mental disorder, as demonstrated by a threat to commit a violent crime against another person or by an actual crime committed by the client; or (4) a duty to report elder abuse or abuse of an at-risk adult with intellectual and developmental disability exists, as discussed in Section 2.14.

This area is one where a psychotherapist should give advance notice of the possibility of disclosure and obtain a client's written acknowledgment and a waiver of confidentiality prior to commencing therapy.

As stated in the statute, a person who discloses information concerning a suspected crime to law enforcement or to an intended victim, when acting in good faith, will be immune from civil liability. "Good faith" immunity means that the reporting person must have a factual basis for his or her suspicions that a crime has occurred, whether that factual basis results from personal observations, statements by the victim, or statements made by the suspected perpetrator.

2.14 Duty to Report Elder Abuse and Abuse of At-Risk Adults with Intellectual and Developmental Disability (IDD)

Reporting Elder Abuse

C.R.S. § 18-6.5-108 requires the reporting of abuse and exploitation of elders 70 years of age or older.

The mandated reporters of elder abuse include physicians, medical doctors, registered nurses, psychologists, mental health professionals, and hospital personnel, as well as long-term care facility personnel engaged in the admission, care, or treatment of patients. Other professionals who must report elder abuse pursuant to this statute include dentists; law enforcement personnel; court-appointed guardians and conservators; pharmacists; Community-Centered Board staff; personnel of banks, savings and loan associations, and other financial institutions; caretakers at care facilities; and caretakers who provide home health care.

The types of abuse or exploitation of elders 70 years of age or older that must be reported pursuant to the definitions contained in C.R.S. § 18-6.5-102 are as follows:

1. Abuse means the "nonaccidental infliction of bodily injury, serious bodily injury, or death; confinement or restraint that is unreasonable under generally accepted caretaking standards; [sexual conduct or contact; and] caretaker neglect."
2. Exploitation for purposes of this statute means an act or omission committed by a person who "uses deception, harassment, intimidation, or undue influence to permanently or temporarily deprive an at-risk elder of the use, benefit, or possession of anything of value"; who, in the absence of legal authority, "employs the services of a third party for the profit or advantage of the person or another person to the detriment of the at-risk elder"; who "forces, compels, coerces, or entices an at-risk elder to perform services for the profit or advantage of the person or another person against the will of the at-risk elder"; or "misuses the property of an at-risk elder in a manner that adversely affects the at-risk elder's ability to receive health care or health care benefits or to pay bills for basic needs or obligations."
3. Caretaker neglect means "neglect that occurs when adequate food, clothing, shelter, psychological care, physical care, medical care, habilitation, supervision, or any other treatment necessary for the health or safety of an at-risk person is not secured for an at-risk person or is not provided by a caretaker in a timely manner and with the degree of care that a reasonable person in the same situation would exercise, or a caretaker knowingly uses harassment, undue influence, or intimidation to create a hostile or fearful environment for an at-risk person"; except that "the withholding, withdrawing, or refusing of any medication, any medical procedure or device, or any treatment, including but not limited to resuscitation, cardiac pacing, mechanical ventilation, dialysis, and artificial nutrition and hydration, in accordance with any valid medical directive or order or as described in a palliative plan of care, is not deemed caretaker neglect."

Reporting Procedures for Elder Abuse

In compliance with C.R.S. § 18-6.5-108, a person "who observes the mistreatment of an at-risk elder or an at-risk adult with IDD, or who has reasonable cause to believe that an at-risk elder or an at-risk adult with IDD has been mistreated or is at imminent risk of mistreatment, shall report such fact to a law enforcement agency not more than twenty-four hours after making the observation or discovery." Thus, pursuant to this law, those required to report elder abuse or exploitation are those professionals who have witnessed it or who have "reasonable cause to believe" that an elder 70 years of age or older has been abused or exploited or is at risk of imminent abuse or exploitation. There is no requirement to report suspected abuse or neglect of an elder.

A best practice would be to disclose to the elder that a report will be made, and to obtain written acknowledgement, if possible, from the elder that a report is going to be made. A professional making the report should document carefully all of the information obtained regarding the abuse or exploitation reported, the identities of witnesses to the abuse or exploitation, and all information concerning the reporting process, including the name of the law enforcement official to whom the report was made.

Failure to report abuse or exploitation of a senior who is 70 years of age or older is a misdemeanor criminal offense. C.R.S. § 18-6.5-108(1)(c).

Mandatory Duty Also Exists to Report Abuse of At-Risk Adults with IDD

In enacting C.R.S. § 18-6.5-108, which mandates that designated individuals report abuse, exploitation, and caretaker neglect of elders 70 years of age or older, the legislature revised statutes regarding at-risk adults. In compliance with the provisions of C.R.S. § 26-3.1-102(1)(a.5), mental health professionals and other healthcare providers are now required to report abuse of at-risk adults with IDD. An "at-risk adult with IDD" means a person who is 18 years of age or older and is a person with an intellectual and developmental disability, as defined in C.R.S. § 25.5-10-202(26)(a). According to C.R.S. § 25.5-10-202(26)(a), "intellectual and developmental disability" means "a disability that manifests before the person reaches twenty-two years of age, that constitutes a substantial disability to the affected person, and that is attributable to mental retardation or related conditions, which include cerebral palsy, epilepsy, autism, or other neurological conditions when those conditions result in impairment of general intellectual functioning or adaptive behavior similar to that of a person with mental retardation."

Reporting Requirements for At-Risk Adults with IDD

A mental health professional must report the mistreatment of an at-risk adult with IDD if they have observed the mistreatment or have reasonable cause to believe that an at-risk adult with IDD has been mistreated or is at imminent risk of mistreatment. This report shall be made to a law enforcement agency not more than twenty-four hours after making the observation or discovery. A failure to make such a mandated report constitutes a misdemeanor criminal offense.

Exception to the Reporting of Abuse to At-Risk Adults

C.R.S. § 26-3.1-102 is designed to provide protective services for adults at risk of mistreatment or self-neglect. There is no mandatory duty for mental health professionals to report when they have a professional relationship with a client who may be an at-risk adult but who is not an elder 70 years of age or older or an at-risk adult with IDD. At-risk adults are defined, in general, as those with physical or mental disabilities, including adults who are developmentally disabled, are mentally ill, or have physical disabilities. In the case of these individuals, who are not at-risk elders 70 years of age or older and are not at-risk adults with IDD, no mandatory duty exists to report abuse. C.R.S. § 26-3.1-102(1)(a) states that a healthcare provider, including a mental health professional "who observes the mistreatment or self-neglect of an at-risk adult or who has reasonable cause to believe that an at-risk adult has been mistreated or is self-neglecting and is at imminent risk of mistreatment or self-neglect is urged to report such fact to a county department not more than twenty-four hours after making the observation or discovery." The fact that mental health professionals are "urged" to make a report means that the report is not required. If a therapist has a professional relationship with an at-risk adult, other than an elder 70 years of age or older or one with IDD, no mandatory duty exists to report the abuse without client consent. In fact, the mental health professional must have client consent to make a report due to the duty of confidentiality.

2.15 Waiver by Client

The statutory privileges and duties of non-disclosure and confidentiality can be waived by a client in three ways:

1. The client's express waiver by the execution and delivery of a signed and dated waiver or authorization to release information. You should require that any such release be notarized and contain an original signature. A client who has signed an authorization to release information or records may limit the scope of information to be disclosed and may revoke the authorization at any time. (Practice pointer: Your form for release of information must disclose to the person signing it: "You may revoke this authorization at any time.")
2. The client's commencement of a lawsuit against a therapist or the initiation of a complaint by a client to the Board of Registered Psychotherapists or to a licensing board. In such a situation, therapists must be able to defend themselves by disclosing information to their attorneys, to the board involved, and to their professional liability insurance carriers.

3. When the communication is made in the presence of a third party who does not enjoy the statutory privilege or who does not have the duty of non-disclosure and confidentiality. The reason for this rule is that the communication is deemed to be outside the therapeutic relationship if made in the presence of someone whom the law deems non-essential to that relationship.

Client waiver solves the problems of breaching confidentiality in the following circumstances: (1) child abuse; (2) "duty to warn" cases; (3) harm to self or others;(4) at-risk adults; and (5) reporting of crimes. If a therapist notifies the client of the possibility of disclosing information in these circumstances, prior to commencing therapy, and obtains a written acknowledgment and waiver of confidentiality in these circumstances, most of the problems outlined above are eliminated.

2.16 Care and Treatment of the Mentally Ill

The information and records prepared in the course of rendering services to individuals under any provision of C.R.S. §§ 27-65-101, *et seq.*, "Care and Treatment of Persons with Mental Illness," are confidential and privileged. According to C.R.S. § 27-65-121, such records and information are subject to disclosure only in the following circumstances:

1. In communications between qualified professional personnel in the provision of services or appropriate referrals; *e.g.*, treatment team staffings or treatment plan review by an interdisciplinary team.
2. When the recipient of services designates persons to whom the information or records may be released.
3. To make claims for aid, insurance, or medical assistance.
4. For research purposes, provided all identifying information has been expunged and the researchers have signed a confidentiality oath.
5. To the courts as necessary.
6. To persons authorized by the courts after notice and hearing to the person to whom the records pertain.
7. To adult family members (spouse, parent, adult child, adult sibling) with respect to the location and fact of admission of a person with a mental illness receiving care and treatment, unless the treating professional decides after an interview with the person with a mental illness that such disclosure would not be in the best interest of the person with a mental illness.

8. To adult family members actively participating in the care and treatment of a person with a mental illness with respect to the following: the diagnosis, the prognosis, the need for hospitalization and anticipated stay, the discharge plan, the medication administered and side effects, and the short-term and long-term treatment goals.
9. In accordance with state and federal law to the agency designated pursuant to the federal "Protection and Advocacy for Mentally Ill Individuals Act," 42 U.S.C. §§ 10801, *et seq.*, as the governor's protection and advocacy system for Colorado.
10. To a parent concerning his or her minor child.

Such information may be released only if the treating professional determines that: (1) the mentally ill person is capable of making a rational decision regarding his or her interests; (2) the mentally ill person consents to such release; and (3) the treating professional believes it would be in the best interest of the mentally ill person to so release the information. If the mentally ill person is determined to be capable of making rational decisions regarding his or her interest and objects to the release, the information will not be disclosed. If the treating professional determines that the mentally ill person is incapable of making a rational decision regarding his or her interests and the patient objects to the release, the treating professional may disclose the information if that would be in the best interests of the mentally ill person. These decisions are subject to administrative review.

C.R.S. § 27-65-121(3)(a) specifically provides that information is not privileged or confidential when it consists of "observed behavior that constitutes a criminal offense committed upon the premises of any facility" providing mental health services or "any criminal offense committed against any person while performing or receiving services" in a mental health facility.

Retention of Facility Records

Outpatient mental health care facilities shall retain all records for a minimum of seven years after termination of treatment, for persons who were 18 years of age or older. Inpatient or hospital facilities shall retain all records for a minimum of 10 years after discharge from the facility for persons who were 18 years of age or older when admitted to the facility, or until 28 years for persons who were under 18 years of age when admitted to the facility.

2.17 Treatment of Adolescents

Several important issues must be considered in treating adolescents. Adolescents 15 years of age and older have the authority to consent to treatment *by a licensed mental health professional* pursuant to C.R.S. § 27-65-103. This statute does not allow minors who are 15 years of age or older to consent to treatment by a registered psychotherapist in a private practice setting. When adolescents consent to treatment, parents are still entitled to information, with or without the consent of the adolescent, concerning the services given and the services needed. This simply means the type of services that are being provided to an adolescent, or the fact that the client may require a referral to another treatment provider for services needed.

In addition to consenting to treat with a licensed physician or mental health professional, an adolescent who is 15 years of age or older also has the authority to consent to treatment at a facility, such as a public hospital, a licensed private hospital, a clinic, a community mental health center or clinic, or a treatment facility in Colorado operated by the Armed Forces of the United States, the United States Public Health Service, or the United States Department of Veterans Affairs.

When the client is 15 years of age or older, that client is the privilege holder for himself or herself. Therefore, before disclosing treatment information concerning an adolescent 15 years of age or older, you must obtain the adolescent's consent in writing.

In divorce and custody cases, a therapist cannot disclose information to a parental responsibility evaluator, custody evaluator, or CFI concerning an adolescent who is 15 years of age or older, unless the therapist has the written consent of that adolescent. Parental consent in such a situation is not sufficient.

From a clinical perspective, therapists need to ensure that parents do not intrude into the process of treating adolescents. Parents need to be informed of the privacy rights of adolescents who are 15 years of age or older, and they need to understand that they should respect the adolescent's privacy, since it is integral to effective treatment.

Consent for Outpatient Treatment by 12-Year-Olds

Children who are 12 years of age or older have the authority granted by HB 19-1120 to consent to outpatient mental health treatment provided by a licensed mental health professional, an LPC Candidate, an LSW, a psychologist candidate or a licensed school social worker, if the mental health professional determines that: (a) the minor is knowingly and voluntarily seeking mental health services; and (b) the provision of psychotherapy services is clinically indicated and necessary for the minor's well-being. Specific provisions regarding the disclosures that may be given with client consent to the 12-year-old's parents regarding these outpatient services, and other provisions of this law, are contained in Section 4.14.

2.18 Welfare Checks by Law Enforcement

When therapists are concerned about the safety of clients who may be suicidal or threatening harm to themselves, a generally accepted practice nationwide is to contact a law enforcement agency in order to request a welfare check. In order to avoid an accusation that requesting a welfare check by a therapist constitutes a breach of confidentiality or a Health Insurance Portability and Accountability Act (HIPAA) violation, a Client Disclosure Statement is available in Appendix A as Form 2. This Client Disclosure Statement informs the client that the therapist's policy is to request a welfare check through law enforcement in the event that the therapist becomes concerned about the client's safety or welfare. The Disclosure Statement is designed to obtain the client's consent to the therapist's practice of obtaining a welfare check, as needed, from law enforcement. When the client signs the Disclosure Statement, providing informed consent for a welfare check to be conducted, the therapist need not worry about a potential breach of confidentiality. This enables the therapist to explain his or her specific concern to law enforcement while requesting the welfare check.

2.19 Disclosure of Information to Coroners

County coroners are authorized by law to make determinations concerning a person's cause of death, to conduct autopsies, and to issue death certificates. C.R.S. § 30-10-606(6) authorizes a county coroner performing his or her duties to request and receive a copy of "[a]ny information, record, or report related to treatment, consultation, counseling, or therapy services from any licensed psychologist, professional counselor, marriage and family therapist, social worker, or addiction counselor, certified addiction counselor, [or] registered psychotherapist . . . if the report, record, or information is relevant to the inquest or investigation."

Whenever a psychotherapist receives a request from a county coroner for treatment records or information regarding a client who is deceased, the therapist may cooperate with the coroner and provide the information requested. The therapist does not need to have a release or authorization for disclosure of information signed by the client prior to death or signed by a client representative.

Immunity

This statute confers immunity upon any therapist who provides treatment information requested by a coroner and states: "Any person who complies with a request from a coroner pursuant to . . . this subsection . . . shall be immune from any civil or criminal liability that might otherwise be incurred or imposed with respect to the disclosure of confidential patient or client information." C.R.S. § 30-10-606(6)(d).

2.20 Waiver of Privilege for Insanity Pleas or Issues of Competency in Criminal Cases

Rarely, but on occasion, a therapist might receive a subpoena for records from a prosecutor or from a defense attorney in a criminal case in which the defendant has pleaded not guilty by reason of insanity or in which issues of competency have been raised. C.R.S. § 16-8-103.6 provides that a defendant who places his or her mental condition at issue by pleading not guilty by reason of insanity pursuant to C.R.S. § 16-8-103 "waives any claim of confidentiality or privilege" as to any mental health treatment records in the possession of a physician or mental health professional. Colorado appellate courts have ruled that this waiver applies to all mental health records, not just records or reports relating to communications made by the defendant in the course of a sanity evaluation for the purposes of the criminal proceeding.

Pursuant to the provisions of C.R.S. § 16-8-103.6, this waiver of any claim of confidentiality or privilege also applies when a defendant has raised the defense of impaired mental condition pursuant to C.R.S. § 16-8-103.5.

This statutory waiver of confidentiality requires a mental health professional to comply with a subpoena *duces tecum* seeking records of treatment for a criminal defendant when the therapist has ascertained that (1) the defendant has, in fact, raised the defense of not guilty by reason of insanity or the defense of impaired mental condition; or (2) where issues have been raised with the court concerning the defendant's competency to proceed.

Practice Pointer

In compliance with C.R.S. § 16-8-103.6, a mental health professional does not need an authorization for disclosure of confidential treatment information in order to produce the defendant's records in compliance with a subpoena or court order. The best practice for compliance with the request for records is to make a copy of the entire chart, to seal the records in an envelope marked "Private and Confidential," and to deliver the records sought to the court at the date, time, and place indicated in the subpoena *duces tecum*.

PART III: PRACTICE POINTERS

2.21 Duty to Report Youth Missing from Out-of-Home Placement

C.R.S. § 19-1-115.3 mandates that a report be made to law enforcement immediately, within 24 hours, whenever any minor child or adolescent is missing from an out-of-home placement. This includes youths who may be runaways from a residential treatment facility, from a Division of Youth Corrections Facility, from foster care, or from any other health care facility or out-of-home placement. In addition to notifying law enforcement officials, a report concerning the missing youth must be made to the National Center for Missing and Exploited Children.

2.22 Releasing Files and Records

The Problem

Occasionally, clients request copies of their files, test reports, and progress notes. Some therapists feel uncomfortable allowing clients to have access to this information. For others, allowing access is not a problem.

Health Care Facility Records

C.R.S. § 25-1-801 requires health care facilities to allow a patient or a patient's personal representative to inspect, at reasonable times and upon reasonable notice, the patient's medical records. However, records pertaining to mental health problems may be withheld from a patient, and a summary of records pertaining to a patient's mental health problems may, upon written, signed, and dated request, be made available to the patient or his or her personal representative following termination of the treatment program.

The health care facility must note all requests by patients for inspection of their medical records, including the time and date of the patient's request, and the time and date of inspection. The patient or personal representative must acknowledge the fact of inspection by dating and signing the record file.

Records of Individual Healthcare Providers

C.R.S. § 25-1-802 requires chiropodists, podiatrists, chiropractors, dentists, medical doctors, osteopathic doctors, nurses, optometrists, audiologists, acupuncturists, direct-entry midwives, and physical therapists who are licensed under Title 12 of the Colorado Revised Statutes to make available to a patient or a patient's personal representative that patient's records upon receipt of a written authorization for inspection of records. However, records pertaining to a client's mental health problems maintained by a psychotherapist need not be made available to a patient or a patient's personal representative. Instead, a summary of records concerning mental health problems may, upon request and signed and dated authorization, be made available to the patient or a designated representative.

All requests by patients for inspection of their records must be noted with the time and date of the patient's or patient's personal representative's request, and the time and date of inspection must be noted by the healthcare provider. The patient is required to acknowledge the fact of inspection by dating and signing the record file.

2.23 Office Management

To ensure that a client's confidentiality is protected and to comply with HIPAA Standards, a psychotherapist should undertake the following steps within the office:

1. Written policies and procedures should be developed and distributed to all staff members concerning client confidentiality.
2. All staff members should receive training on client confidentiality and sign a written statement acknowledging their duty and obligation to maintain client confidentiality.
3. Client confidentiality should be the topic of discussion with appropriate frequency at staff meetings.
4. Client files should be stored in locked filing cabinets with access limited to certain persons and checked out only to authorized persons. A record of who has the file should be maintained at all times.
5. Client information should only be released after receipt of a court order or signed release from the client specifying the information to be released and to whom such information may be given.
6. A written record should be maintained in the client file, identifying the date of any release of client information, the person receiving the information, and the specific information released.
7. Any release of client information should be stamped "Private and Confidential" and should be accompanied by a statement that outlines that the released information may not be released by the recipient.
8. All staff members should be advised that detailed messages about a client should not be left on any answering machine and that conversations about clients should not occur over any radio medium such as portable or cellular telephones.

9. Staff discussions about clients should not occur in public areas of the office such as the restroom or lunchroom.
10. Staff should not send faxes containing sensitive information unless a reasonable precaution is made to ensure that the confidentiality of the information is maintained.
11. Staff should not discuss confidential matters on a cellular telephone.
12. A client's informed consent to treatment should be obtained in writing prior to commencing treatment. The consent should include disclosures concerning exceptions to confidentiality addressed in section 6.02 of this book.

2.24 Responding to Subpoenas and Requests for Client Records

HIPAA practices have created confusion regarding the appropriate response by mental health professionals to requests for treatment records. While HIPAA practices require that patients have access to their medical records, an exception exists for "psychotherapy notes." According to the HIPAA Privacy Rule, found at 45 C.F.R. § 164.524, counseling clients do not have a right to access a therapist's "Session Notes," *i.e.*, psychotherapy notes, which should be kept in a separate section of the client's chart. In addition, state laws, which require medical professionals to turn over a copy of all client records when authorized by a signed, dated request for records by a client, generally contain exceptions for psychiatric, psychological, and mental health records. Therapists, therefore, need to make themselves aware of state laws concerning the access to therapists' notes and records that clients are entitled to receive. This information can often be obtained from licensing board representatives, local professional associations, or attorneys specializing in health care law.

Service of a Subpoena

Legal service of a subpoena requires that a process server hand a subpoena to the person being served. To be effective, service of the subpoena must occur at least two business days prior to the date of the hearing or deposition identified in a subpoena requesting that the person served appear and testify. If a subpoena demands production of records, then the subpoena must be served with an authorization for release of any confidential or privileged records, signed by the privilege holder or holders. A subpoena may be sent by e-mail, fax, or mail, accompanied by a Waiver of Service, but mental health professionals should not "waive" service by signing and returning the Waiver, unless they know that their client consents to testimony by the therapist whereby the therapist discloses treatment information to those present in court. A written Release of Information (ROI) signed by the client or clients involved, or by client representatives who may hold the privilege, is required in order to testify. It is appropriate for a therapist who is subpoenaed to testify regarding treatment information, with client consent, to be paid for the professional's time to prepare for court, travel to court, and appear in court for testimony. A Fee Policy form is included as Form 9 in Appendix A.

Therapists must remember that the service of the subpoena only compels attendance at a specific time and location for an appearance. A subpoena does not compel a therapist to testify regarding confidential treatment information or to produce privileged treatment records. Client consent is needed before a mental health professional can disclose treatment information or records. A court order signed by a judge requiring testimony or the production of records should be honored.

Responding to Subpoenas

Whenever a therapist receives a subpoena for testimony or a subpoena *duces tecum* requiring the production of treatment records, an informed consent process should begin. In this process, contact the client to determine if he or she consents to courtroom testimony and will give written authorization for disclosure of confidential information to the judge, attorneys, and all others present in court. Similarly, when a therapist receives a subpoena to produce for production of treatment records, the therapist needs to contact the client involved to determine if the client is willing to authorize the disclosure of a copy of all records subpoenaed—usually the entire client chart—at the time and place commanded by the subpoena.

This is an informed-consent process because clients generally do not know the content of the information in their records, and may not remember what history was provided to a therapist during the assessment conducted at the inception of treatment. When a client is informed of the nature of the information contained in the therapist's chart and the specific history contained in notes, the client may then authorize disclosure of that information.

If an authorization signed by the client for release of treatment information accompanies written correspondence from an attorney or healthcare professional who has been authorized to receive the information, the generally accepted standard of practice is to comply with state law in producing the records sought. However, the best practice is to inform the client of the information contained in the chart, and ensure that the client is willing to authorize the disclosure of the records knowing their contents. After being apprised of the information contained in the chart, the client has the choice of whether to revoke the previously signed written authorization for disclosure of records.

During this informed-consent process, a client may object to any release of treatment information when notified of the subpoena served by an opposing party's attorney in litigation involving the client. If a client does not authorize the disclosure and production of treatment records or testimony by a therapist, then the client should instruct his or her attorney to oppose the subpoena and seek to have it quashed or file a motion for a protective order requesting protection of the confidential information contained in the mental health records. It should be the client's attorney who engages in legal procedures, at the client's expense, to protect the client's privacy and the confidentiality of treatment information. It is not the therapist's obligation to retain counsel at the therapist's expense to file a motion for protective order. However, if the client has no attorney, therapists can contact their professional liability insurer to determine if their insurance policy provides coverage to retain an attorney for this purpose.

If a therapist is employed by a mental health center or agency, then the therapist's supervisor should be notified immediately of the subpoena. The agency's counsel can then assist in protecting the client's privacy and the privileged information contained in records when the client does not consent to a therapist's testimony or objects to the production of records. A form motion for protective order is contained in Appendix A at Form 1.

Therapists, of course, are entitled to be paid for their time for testifying in court (if called as an expert witness) and for conferring with a client's attorney, when authorized to do so, to prepare for testimony as an expert.

In situations when a therapist has received a subpoena to testify in court or to produce records, the professional cannot ignore the subpoena and must appear. If the client has not waived the therapist-client privilege and has not consented to testimony or disclosure of treatment information, the therapist should inform the court before testifying or turning over records that no client has authorized any waiver of the privilege or has consented to disclosure of treatment information.

In addition, a therapist may inform the judge that any information in the therapist's possession would be personal, private, and harmful if disclosed. This can be done without acknowledging that a professional relationship has existed in the past with any person in the courtroom. If the judge then directs that the therapist take the witness stand or produce records that have been subpoenaed, the therapist should ask, "Your Honor, are you ordering me to comply with the subpoena?" If the judge responds in the affirmative, then the therapist should comply with the court's order, trusting that the judge is properly applying and enforcing the applicable law.

The malpractice insurance policies for mental health professionals generally provide coverage for legal fees incurred in responding to a subpoena for client records. Professional liability insurers want therapists to be able to retain an attorney to assist in responding to a subpoena so that they can avoid pitfalls, and can prevent worse problems.

What issues and questions should a therapist discuss with his or her own attorney after receiving a subpoena for testimony in court or for client records? First, was service of the subpoena proper, or can a motion to quash the subpoena be filed? Has the client or the client's legal representative consented in writing to disclosure of treatment information in court or to release of treatment records, or should a motion for protective order be filed with the court to protect against a breach of confidentiality, which would occur if treatment information were disclosed without the client's consent? Does the subpoena comply with court rules, providing enough time to the therapist to rearrange scheduled appointments before the court appearance? Do the court rules require the therapist to travel the distance involved, especially if it is outside the county where the therapist was served? These are legal issues and questions that require legal assistance.

In what other ways can an attorney help a therapist who has received a subpoena? First and foremost, an attorney can confer with the attorneys who issued the subpoena to advise, "My client cannot help you." An attorney can also demand the expert fee that would be required, if the therapist is not released from the subpoena. And in many cases these days, an attorney can inform the attorney who issued the subpoena that the client signed a promise not to subpoena the therapist and not to request the therapist's testimony in court. In many instances, attorneys have released my clients from subpoenas, either having been confronted with a motion to quash or a motion for protective order, or when the attorney who issued the subpoena has been confronted with the ultimate reality, "You are going to be wasting your money in this case, because you will have to pay my client an expert fee, and my client's testimony will not help you."

In terms of basic practical advice regarding subpoenas, keep in mind that a subpoena does not authorize the disclosure of confidential, privileged treatment information; it only compels you to be present at the place and time listed in the subpoena. If you receive a subpoena in the mail, which is accompanied by a card that you are asked to sign and send back, do not send the card back unless you want to appear in court and testify. The card is a waiver of service. Signing the card and returning it means that you will be required to appear in court.

So what is the first step that you should take in responding to a subpoena? Let your insurance company know that you have received a subpoena and want to hire legal counsel.

Requests for Information from Court Investigators

Judges recognize the value of recommendations by mental health professionals to assist courts in handling divorce and custody cases, sentencing defendants in criminal cases, imposing conditions of probation for drug- or alcohol-related offenses, and ordering treatment for juveniles who have broken the law. Family court cases involving divorce and custody litigation provide the most frequent opportunity for mental health professionals to have contact with the courts. Therapists for the husband, the wife, or the children of the parties are frequently contacted by court investigators, custody evaluators, or court-appointed special advocates (CASA advocates) seeking information for use in making recommendations to the court. These recommendations concern the award of custody, joint custody, the allocation of parental responsibilities by the court, and visitation or "parenting time."

Courts use mental health professionals as well as attorneys to conduct these investigations and to make such recommendations to the court. These investigations facilitate the judicial process, making it more efficient, so that judges do not need to spend days in court hearing the testimony of witnesses in order to rule upon disputed issues. When therapists are contacted by investigators for the court, CASA advocates, or custody evaluators, but have not received any written authorization from clients to disclose information to these individuals, they should do the following:

1. Contact the court representative without disclosing that a professional relationship has existed with anyone involved in the domestic litigation.
2. Inform the court representative that a signed, written authorization for treatment information must be received before any discussion can occur or any information can be disclosed. Usually, the custody evaluator is being paid to conduct an investigation, and can obtain the written authorization needed from the client. In these situations, courts frequently order the parties to sign authorizations so that professionals involved with the family can provide information needed by the custody evaluator and the court. Often the court representative will have signed authorizations from the parties, which can be easily transmitted to a therapist.

3. In conferring with a court representative after having been authorized to do so, do not advocate for the client. It is the therapist's duty to provide factual information in response to questions.

When authorized to provide information to a custody evaluator, provide the least amount of information needed to satisfy the court representative's purpose. If questions are asked of the therapist concerning which parent would make the better custodian, the therapist needs to acknowledge limitations on his or her ability to respond, and acknowledge any bias or lack of objectivity that would affect the therapist's judgment in answering the questions posed. If the therapist is subsequently called as a witness to testify in a divorce or custody action, he or she should discuss the facts and not express opinions or recommendations regarding custody, parenting time, or issues that the therapist has not had an opportunity to evaluate, and not make assessments of a party whom the therapist has never met, much less assessed.

Motion for Protective Order

The Colorado Supreme Court issued a ruling that reaffirms a therapist's duty to oppose a subpoena *duces tecum* for treatment records in a situation where the client has not consented to the disclosure of the records. In *People v. Sisneros*, 55 P.3d 797 (Colo. 2002), the Colorado Supreme Court considered a criminal case in which charges of sexual assault on a minor had been filed and in which the defendant's attorney had issued a subpoena to produce to the victim's psychologist, demanding that the victim's treatment records be turned over. When the psychologist refused to turn over the records and sought a protective order from the Pueblo District Court, the judge initially ruled that he wanted to inspect the records *in camera* (in private) to see if any records should be turned over to the defendant. The psychologist took an immediate appeal to the Colorado Supreme Court, seeking to protect the confidential and privileged information contained in the treatment records.

The Colorado Supreme Court discussed the therapist-client privilege set forth in C.R.S. § 13-90-107. Pursuant to this privilege, a therapist may not testify in court or turn over records concerning a client's treatment without the client's consent. In its decision, the Colorado Supreme Court ruled that the trial court judge did not have the discretion to order the victim's records to be disclosed, even for the judge's *in camera* review. The Colorado Supreme Court also determined that the victim did not waive her privilege by testifying in court that she had received treatment from the psychologist.

This decision applies in any situation where treatment records have been subpoenaed and the client (or clients in the case of couples or family therapy) has not consented to the disclosure of treatment information. In any criminal case in which charges of sexual assault, domestic violence, or other crimes against a person have been charged, the decision in *Sisneros* should establish a precedent to be followed by the trial court. Unless the court finds that the privilege has been waived or that the client has consented to disclosure of treatment information, the court should issue a protective order, protecting against disclosure of the confidential, privileged information.

What is the duty of a therapist who receives a subpoena to testify in court or a subpoena to produce to turn over treatment records? To oppose the request by seeking a protective order from the court. If your client is a party to the case in which the subpoena has been issued, your client's attorney should be able to raise the issue in an appropriate manner. If it is a criminal case, then the district attorney ordinarily should be willing to raise the issue with the court in order to protect the victim's privacy. If necessary, a therapist can provide the judge hearing the case with a motion for protective order, being careful not to disclose the fact that a professional relationship exists. Keep in mind that you cannot refuse to obey a court order. If a judge orders you to testify or to disclose records in a case, the prevailing practice among therapists is to trust that the judge's ruling is legally correct and comply with it, unless an appeal is filed.

A Motion for Protective Order form is included in Appendix A as Form 1. This motion contains a discussion of Colorado statutes regarding confidentiality and privilege, and summarizes the legal principles regarding client confidentiality discussed in decisions issued by both the United States Supreme Court and the Colorado Supreme Court.

2.25 HIPAA Business Practices

When the Health Insurance Portability and Accountability Act (HIPAA, Pub. Law 104-191 (1996)) went into effect on April 14, 2003, it established procedures for compliance with standards to protect confidential health information by healthcare professionals who transmit treatment information or billing information electronically. The primary purpose of this Act was to require insurance companies, HMOs, PPOs, and third-party payors to protect the confidentiality of the information sent to them for billing purposes. These protections are assured through identity codes, which are used instead of a client's name. In addition, diagnostic codes are used (as had been the practice in the past), along with procedure or intervention codes.

In part, the law was enacted to prevent entities that pay for healthcare treatment from creating data banks of information concerning consumers and their problems. Fears had existed and myths were prevalent regarding the prospect that companies were setting up data banks concerning patients who were depressed or HIV-positive, so that this information could be used to deny life insurance applications or applications for health insurance.

Confusion abounds regarding HIPAA, its applications, and its effect in relation to state law. State laws preempt HIPAA when they are more stringent than HIPAA procedures and the state laws provide for greater protection of confidential health information. For example, some state laws allow therapists to use their discretion in responding to a request for records and to provide a treatment summary – rather than a copy of the actual records – when therapists believe that a client might be harmed by the disclosure of the records or unable to process the data in them appropriately. Such laws and the procedures they authorize preempt HIPAA regulations and procedures.

In some jurisdictions, therapists are allowed to exercise their professional judgment and refuse a request for records. Again, such laws take precedence over HIPAA regulations. The Act recognizes that state laws that are more stringent than HIPAA standards take precedence. In practice, this means that the protections for confidential health information that existed before HIPAA went into effect still applied after HIPAA went into effect. Essentially, HIPAA did not change the procedures for protecting mental health records established by state law; it changed the amount of paperwork used by professionals.

The regulations adopted by the U.S. Department of Health and Human Services to implement HIPAA contain privacy standards, found at 45 C.F.R. §§ 164.500 to 164.534. As every consumer of healthcare services knows, patients (and even customers at pharmacies) were provided a HIPAA Privacy Notice, which explains the uses and disclosures of confidential health information.

In addition, providers who are HIPAA-compliant are required to have the business associates who receive patients' confidential health information sign a Business Associate Contract, agreeing to maintain the confidentiality of all information that the business associate may receive. For example, a contractor who conducts a billing service for mental health professionals or physicians comes into contact with extremely personal information relating to patients and their diagnoses. Pursuant to a HIPAA Business Associate Contract, the individual or billing service must agree to return or destroy all confidential information when it is no longer needed.

Other business practices required by HIPAA include providing an accounting to clients of the disclosures made by a provider, if such an accounting is requested by a patient or client. When an accounting is requested, therapists are required to provide a statement containing the following information: (1) the date of the disclosure, (2) the recipient of the information, (3) the purpose of the disclosure, (4) the nature of the information requested, and (5) a statement regarding the specific information that was disclosed.

When a request for an accounting is made by a client, providers have 60 days within which to comply with that request. In providing an accounting, professionals do not need to go back before April 14, 2003. An exception to this procedure states that healthcare professionals do not need to account for the disclosure of information made in billing for services or for disclosures of information made with client consent to other healthcare professionals.

HIPAA regulations also require that authorization forms to be signed by patients or clients when authorizing the disclosure of treatment information contain specific statements and elements in order to be HIPAA-compliant. These are discussed thoroughly in the next section. One requirement for a professional's authorization form is that it contain a statement that the authorization may be revoked, in writing, by the client at any time.

The most important standard for mental health professionals adopted by HIPAA is the requirement that when professionals receive a request for disclosure of confidential health information with client consent, they are to disclose the least amount of information possible to comply with the request. This new standard is important because in the past, insurers and government healthcare programs, such as CHAMPUS/TRICARE, at times requested a copy of the entire client chart in order to justify the reasonableness and necessity of bills for treatment as part of a utilization review. These requests were extremely invasive of clients' privacy rights. The idea that a psychologist or other mental health professional might be required to provide an entire chart with all notes to justify payment of bills was troubling because it was potentially violative of the clients' right to privacy.

Appendix A contains basic HIPAA business forms for use in complying with procedures for professionals who are required to be HIPAA-compliant. The HIPAA Privacy Statement (Form 3-1 in Appendix A) should be provided to new clients as part of the informed-consent process. It is not intended as a substitute for any client disclosure statement or informed-consent form required by state law, and does not include all of the disclosures required by the national professional associations for mental health therapists. Form 3-5 also contains a

HIPAA-compliant authorization form for disclosure of confidential, privileged treatment information.

When HIPAA was enacted by Congress, its purpose was, in part, to establish national standards for the protection of confidential health information. As stated above, this statute and its regulations do not preempt state law to the extent that state standards for confidentiality and privilege may be more rigid and provide more protections than HIPAA standards. The basic exceptions to confidentiality contained in codes of ethics for mental health professionals, and also mandated by state law, are incorporated into the federal statute. For example, reports of child abuse or neglect, reports of imminent threats of physical violence made by clients, and procedures to hospitalize patients who are imminently dangerous to self or others were recognized under HIPAA as being exceptions to confidentiality.

One additional exception to confidentiality was created: a duty to report threats to the national security of the United States. Consistent with state laws and ethical codes, mental health professionals can comply with HIPAA by including in their disclosures to clients, in writing, a statement that the professional will report information concerning suspected threats to national security to federal officials. This disclosure would be contained in the same informed-consent form that discloses to clients the limitations on confidentiality – that treatment information is confidential, except that a mental health professional has a duty to report suspected child abuse or neglect, to warn potential victims concerning imminent threats of violence, to initiate hospitalization of clients who are imminently dangerous to self and others, and to report threats to national security to federal officials. In this way, clients give informed consent to a professional to make these reports when necessary.

Insurers, HMOs, and others who violate clients' privacy rights by improperly disclosing treatment information can have monetary sanctions imposed against them. The regulations adopted by the U.S. Department of Health & Human Services (HHS) recommend that healthcare providers initiate commonsense practices to protect against the inadvertent disclosure of treatment information by keeping client records in locked file cabinets. Information maintained on computers must be password-protected. Other recommendations include positioning computer screens so that they are not visible to people walking by, and not leaving confidential reports, records, and files face up on a desk where they can be seen by clients entering the office.

Therapists are required to be HIPAA-compliant if they transmit treatment information electronically, either in billing for services or in transmitting information over the internet. Be assured that if you do insurance billing, the insurer will require you to maintain compliance with all HIPAA standards and will advise you of procedures that do so. If you do not transmit billing information to third-party payors electronically, then, in all likelihood, you do not need to be HIPAA-compliant. Sending a fax containing client information or confidential health information does not subject a therapist to HIPAA procedures.

In order to comply with the national standard of care for providing mental health treatment, therapists are required to provide treatment in accordance with the "generally accepted standards of practice." HIPAA provisions are rapidly becoming the generally accepted standards of practice for mental health professionals.

The HIPAA Privacy Rule and C.R.S. § 25-1-802

Mental health counselors are generally familiar with the HIPAA Privacy Rule, even if they cannot cite the federal regulation regarding it. The HIPAA Privacy Rule is contained in 45 C.F.R. § 164.524, and provides that "psychotherapy notes" should not be disclosed in response to a request for client records. "Psychotherapy notes" are defined as notes recorded by a mental health professional, documenting or analyzing the contents of private conversations with a client during a private counseling session.

This Privacy Rule is comparable to C.R.S. § 25-1-802, which concerns requests for client healthcare records. This Colorado law states that all healthcare providers except for mental health counselors must provide a complete set of records upon receipt of a signed, dated request from the client. However, when a request is made for mental health treatment records, a mental health professional may provide a treatment summary and not the psychotherapy notes and records maintained by the therapist.

The purpose of both the HIPAA Privacy Rule and this Colorado law is to protect against disclosure of information that may be extremely personal and private, and not pertinent to a request for records. Providing a treatment summary in compliance with these legal standards is consistent with another HIPAA standard. HIPAA requires that when therapists comply with requests for treatment information, they should supply the least amount of information needed to satisfy the request. This principle applies, for example, when an insurance company that is paying for client treatment asks for records to justify the need for counseling.

When a therapist receives a court order, however, requiring the disclosure of all treatment records in the therapist's possession, it means exactly that, and therapists are bound to comply with the court order, since doing so is a generally accepted standard of practice.

2.26 HIPAA Standards Concerning Authorizations to Disclose Confidential Health Information

The regulations adopted by HHS contain specific requirements for the inclusion of elements and statements used in professionals' forms to be signed by clients in authorizing the disclosure of confidential treatment information. According to 45 C.F.R. § 164.508(c), authorization forms must contain the following elements (along with any additional requirements required by state law):

- "A description of the information to be used or disclosed that identifies the information in a specific and meaningful fashion."
- "The name or other specific identification of the person(s), or class of persons, authorized to make the requested use or disclosure."
- "The name or other specific identification of the person(s), or class of persons, to whom the covered entity may make the requested use or disclosure."
- "A description of each purpose of the requested use or disclosure. The statement 'at the request of the individual' is a sufficient description of the purpose when an individual initiates the authorization and does not, or elects not to, provide a statement of the purpose."
- "An expiration date or an expiration event that relates to the individual or the purpose of the use or disclosure. The statement 'end of the research study,' 'none,' or similar language is sufficient if the authorization is for a use or disclosure of protected health information for research, including the creation and maintenance of a research database or research repository."
- "The signature of the individual and date. If the authorization is signed by a personal representative of the individual, a description of such representative's authority to act for the individual must also be provided."
- A statement adequate to place the individual on notice of the individual's right to revoke the authorization in writing, and either: (1) the exceptions to the right to revoke and a description of how the individual may revoke the authorization; or (2) to the extent that the information in (1) is included in the Notice of Privacy Practices, a reference to the covered entity's notice.

- A statement adequate to place the individual on notice of the ability or inability of the covered entity to condition treatment, payment, enrollment, or eligibility for benefits on the authorization, by stating either: (1) The covered entity may not condition treatment, payment, enrollment, or eligibility for benefits on whether the individual signs the authorization when the prohibition on conditioning of authorizations in the Privacy Regulation applies; or (2) the consequences to the individual of a refusal to sign the authorization when the covered entity can condition treatment, enrollment in the health plan, or eligibility for benefits on failure to obtain such authorization.
- A statement adequate to place the individual on notice of the potential for information disclosed pursuant to the authorization to be subject to re-disclosure by the recipient and no longer be protected by the rule.
- The authorization must be written in plain language.
- A copy must be given to the individual. If a covered entity seeks an authorization from an individual for a use or disclosure of protected health information, the covered entity must provide the individual with a copy of the signed authorization.
- If the authorization is for a marketing purpose that involves direct or indirect remuneration to the covered entity from a third party, the authorization must state that such remuneration is involved.

The statement that HIPAA-compliant authorizations for disclosure of treatment information "must be written in plain language" is ironic; if only the HIPAA regulations were written in plain and intelligible language!

The last element on this checklist for authorization forms is problematic. Professionals who seek testimonials from clients for marketing purposes, requiring them to obtain client authorization for this purpose, could easily be seen as exploiting the client for the benefit of the professional. A word to the wise: this is not a generally accepted practice among mental health professionals, and a licensing board might consider the use of client testimonials for marketing as a boundary violation.

2.27 Questions and Answers about HIPAA and Mental Health

The U.S. Department of Health and Human Services has published "Questions and Answers about HIPAA and Mental Health." The following FAQs and the responses are direct quotes from the website at https://www.hhs.gov/hipaa/for-professionals/special-topics/mental-health/index.html.

Questions and Answers about HIPAA and Mental Health

Question: Does HIPAA allow a health care provider to communicate with a patient's family, friends, or other persons who are involved in the patient's care?

"Yes. In recognition of the integral role that family and friends play in a patient's health care, the HIPAA Privacy Rule allows these routine—and often critical—communications between health care providers and these persons. Where a patient is present and has the capacity to make health care decisions, health care providers may communicate with a patient's family members, friends, or other persons the patient has involved in his or her health care or payment for care, *so long as the patient does not object*. [Emphasis added.] *See* 45 CFR 164.510(b). The provider may ask the patient's permission to share relevant information with family members or others, may tell the patient he or she plans to discuss the information and give them an opportunity to agree or object, or may infer from the circumstances, using professional judgment, that the patient does not object. A common example of the latter would be situations in which a family member or friend is invited by the patient and present in the treatment room with the patient and the provider when a disclosure is made.

* * *

"In all cases, disclosures to family members, friends, or other persons involved in the patient's care or payment for care are to be limited to only the protected health information directly relevant to the person's involvement in the patient's care or payment for care."

Best Practice: You should get written consent from a client before disclosing any treatment information to family and friends, notwithstanding the guidance from the U.S. Department of HHS. Also be certain to discuss with the client the basic information that you would provide to family members and friends regarding the client's situation, and obtain written consent from the client to do so.

Question: Does HIPAA provide extra protections for mental health information compared with other health information?

"Generally, the Privacy Rule, 45 C.F.R. § 164.524, applies uniformly to all protected health information, without regard to the type of information. One exception to this general rule is for psychotherapy notes, which receive special protections. The Privacy Rule defines psychotherapy notes as notes recorded by a health care provider who is a mental health professional documenting or analyzing the contents of a conversation during a private counseling session or a group, joint, or family counseling session and that are separate from the rest of the patient's medical record. . . .

"Psychotherapy notes are treated differently from other mental health information both because they contain particularly sensitive information and because they are the personal notes of the therapist that typically are not required or useful for treatment, payment, or health care operations purposes, other than by the mental health professional who created the notes. Therefore, with few exceptions, the Privacy Rule requires a covered entity to obtain a patient's authorization prior to a disclosure of psychotherapy notes for any reason, including a disclosure for treatment purposes to a health care provider other than the originator of the notes."

Question: Is a health care provider permitted to discuss an adult patient's mental health information with the patient's parents or other family members?

"In situations where the patient is given the opportunity and does not object, HIPAA allows the provider to share or discuss the patient's mental health information with family members or other persons involved in the patient's care or payment for care. For example if the patient does not object:

- "A psychiatrist may discuss the drugs a patient needs to take with the patient's sister who is present with the patient at a mental health care appointment.
- "A therapist may give information to a patient's spouse about warning signs that may signal a developing emergency.

"BUT:

- "A nurse may not discuss a patient's mental health condition with the patient's brother after the patient has stated she does not want her family to know about her condition.

"In all cases, the health care provider may share or discuss only the information that the person involved needs to know about the patient's care or payment for care. *See* 45 CFR 164.510(b). Finally, it is important to remember that other applicable law (e.g., State confidentiality statutes) or professional ethics may impose stricter limitations on sharing personal health information, particularly where the information relates to a patient's mental health."

Practice Pointer

Due to the fact that Colorado law constitutes a stricter standard than the HIPAA standard, therapists in Colorado must comply with state confidentiality and privilege statutes, maintaining the confidentiality of treatment information and only disclosing it in compliance with a client's written authorization for disclosure of specific treatment information to specific individuals.

Question: Does a parent have the right to receive a copy of psychotherapy notes about a child's mental health treatment?

"No. The Privacy Rule distinguishes between mental health information in a mental health professional's private notes and that contained in the medical record. It does not provide a right of access to psychotherapy notes, which the Privacy Rule defines as notes recorded by a health care provider who is a mental health professional documenting or analyzing the contents of a conversation during a private counseling session or a group, joint, or family counseling session and that are separate from the rest of the patient's medical record. *See* 45 CFR 164.501. Psychotherapy notes are primarily for personal use by the treating professional and generally are not disclosed for other purposes. . . . *See* 45 CFR 164.524(a)(1)(i).

"However, parents generally are the personal representatives of their minor child and, as such, are able to receive a copy of their child's mental health information contained in the medical record, including information about diagnosis, symptoms, treatment plans, etc. *Further, although the Privacy Rule does not provide a right for a patient or personal representative to access psychotherapy notes regarding the patient,* HIPAA generally gives providers discretion to disclose the individual's own protected health information (including psychotherapy notes) directly to the individual or to the individual's personal representative. [Emphasis added.] As any such disclosure is purely permissive under the Privacy Rule, mental health providers should consult applicable State law for any prohibitions or conditions before making such disclosures."

Question: Does HIPAA prevent a school administrator, or a school doctor or nurse, from sharing concerns about a student's mental health with the student's parents or law enforcement authorities?

"Student health information held by a school generally is subject to the Family Educational Rights and Privacy Act (FERPA), not HIPAA. HHS and the Department of Education have developed guidance clarifying the application of HIPAA and FERPA.

"In the limited circumstances where the HIPAA Privacy Rule, and not FERPA, may apply to health information in the school setting, the Rule allows disclosures to parents of a minor patient or to law enforcement in various situations. For example, parents generally are presumed to be the personal representatives of their unemancipated minor child for HIPAA privacy purposes, such that covered entities may disclose the minor's protected health information to a parent. *See* 45 CFR 164.502(g)(3). In addition, disclosures to prevent or lessen serious and imminent threats to the health or safety of the patient or others are permitted for notification to those who are able to lessen the threat, including law enforcement, parents or others, as relevant. *See* 45 CFR 164.512(j)."

Practice Pointer

School counselors should consult the school's legal counsel to obtain legal advice concerning the application of FERPA to any release of mental health information to family members.

2.28 Preparing a Professional Will: Protecting Clients and Their Treatment Information After a Therapist's Retirement, Disability, or Death

State licensing board rules and ethical codes for mental health professionals are beginning to require therapists to appoint an executor for their professional estate so that arrangements can be made for the proper disposition of client records or for the referral of clients in the event of a therapist's retirement, disability, or death. The American Association for Marriage and Family Therapy (AAMFT) Code of Ethics Principle 2.5 provides, "Subsequent to the therapist moving from the area, closing the practice, or upon the death of the therapist, a marriage and family therapist arranges for the storage, transfer, or disposal of client records in ways that maintain confidentiality and safeguard the welfare of clients." In Ohio, mental health counselors applying for or renewing their license must identify the professional executor who has been appointed to wind up a therapist's practice in the event of death or disability. Just as estate planning is important so that an individual's property can be disposed of through a will, which designates an executor to carry out the provisions of the will, mental health professionals are being required or encouraged to designate another therapist to be the executor of their professional estate.

Currently, a need exists for counselors in private practice to make appropriate arrangements to avoid the prospect that family members will be going through dusty old boxes of client files, found in a corner of the garage, after a therapist has died. Just as a therapist making plans for retirement should make arrangements for appropriate storage and disposition of client records, payment of bills, collection of fees, and referral of clients to ensure continuity of care, all private practitioners should also make basic contingency plans to protect clients' interests and the privacy of their treatment information in the event of a counselor's incapacity or death.

Practical Considerations

Form 6 in Appendix A is a form to use in creating a professional will. This form is adapted from a template created by the San Diego Psychological Association for use by mental health professionals. In reviewing the form professional will, you will see that a great deal of the information to be included in the document concerns logistical information, such as the location of bank accounts, account numbers for any business accounts, the location of keys for your office, and passwords for access to office computers or voice mail. The professional will is like a power of attorney, in that it grants authority to the professional executor to conduct business, as needed, and to close a therapist's practice. A HIPAA Business Associate Contract should be signed by the professional executor, agreeing to maintain confidentiality of all treatment information to which the professional executor will have access. The therapist's personal will needs to reference the fact that a professional will has been created, so that the personal representative of the therapist's estate can coordinate activities with the professional executor, and grant authority to the professional executor to transact business in the event of a therapist's death.

The first step is to select a colleague who would be entrusted with the responsibility for winding up your practice and either taking over your caseload or making referrals, as needed. You should determine that this colleague is willing to serve as the executor of your professional estate. In making these arrangements, you may want to reciprocate and agree to be the executor for your colleague. So that confidential treatment information may be shared with the executor in the event of an emergency, you should have the professional executor sign a HIPAA Business Associate Contract. By signing this contract, the business associate agrees to maintain clients' records and confidential treatment information appropriately within the scope of the therapist-client privilege. Then a power of attorney form should be filled out to convey to the executor the authority to take care of business matters.

The next step is to prepare a professional will, which directs the executor as to his or her duties in the event of your death or disability. The professional will need not be legalistic, nor does it require specific language. It can simply begin with the statement, "I hereby appoint my trusted professional colleague, Jane Designee, to be the executor of my professional estate." The professional will then would detail the duties to be performed and the information needed for performance of those duties.

The will should contain an appropriate checklist of matters that would require the executor's attention, such as paying any business debts, collecting fees owed by clients, providing appropriate notice to clients concerning the therapist's unavailability, and at the same time providing information to clients concerning who to contact for a referral or for continuity of care. The logistics involved in providing the executor with information and access to business records, client files, and computers require. the therapist to make the following available to the executor: (1) keys to the office and to file cabinets; (2) passwords for computers and e-mail accounts; and (3) the location of appointment calendars, billing records, client files, mailboxes, and bank accounts, along with the information specifically needed to access bank accounts, voice mail, and storage areas containing client records that have been securely stored off-site. Obviously this is a thorough planning process. We can all understand that this process is extremely important for the sake of clients to ensure continuity of care, so that no client is abandoned in the event of an emergency.

What provisions does a therapist's professional will contain? It will contain all of the logistical information described above and any additional information concerning office staff or billing clerks who can help an executor perform all these duties. It would be advisable to attach to the professional will the business associate contract and the power of attorney forms discussed above. Then the will and its attachments can be given to the professional executor for safekeeping, to use in the event that it is needed. A website that provides practical information regarding the logistics involved in the contingency planning process is www.psychotherapy.net, which posts an excellent article by Ann Steiner, Ph.D., entitled, "The Empty Chair: Making Our Absence Less Traumatic for Everyone."

2.29 Closing Your Practice

As discussed in the preceding section, a professional will enables therapists to dispose of client treatment records and make arrangements for transition of clients' care in the event of a therapist's death or disability. When mental health professionals are retiring and closing their practice, arrangements must be made to safeguard treatment records and to plan for the continuity of care for both current and former clients, who may need services in the future.

1. Notification to Current Clients

Provide current clients with a written notification regarding the fact that you will be closing your practice and providing current clients with referrals to other therapists. Give the client this written notification approximately 60 days before the closing of the practice, and include in it the names and contact information for therapists to whom you will be referring clients. Of course, you can provide guidance to each individual client in terms of a therapist whose area of specialty and professional experience would be appropriate for the client, who will be transitioned.

2. Client Records

As current clients are being transitioned to new therapists, you can offer to provide a copy of your file to the new therapist. In order to do this, you will need a signed authorization for disclosure of treatment information, signed by the client, authorizing you to provide the client's clinical records to a specific therapist, in order to facilitate continuity of care. The same signed authorization should enable you to consult with the new therapist, in order to provide your insights concerning the client's treatment needs and current problems.

3. Retention of Client Records

Keep a copy of all client records that you may be providing to your client's new therapist. In Colorado, records must be kept for a specific period of time, depending on your regulatory board's record-keeping rule. You must continue to maintain the security of all records that you will be storing by keeping them in locked file cabinets. This will include, of course, the records of former clients, who may contact you at some time in order to obtain treatment information or records for various purposes.

4. Maintaining Contact Information

It is a good idea to keep your office telephone number, unless a new therapist is going to take over your practice, your office, and your phone line. By keeping your office telephone number, you will be able to transition former clients who call because they need treatment, records, or other information.

Keeping your professional e-mail would provide the same opportunity for you to be contacted by those former clients who have used e-mail in the past to schedule appointments. This would enable you to make referrals of former clients to a new therapist, or to send to the former client the same notification letter that you provided to your current clients before closing your practice.

5. Insurance

Notify your professional liability insurance carrier that you are closing your practice before you do so. The insurer may offer you "tail" coverage, which would prevent your malpractice coverage from lapsing and should cover you for future claims arising from the provision of services prior to the closing of your practice.

6. Contracts with Insurance Panels or Referral Services

If you have contracts to provide services through insurance panels or contracts with referral services, review those contracts and any clauses concerning termination of the contract. Comply with the contractual provisions regarding termination, so that you can inform the health insurer or referral service that you are closing your practice and will not be accepting any future referrals. As a professional courtesy, inform any doctors, therapists, colleagues, or individuals who have provided referrals of clients to you in the past regarding the fact that you will be closing your practice so that you can thank them all for the referrals that you have received and notify them that you are not going to be accepting new referrals.

7. Consultations Regarding the Closing of Your Practice

In order to ensure that you are complying with all ethical and legal standards, consult with a professional colleague or an attorney who specializes in health law to ensure that you are complying with all clinical, ethical, and legal requirements. For example, if you have set up a corporation, under which you practice, confer with the attorney or accountant who set up this corporation to determine what you may need to do, either to maintain the corporation or to terminate it.

Complying with the process discussed above will enable you to comply with clinical and ethical best practices for the coordination of care for your clients as you are closing your practice.

2.30 Colorado Law Regarding D&N Cases

In January 2013, the Colorado Supreme Court issued a decision in L.A.N. v. L.M.B., 292 P.3d 942 (Colo. 2013), in which the court ruled that a guardian *ad litem* (GAL), appointed by the court in a dependency and neglect (D&N) case, holds the privilege for children who have been removed from their parents' custody and whose custody has been transferred to the Department of Human Services (DHS). In the past, the DHS caseworker was the individual who held the privilege for children in the custody of DHS, so that the caseworker, not the children's parents, had the authority to consent to treatment or to authorize the release of treatment information. In its decision, the Colorado Supreme Court noted that in every D&N case, the court is required to appoint a GAL for the parties' children.

The role of the GAL in a D&N case is to represent the family's children and to make recommendations to the court concerning their best interests. In ruling that the GAL holds the privilege for children involved in a D&N case who are in the custody of DHS, the supreme court specifically ordered that the GAL is the individual best situated to make decisions concerning release of the children's treatment information. As the privilege holder for children, it is the GAL who now has the authority to select treatment providers for children in the custody of DHS, not the caseworker. So, the GAL would need to sign the Client Disclosure Statement for treatment.

Already, questions are being posed regarding this supreme court decision and its application. For example, if a GAL in a D&N case sends a signed Release of Information (ROI) form to you seeking treatment records from your child client, you should provide the same information in response that you would ordinarily provide to a parent who is requesting a child's treatment record: a treatment summary in compliance with HIPAA standards and C.R.S. § 25-1-802. The reason for this is that most GALs will share any treatment records with attorneys for other parties in the D&N case, which may foreseeably result in harm to the child.

Keep in mind that if you are providing services to children involved in a D&N case, possibly under a contract with DHS, and if you are subpoenaed to testify in court at a hearing to determine an appropriate treatment plan for family members, to determine if parental rights should be terminated, or to determine an appropriate placement for the children, you will need the consent of the GAL/privilege holder, in writing, in order to testify and disclose treatment information at the hearing.

To clarify, this ruling by the Colorado Supreme Court only applies to D&N cases where children have been removed from parents' custody and where custody has been transferred to DHS. It does not apply to divorce or custody actions in which the court may have appointed a GAL or a Child Legal Representative (CLR).

2.31 Service Animals

In 2016, the Colorado General Assembly passed a law making it a crime if a person intentionally misrepresents that he or she is entitled to a service animal or that a pet is a service animal or an assistance animal, when the individual knows that is not true. *See* C.R.S. § 18-13-107.3.

Definitions of Service Animal and Assistance Animal

The term "service animal" is defined as "a dog or miniature horse trained to do work or perform tasks for the benefit of an individual with a disability and whose work or task is directly related to the individual's disability. Under the law, the provision of emotional support, well-being, comfort, or companionship does not constitute the work or tasks of a service animal." An "assistance animal" is defined under the Federal Fair Housing Act as an animal, such as a cat, dog, or other type of companion animal, which provides emotional support or comfort, as well as physical benefits from the animal living in the home. In general, a letter from a medical doctor or therapist is all that is needed to classify the animal as an assistance animal. The Federal Fair Housing Act, 42 U.S.C. § 3601 provides that landlords need to make reasonable accommodations to tenants by allowing them to possess an assistance animal in order to accommodate a tenant's mental health needs. In addition, the Air Carrier Access Act applies to persons with disabilities who are traveling with a service animal or with an emotional support animal.

Whenever a customer brings an animal that is represented to be a service animal into a public accommodation, only two questions are allowed to be asked of the customer in order to protect the privacy of individuals with disabilities: (1) Is the dog or miniature horse a service animal required because of a disability; and (2) What work or task has the dog or miniature horse been trained to perform?

Therapists' Duties Relating to Assistance Animals

C.R.S. § 12-245-229 authorizes mental health professionals to make a finding regarding whether an individual has a disability and whether, as a result of the disability, that person needs an assistance animal. This statute provides that a therapist

> who is approached by a patient seeking an assistance animal as a reasonable accommodation in housing shall either: (a) make a written finding regarding whether the patient has a disability and, if a disability is found, a separate written finding regarding whether the need for the animal is related to that disability; or (b) make a written finding that there is insufficient information available to make a finding regarding disability or the disability-related need for the animal.

This statute further provides that the therapist shall not make any determination unless the therapist: "(a) [h]as met with the patient in person; (b) [i]s sufficiently familiar with the patient and the disability; and (c) [i]s legally and professionally qualified to make the determination." Medical doctors are also authorized to make the same determinations according to C.R.S. § 12-240-144, contained in the Medical Practice Act.

The term "disability" in this statute is defined under the Americans with Disabilities Act as a temporary or permanent "physical or mental impairment that substantially limits one or more major life activities." 42 U.S.C. § 12102.

2.32 Advance Directives for Behavioral Health Care

On March 28, 2019, Gov. Polis signed a law, HB 19-1044, which established "behavioral health orders for scope of treatment" (Advance Directives for Behavioral Health Care) by adding a Part 2 to Title 15, article 18.7, C.R.S. This law requires that health care providers, including all mental health professionals, comply with Advance Directives for behavioral (mental health) care signed by an adult client. These directives may limit the scope of treatment; express a preference not to take specific medication; or express a preference not to receive alternative treatment. An exception to this requirement exists if compliance with the behavioral health orders "will cause substantial harm to the adult," to emergency medical service personnel, to the health care provider, or to others at a health care facility. Other exceptions include an Advance Directive that "exempts the adult from an involuntary emergency procedure or commitment", such as a 72-hour hold for hospital evaluation and treatment. In addition, an Advance Directive does not compel or authorize a care provider to administer treatment or medication that is prohibited by State or Federal law.

Immunity exists for any professional "authorized to perform an involuntary emergency procedure or commitment" who complies with the requirements of the emergency procedure or commitment, so that the treatment provider "is not subject to civil or criminal liability or regulatory sanction." The patient cannot sue the provider and any regulatory board complaint must be dismissed.

The law further provides that the adult can assign an agent, who may be authorized to enforce the behavioral orders, or who may receive power of attorney to make health care decisions for the adult. An Advance Directive is in effect for two years, unless it is revoked or renewed.

What are the duties of a mental health professional in order to comply with HB 19-1044 (C.R.S. §§ 15-18.7-201, *et seq.*)? The following protocols discuss recommended procedures for therapists to follow and detail specific requirements of the law.

2.33 Protocols for Compliance with HB 19-1044

At the initial session with an adult client, ask: "Do you have an Advance Directive for Behavioral Health Care?" If the client asks, "What is that?" then respond: "It is a document that anyone can write up which states their preferences for behavioral health treatment."

If the client responds, "No," then document the fact that this question was asked and the adult client answered "No." If the client answers, "Yes," then request a copy of the Advance Directive and ask the client, "Have you appointed an agent to assist you in this process?" Document this discussion and if the client has appointed an agent, record the contact information for that person, and have the client sign a Release (ROI) for the agent to provide you with a copy of the Advance Directive; and have the client sign a ROI for you to discuss treatment information with the agent. Follow up by contacting the agent and informing that person of the fact that you are a therapist, providing mental health treatment to the client. Provide copies of the ROIs signed by the client to the agent, and ask the agent for a copy of the Advance Directive for Behavioral Health Care and get a copy of the paperwork signed by the client appointing the agent, so you can determine the agent's powers and authority. Also, ask the agent to inform you if any change is made in the future to the directives.

Review the Advance Directive when it is provided, and ensure that it complies with Colorado law. It must be witnessed by two people who are "disinterested witnesses"; *i.e.*, individuals who are not related by blood or marriage to the client, are not heirs of the client; and can attest that the adult client was "of sound mind and free of coercion when the client signed the Advance Directive."

You should discuss the Advance Directive with the client to ensure that you understand its meaning. If you can, assure the client that you will comply with the treatment preferences made in the orders. If substantial harm to the client will occur, then you should "make a good faith effort to consult with the client's agent, if applicable, and offer an alternative course of treatment."

If the client indicates that they refuse behavioral health care and will not consent to individual counseling or group therapy, the client's right to refuse treatment must be respected. If treatment is court-ordered, *e.g.*, in a criminal case or dependency and neglect action, then inform the client that advice should be sought from their attorney regarding the consequences which might result from refusing to comply with a court order for treatment.

Chapter 3: Testifying as an Expert

Psychotherapists are often called to testify about their knowledge or opinion of their clients. When this occurs, what can a psychotherapist expect to occur in the process of testifying? What is expert witness testimony? Is there a right to compensation for the time involved in preparing for and actually testifying? Who is responsible for paying that compensation? What happens in a deposition? What happens at trial? What rights does a witness have? The answers to these and other questions are set forth in this chapter.

3.01 Expert Witness Testimony

In general, an expert is a person who possesses special knowledge, skill, education, experience, or training in a particular field. This broad definition certainly encompasses most psychiatrists, psychologists, social workers, professional counselors, marriage and family therapists, and other mental health workers.

Rule 702 of the Colorado Rules of Evidence sets forth the admissibility of expert witness testimony as follows:

> If scientific, technical, or other specialized knowledge will assist the trier of fact to understand the evidence or to determine a fact in issue, a witness qualified as an expert by knowledge, skill, experience, training, or education, may testify thereto in the form of an opinion or otherwise.

3.02 Offered Testimony Must Be Helpful

Rule 702 requires that the court first determine whether there is a need for expert witness testimony. Thus, before a psychotherapist can testify in a trial, the court must be convinced that the testimony will help the jury or the judge to understand some factual issue in dispute.

In *People v. Beaver*, 725 P.2d 96 (Colo. App. 1986), the court excluded the testimony of a psychologist concerning certain factors that affect eyewitness testimony. A similar ruling excluding the testimony of a psychotherapist was made in *People v. Campbell*, 785 P.2d 153 (Colo. App. 1989). In these two cases, the courts determined that such testimony from a psychologist was not helpful in resolving issues, since such factors were within the realm of a juror's everyday experience.

The requirement that psychological testimony be helpful to the trier of fact was reiterated in *People v. Lomanaco*, 802 P.2d 1143 (Colo. App. 1990). In this case, the court excluded psychological testimony on the issue of irresistible impulse and heat of passion, since such issues were found to be within the experience of average laypersons.

Although the foregoing cases suggest that the testimony of psychotherapists may not be deemed helpful to the trier of fact, this is generally not the case. In practice, the courts are interested in the opinions and insights of such professionals, particularly in adoption, juvenile, child custody, mental competence, and emotional distress cases.

For example, in *People v. District Court*, 647 P.2d 1206 (Colo. 1982), the Colorado Supreme Court held that a psychiatrist could testify to the incompetence of a witness based on a review of a videotaped testimony of the witness. Also reflective of this practice are the following cases that hold that rape counselors, social workers, and others may qualify as experts, despite the fact that their testimony may be limited by application of other rules: *Farley v. People*, 746 P.2d 956 (Colo. 1987); *People v. Hampton*, 746 P.2d 947 (Colo. 1987); *People v. Snook*, 745 P.2d 647 (Colo. 1987); and *People v. Koon*, 724 P.2d 1367 (Colo. App. 1986).

In further recognition of this practice, one should note that an expert may not give an opinion on whether another witness is being truthful. *People v. Guilbeaux*, 761 P.2d 255 (Colo. App. 1988). However, according to *People v. Deninger*, 772 P.2d 674 (Colo. App. 1989), psychologists have been allowed to testify regarding the capacity of a child to fabricate sex abuse claims. *People v. Mathes*, 703 P.2d 608 (Colo. App. 1985); *People v. Koon*, 713 P.2d 410 (Colo. App. 1985); and *People v. Ashley*, 687 P.2d 473 (Colo. App. 1984).

In *People v. Gillispie*, 767 P.2d 778 (Colo. App. 1988), the Colorado Court of Appeals held that in sexual assault situations, especially where a child is very young, an opinion by a psychologist as to credibility of the witness is admissible if the testimony relates to general characteristics only.

The foregoing cases were preceded by *People v. Ortega*, 672 P.2d 215 (Colo. App. 1983), which held that the trial court erred by admitting the testimony of a clinical psychologist that a child sexual assault victim was not fabricating the incident. This case seems to conflict with those cited above. A reasonable legal prognosis is that psychotherapists will not be allowed to testify concerning the credibility of a witness or of a victim's account.

3.03 Qualifying as an Expert

Once the court has determined that expert witness testimony from a psychiatrist, psychologist, social worker, counselor, or other psychotherapist would be helpful to the trier of fact, the witness must qualify as an expert by convincing the court that he or she has the knowledge, skill, experience, training, or education to be an expert in the particular field.

This process involves the expert's recitation of his or her credentials, which should include, but not be limited to, the following:

1. Academic degrees by year, field of study, and granting institution(s);
2. Academic honors;
3. Publications by title, year of publication, and publisher;
4. Relevant professional history, stressing work related to the anticipated testimony;
5. Affiliations with relevant professional associations;
6. Licenses held, by date of issuance and body granting such licenses;
7. Professional honors;
8. Speaking appearances on topics in the field of expertise; and
9. Prior qualifications as an expert witness in other trials.

It is important that the credentials be presented in a manner that is forthright and professional. This is not the time to be humble. On the other hand, one must not become self-absorbed and egotistical. Do not forget that if a psychotherapist is testifying to a jury, it is likely that his or her qualifications and educational background will exceed those of the average juror. The psychotherapist must not alienate the jury with his or her qualifications, but must convince them that he or she is qualified and has opinions that are reasonable and consistent with all the known facts.

3.04 Types of Testimony

The testimony of a psychotherapist can be divided into three classes. First, it may relate solely to the psychotherapist's personal firsthand observations of the client, which would include events witnessed by the therapist and statements made directly to the therapist by the client. Second, it may relate solely to the psychotherapist's opinion of the mental status of the client or some other opinion, such as the therapist's assessment of the client or treatment recommendations. Third, the testimony may involve both first-hand observations and expert opinions.

Rules 702 and 704 of the Colorado Rules of Evidence specifically allow all three types of expert witness testimony from psychotherapists. However, if the case is a federal criminal matter governed by the Federal Rules of Evidence, then FRE 704(b) does not allow a psychotherapist to testify with respect to whether the defendant had the mental state or condition constituting an element of the crime charged or a defense to it. The Colorado courts do not follow this federal restriction, and psychotherapists are allowed to render opinions on the ultimate issue in a case according to CRE 704.

3.05 Basis of Testimony

What can a psychotherapist's expert witness testimony be based upon? Rule 703 of the Colorado Rules of Evidence provides the answer as follows:

> The facts or data in the particular case upon which an expert bases an opinion or inference may be those perceived by or made known to the expert at or before the hearing. If of a type reasonably relied upon by experts in the particular field in forming opinions or inferences upon the subject, the facts or data need not be admissible in evidence. . . .

This rule allows a psychotherapist to base his or her opinion testimony on facts or data gathered from a variety of sources. Consequently, the psychotherapist is not limited to his or her own personal observations of the client.

Additionally, if the facts or data used by the psychotherapist are of a type reasonably relied upon by other experts in the field, then such facts themselves need not be admissible in evidence.

Under this rule, a psychotherapist may base his or her opinion on the following:

1. Personal observations of the client or subject;
2. Reports of other professionals who examined the client or subject;
3. Results of professional tests administered by the mental health professional or others;
4. Reports of family members, close friends, co-workers, etc., of the client or subject, provided such are customarily relied upon by other experts;
5. Sworn testimony of the client or subject or others;
6. Facts made known to him or her, at or before the hearing, which may include briefings by counsel, review of depositions, written interrogatories, and other information;

7. Opinions of other experts; and
8. Professional and academic literature, such as surveys, reports, books, learned treatises, articles, etc.

3.06 Disclosure of Underlying Facts or Data

Rule 705 of the Colorado Rules of Evidence allows an expert witness to testify in terms of opinion or inference and give the reasons therefor without prior disclosure of the underlying facts or data unless the court requires otherwise. However, Rule 705 does require disclosure of such facts and data upon cross-examination.

This rule no longer requires the expert to lay out at trial all of the facts and data that were used in developing his or her opinion. Thus, an expert may simply testify as to his or her opinion and the reasons for it.

Generally, the lawyer calling the expert witness will decide whether it is advisable to disclose all of the facts and data before the opinion is rendered. However, the expert witness should be prepared to reveal all of the facts and data upon which he or she relied during cross-examination. Further, the expert should offer his or her opinions to the lawyer regarding whether such prior disclosure aids in the effective presentation of his or her opinion at trial.

3.07 Being Retained

Psychotherapists become involved in lawsuits as experts in a variety of ways. Some have developed a reputation in a particular area and are frequently called upon by lawyers to review a case and render an opinion. For example, many psychologists and licensed therapists perform custody evaluations and are hired by a lawyer seeking such an evaluation for his or her client. Psychiatrists and psychologists are frequently involved in issues of criminal insanity and competency to stand trial and are sought out by criminal defense lawyers or prosecutors.

Psychotherapists also become involved as experts when their own clients are litigants and there is an issue as to the client's emotional or mental health. In such cases, the psychotherapist is usually contacted by the lawyer for the client and asked for his or her input regarding the specific issue. If the lawyer believes the opinion of the therapist would be helpful to the case, the lawyer will not hesitate to call the therapist at trial. This of course will result in a waiver of the therapist-client confidentiality privilege. Any authorization for disclosure of treatment information, authorizing courtroom testimony by a client's therapist, should authorize disclosure to all persons present in court, as well as all persons who may review a transcript of the testimony.

Regardless of how or why the psychotherapist becomes involved, there are certain aspects of the involvement that should immediately be clarified by the psychotherapist. These include the following:

1. The client should sign a specific release prior to any substantive discussions with any third party.
2. An understanding should be reached between the psychotherapist, client, and lawyer as to the handling of the psychotherapist's fees. For example, is the psychotherapist to look to the client for payment of his or her expert witness fees, or to the lawyer? Is an advance payment required by the psychotherapist? If so, how much? How is the fee to be determined and when is it due and payable?
3. The understanding regarding fees should be reduced to writing by the psychotherapist and signed by the client, lawyer, and psychotherapist.
4. The understanding regarding fees should include a recital of what is expected from the psychotherapist in terms of consultation, written reports, participation in depositions, and trial testimony.
5. An understanding should be reached with the lawyer as to how to handle inquiries from the opposing counsel and others involved in the litigation.

It is the responsibility of all parties to see that the foregoing items are covered. If the lawyer fails to initiate a conversation regarding these items, the psychotherapist should do so in the first conversation. For some reason, people are reluctant to discuss such matters, and assumptions are frequently made that ultimately prove to be in error. Hence, it is the better practice to confirm all business matters in writing.

Most expert witnesses are compensated at an hourly rate that is set by them. Occasionally, a witness will render his or her services for a flat fee. It is always prudent to request an advance retainer for services to be performed. Most competent and successful attorneys follow this practice, and there is no reason why a psychotherapist who has been retained as an expert should not similarly expect such treatment.

3.08 Preparing a Report

On occasion, a lawyer will request a written report from the psychotherapist regarding various aspects of his or her testimony. There is no standard format for these reports, since the contents are dictated by the needs and the particular circumstances of the case.

An attorney should make a verbal request for the report and review in detail the specific information that he or she needs to have covered in the report. This verbal request is not an attempt to dictate an opinion, but rather is simply a means of communicating what the report should cover. For example, in an evaluation of parental responsibilities and parenting time in a domestic case, there are certain statutory issues a court must consider. A good lawyer will request that the evaluation address each of the specific issues. In a case involving emotional damages, the lawyer's request will typically ask for the following kinds of information: patient background, social history, treatment history, diagnosis, prognosis, and estimated cost of future treatment.

The verbal request for a report should be confirmed in writing by the attorney. If this is not done, the psychotherapist should confirm that the lawyer has made the request for the report.

A good lawyer will want to discuss the contents of the report prior to its finalization in writing. This is typically done to ensure that the expert will cover all the required areas of analysis. If this is done, it avoids the necessity of a follow-up report covering areas that were missed.

At times, an expert will feel subtle pressure from the attorney to provide a specific opinion. Lawyers are very skilled at leading witnesses and planting ideas that may not have been there in the first place. A psychotherapist should understand that this may happen and that such efforts by the lawyer should not be allowed to influence his or her ultimate opinion. A competent lawyer will respect an expert's independence, even though disappointment, anger, or frustration may be expressed over the report. But the expert's reputation in the field may be enhanced because other lawyers and judges will come to know that expert as one whose integrity is intact and whose opinion cannot be compromised.

If a psychotherapist has been appointed by the court and is not working for a particular attorney, care should be taken to avoid any appearance of impropriety or bias. The final report should be written and distributed without disclosing its contents prior to distribution. Also, it is an excellent idea to require payment for the report prior to distribution. At times, a disgruntled litigant has been known to refuse to pay for a report once it has been issued.

3.09 Deposition Practice

A deposition is a proceeding that occurs outside of the courtroom whereby one party has the right to interrogate a witness under oath in order to determine what the witness's testimony will be at trial. The attendance of the witness and the production of certain documents can be compelled through subpoena. A court reporter is present and records the entire proceeding.

If any party to a lawsuit wants to depose a psychotherapist, a written agreement should be reached regarding who will pay for the expert's time for preparing, testifying, reading, and verifying the transcribed testimony. The expert should contact his or her client's attorney and seek clarification of this issue.

Typically, it is the opposing side that is responsible for compensating the expert for his or her time in preparing, testifying, and reading the deposition. To avoid controversy regarding this matter, the psychotherapist should obtain clarification from both sides in writing.

Many medical practitioners require that their depositions be taken in their own offices. This is probably a good idea for psychotherapists, provided the office will accommodate the group.

There are several ground rules that should be followed in a deposition. Most lawyers will meet with their own expert prior to the deposition to review these practice tips and anticipated questions. The following are standard instructions given to all witnesses prior to a deposition.

1. A witness takes an oath to tell the truth. Therefore, tell the truth. Do not lie or stretch the truth.
2. Listen carefully to each question that is asked.
3. Think about the answer before responding.
4. Answer only the question that is asked.
5. Do not volunteer any information, even if you think it would be helpful.
6. If you do not understand a question, ask that it be rephrased or terms defined.
7. Never argue with the person asking the question. Simply respond and move along.
8. Ask to take a break when you become tired or need to take care of some other human need, or if you would like to consult with an attorney before responding.
9. Your answers must be verbal. Head nodding or head shaking cannot be recorded by the reporter.
10. Use your notes and refer to the client file in order to be precise in your recollection.

11. Remain calm and take your time.

After the first attorney has completed his or her questioning, the other attorney has the opportunity to ask questions to defend or rehabilitate the witness. Again, listen to the questions carefully and follow the same ground rules.

When the deposition is completed, the court reporter will ask if you would like to waive signature of the deposition. This means that it will be filed directly with the court, without the expert having read it and been given the opportunity to correct mistakes. Never waive signature, even if the attorneys are agreeable to doing so. It is your right to insist that the transcription be verified, and to be paid for the time you spend in reviewing the transcript.

In a few weeks or days, you will receive the transcription of the testimony. It should be carefully reviewed and any errors noted on a correction page. You should request from the lawyer who hired you that you be given a copy for your records. If you have to testify at trial, you will definitely need to review your deposition testimony before you take the stand. Opposing counsel will have abstracted your deposition and will be eagerly waiting for you to contradict yourself at trial. Hence, it is a cardinal rule that you know what you have previously said under oath.

Frequently, at the deposition, a demand will be made for the psychotherapist to produce and allow photocopying of the client file. Generally, this is not favorably received. However, if a subpoena *duces tecum* has been served upon the witness and a protective order has not been obtained, there is little legal justification for withholding the file. Chapter 2 outlines the problems encountered with such disclosure. If copies are requested, the psychotherapist should make the copies. Do not simply turn the file over to someone else for this task. Keep a record of how many copies were made and to whom they were distributed. A reasonable photocopying fee may be charged for this service.

A witness who has been subpoenaed to a deposition has the right to be represented by counsel of his or her own choosing and at his or her expense. Generally, this right is not exercised where the expert is working under a retainer. However, there are cases in which a psychotherapist has been subpoenaed and questions of privilege have not been previously resolved. In such situations, it is wise to retain an attorney immediately and to have him or her present at the deposition.

3.10 Preparation for Trial

The most important aspect of testifying at a trial or hearing is adequate and thorough preparation of the testimony. This should involve (at a minimum) the following:

1. A review of the client file.
2. A review of any deposition testimony given by the expert.
3. A review of any written reports prepared by the expert.
4. Preparation of an outline of what the expected testimony will be.
5. A face-to-face meeting with the attorney at least one day prior to the trial, at which time the testimony will be finalized and rehearsed.
6. Reaching an agreement with the attorney regarding the time the expert should arrive, and the location at which the expert is to appear.
7. Reaching an understanding with the attorney as to any special dress requirements.

Each of the foregoing items is crucial to the effective presentation of trial testimony. The attorney is only as good as the expert who testifies. The first step in presenting persuasive trial testimony is to devote whatever time it takes to know the testimony inside and out. Hence, the psychotherapist's priority should be to prepare himself or herself as thoroughly as possible, in accordance with the items outlined above.

The next step is to organize the testimony in such a way that it can be presented in a clear, cogent, and convincing manner. The attorney is ultimately responsible for this task. However, most good trial lawyers appreciate input from the expert and will seek this out in the face-to-face meeting. The demands of trial work often dictate that the lawyer talk briefly with the expert on the phone or outside the courtroom just prior to trial. This is not a good practice and should be discouraged by the expert. The expert needs to have a road map of the testimony so that the attorney and the expert complement each other during trial. The only way to do this is by preparation and rehearsal.

The notion that testimony should be rehearsed may seem strange to some people. However, the practice of rehearsing simply involves the lawyer's questioning of the expert outside the courtroom, and the expert's answering of those questions as if he or she were actually in the courtroom. This provides both the attorney and the expert with a mental image of how the interrogation will go in the courtroom, as well as an opportunity to rephrase questions or answers in order to develop better timing and pacing of the testimony.

The psychotherapist should ask the lawyer for any suggestions regarding the appropriate dress at trial. This may seem odd to some professionals. However, the frequency of inappropriately dressed experts suggests that not enough attention is paid to this matter when preparing for trial.

Each lawyer and expert will have to decide for themselves the specifics of the dress requirement. However, some general rules are as follows:

1. The traditional business or professional look for both men and women is encouraged. Dark blues, tans, and beige seem to be most appropriate. Busy prints should be avoided.
2. Avoid clothing, jewelry, and makeup that tend to bring attention to the expert. The courtroom is not a place to set and establish fashion trends.

3.11 On the Witness Stand

When called as a witness, your name will be announced and at that time you should rise and walk toward the witness stand. The court clerk or judge will direct you to raise your right hand and ask you if you will swear or affirm to tell the truth. The appropriate response is, "I do." You will then be told to be seated in the witness box or stand.

If you have not been given any directions to the contrary, feel free to take your file and notes with you. You should try to testify without referring to your file; however, this is not always possible, and you should not hesitate to look at your file to refresh your memory. You may not read your testimony into the court record. It should be your own words, formed by you from your memory, after examining your file.

Adhere to the following rules when answering questions from attorneys:

1. Always tell the truth. Do not lie or stretch the truth.
2. Listen carefully to each question that is asked.
3. Think about the answer before responding.
4. Don't be evasive.
5. If you are presented with a yes or no question and you think it cannot be answered that way, tell the lawyer that such a question is hard to answer in that fashion and try to explain. If you are cut off and are given an ultimatum, don't argue. Your choices are to answer the questions with a yes or no, or simply restate that you cannot give a yes or no answer. If the lawyer persists, ask the judge for direction. Follow the judge's ruling.
6. Answer only the question that was asked.

7. Don't volunteer any information, even if you think it would be helpful.
8. If you do not understand a question, ask that it be rephrased or terms defined.
9. Never argue with the person asking the question. Simply respond and move along.
10. Your answers must be verbal. Head nodding or head shaking cannot be recorded by the reporter.
11. Speak slowly and deliberately.
12. Remain calm and take your time.
13. When answering a question, alternately look at the judge, jury, and the attorney doing the interrogation. Establish eye contact with each of these people.
14. Avoid technical or scientific jargon. If you must use such terminology, explain the concept in lay terms.
15. Don't hesitate to use a flip chart or blackboard to explain your testimony.
16. Remember, your goal is to persuade the judge or jury, not to impress them with how much you know. Consequently, don't adopt a superior or egotistical attitude.
17. When asked about your credentials, follow the guidelines described in section 3.03 of this book.

After your direct testimony by the lawyer who called you, the opposing side has the right to cross-examine you. This can be stressful, since the opposing counsel's job is to discredit you and your testimony. You must not take any cross-examination personally. You must suppress your feelings of pride and ego, and simply answer the questions as best you can while following the ground rules described above. Most experts get into trouble when they try to argue with an attorney, or when their emotions take over and they become defensive. Do not let this happen to you. If you understand the process, have done your homework, and follow the rules set forth earlier, you should be able to withstand any cross-examination.

Once the cross-examination has been completed, the attorney who called you as a witness has the opportunity to engage in re-direct examination. This involves questioning you about the areas brought up in the cross-examination. If the attorney has adequately prepared your testimony, he or she will ask you questions that let you explain those areas that the opposing counsel may have obscured or won in the cross-examination.

Listen to these questions very carefully. They will normally be phrased in such a manner that you will remember what you wanted to say to the opposition and were not allowed to do so. On re-direct, a good lawyer will lead you to these areas and give you the opportunity to rehabilitate yourself from any damage that the other side may have inflicted. In essence, it is your job to bolster your testimony on re-direct. The lawyer can only serve up the questions. You have to play them as winners.

3.12 Your Rights as a Witness

While serving as a witness, you have the following rights:

1. To reasonable compensation before consulting with an attorney and in advance of testimony.
2. To request cooperation from everyone regarding the scheduling of your deposition, including the date, time, and location.
3. To counsel during your deposition, at your expense.
4. To read and correct your transcribed deposition testimony.
5. To refresh your memory with the contents of your file or notes.
6. To seek a protective order from the court that declares what you must and must not do regarding confidentiality and privacy issues.
7. To be treated with respect and professionalism.
8. To absolute immunity for your testimony, as discussed in section 3.13 of this book.

3.13 Immunity

All expert witnesses under Colorado law are entitled to absolute immunity for their testimony. An expert is defined in the Colorado Rules of Evidence as a witness qualified "by knowledge, skill, experience, training, or education," whose "specialized knowledge will assist the trier of fact to understand the evidence or to determine a fact in issue." CRE 702. In *Merrick v. Burns*, 43 P.3d 712 (Colo. App. 2001), the Colorado Court of Appeals dismissed a lawsuit that had been filed against an attorney who had prepared a report as an expert in a malpractice case. In its decision, dated November 23, 2001, the court reaffirmed the rule in Colorado that expert witnesses are entitled to immunity for their testimony in court. In its ruling, the court stated: "[W]e agree with the trial court that [the expert's] conduct was protected by the doctrine of absolute immunity." *Id.* at 713.

What does "immunity" mean as a practical matter? It means that if you are sued by anyone because of testimony that you have given as an expert witness, the suit against you must be dismissed.

In *Awai v. Kotin*, 872 P.2d 1332 (Colo. App. 1993), the Colorado Court of Appeals cited cases where therapists have been afforded immunity for their evaluations and recommendations discussed in courtroom testimony. These cases ruled that therapists are entitled to immunity for: (1) their evaluations and recommendations concerning a dependency and neglect case; (2) an evaluation regarding termination of parental rights; (3) a custody evaluation; and (4) a competency and sanity evaluation. The Colorado Mental Health Statutes extend this immunity doctrine to witnesses and consultants involved in grievances or licensing board matters. C.R.S. § 12-43-203 also provides that board members are entitled to immunity for their official acts.

In *Briscoe v. LaHue*, 460 U.S. 325, 103 S. Ct. 1108 (1983), the U.S. Supreme Court held that "considerations of public policy support absolute immunity" for witnesses testifying in a judicial proceeding. 460 U.S. at 343, 103 S. Ct. at 1119. The Court in Briscoe specifically ruled that "witnesses and other persons who are integral parts of the judicial process are entitled to absolute immunity." *See Kurzawa v. Mueller*, 732 F.2d 1456, 1458 (6th Cir. 1984). The rationale for extending absolute immunity to judicial officers, witnesses, and others who serve an important function in the judicial process is to encourage these individuals to perform their duties without fear of retaliation or suit, which "would hamper the duties" of such persons in fulfilling their respective roles "in judicial proceedings." *Id.*

3.14 Testifying Is Fun

Some psychotherapists are terrified of the courts and lawyers. They hate the thought of being called to testify. There are others, however, who have learned the ground rules described in this chapter and have become accomplished expert witnesses. For them, testifying is a challenging, rewarding, and fun aspect of their profession. The same potential exists for any psychotherapist who can perceive the process of testifying in the same manner.

As the expert, you are in control whenever you are testifying in a deposition or in a courtroom setting. Have confidence in the knowledge that you know more about your client and your area of expertise than any attorney questioning you. This mindset—this confidence—should make you more comfortable as you are testifying.

Chapter 4: Malpractice and Professional Liability

We live in a society that has adopted a system of justice that allows for the imposition of civil liability upon a person who, through professional negligence, has caused injury or harm to another. Psychotherapists are not exempt from this potential liability and should be intimately aware of their professional and legal obligations. This chapter outlines the major areas of potential liability for psychotherapists.

4.01 Negligence

The majority of malpractice and professional liability cases against psychotherapists involve negligence on the part of the psychotherapist.

Negligence is a breach of a duty owed to a third party that is the actual and proximate cause of injury, harm, or damage to another. Whether a therapist owes a specific duty to a client is an issue of law for the judge to decide.

Duty Owed

A plaintiff must establish that a psychotherapist owed a specific duty to the client. This is not difficult, since the law provides that all people owe an affirmative duty not to harm others. This is known as the "reasonable man rule."

This rule requires everyone to act as a reasonable person, and to exercise reasonable care in all activities. Hence, a psychotherapist must exercise ordinary and reasonable care in treating the client. But what is ordinary and reasonable care?

In Colorado, ordinary and reasonable care is defined as that which a reasonably prudent psychotherapist would provide, given the particular circumstances of the client. In practice, this means that expert witness testimony is necessary to establish that a psychotherapist owed a particular duty of care to a patient. If a plaintiff can locate a psychotherapist who would testify that most psychotherapists would, or would not, do a particular act in any given situation, then the plaintiff has met the burden of establishing the existence of a particular duty.

There are several sources that outline legal duties or standards of care required of psychotherapists.

The Colorado Mental Health Act, C.R.S. §§ 12-245-201, *et seq.*, states numerous statutory duties and obligations that are required of licensed and registered psychotherapists. See sections 6.07 and 6.08 of this book for elaboration of these duties.

The mental health licensing boards have promulgated numerous rules and regulations that govern the practice of psychotherapy. These rules and regulations set forth certain psychotherapeutic standards of care that also must be followed. See sections 6.04 and 6.05 of this book for an elaboration of these particular duties.

Most professional associations have promulgated practice standards, ethical codes, or guidelines that also set forth specific duties and standards. It is critical that psychotherapists know and follow these professional mandates since they, too, are legal duties psychotherapists owe to clients.

Treatment protocols, as set forth in generally accepted and well-regarded learned treatises, journals, and other professional texts also set forth specific duties that must be followed when treating clients.

Breach of Duty

Once the existence of a duty has been established, a plaintiff must then prove that the applicable standard of care owed to the patient was breached, or not followed, by the psychotherapist.

This is generally a factual question as to what was, or was not, done by the psychotherapist. In most negligence cases, an expert witness will simply testify that the care rendered by the psychotherapist fell below that standard of care required by law. The defendant will defend this claim by putting on an expert witness to rebut the testimony of the plaintiff's expert witness. The jury will determine whether the duty was breached by listening to the testimony of the experts, the parties, and the other witnesses. Having a knowledgeable, respected, and persuasive expert witness is therefore critical to the outcome of the case.

Causation

The breach of duty must be the actual and proximate cause of the injury, harm, or damage suffered by the plaintiff.

Actual cause is defined as that which actually produces the injury, harm, or damage.

Proximate cause is defined as that which, in a natural and continuous sequence, unbroken by any efficient intervening cause, produces the injury and without which the result would not have occurred.

Injury, Harm, or Damage

The plaintiff must also prove that actual injury, harm, or damage has been suffered. The types of injuries, harm, or damages are numerous and include, but are not limited to, the following:

1. Pain and suffering;
2. Emotional distress;
3. Loss of enjoyment of life;
4. Lost wages;
5. Permanent impairment; and
6. Past and future treatment expenses.

Immunity

Immunity is an affirmative defense to a claim of malpractice. Under Colorado law, a therapist should be entitled to immunity in the following circumstances:

1. For reporting suspected child abuse or neglect;
2. For complying with the duty to warn and protect regarding a client's threat of imminent physical violence pursuant to C.R.S. § 13-21-117;
3. For any court-ordered evaluation or treatment recommendation;
4. For any courtroom testimony;
5. For any evaluation or treatment recommendation made to a court in seeking a short-term certification or long-term certification pursuant to C.R.S. §§ 27-65-101, *et seq.*;
6. For any court-ordered sanity or competency evaluation in a criminal case;
7. For any court-ordered evaluation of a domestic violence perpetrator or treatment recommendation made to the court in any juvenile or criminal matter; and
8. Making a report to a school official or to a school district regarding a student who poses a risk of harm to the school or to other students.

Based upon the decision of the U.S. Supreme Court in *Briscoe v. LaHue*, 460 U.S. 325 (1983), therapists should be entitled as a matter of policy to immunity in situations where they are providing treatment pursuant to a court order in domestic litigation, where the therapists' services facilitate the judicial process of resolving conflict or domestic disputes. The interests of judicial economy are served by mental health professionals who may be appointed by the court to assist in the judicial process, thereby entitling therapists to absolute immunity for the functions that they serve. *See Briscoe*. To the extent that therapists, mediators, or court-appointed evaluators assist the court in resolving conflict and avoiding protracted litigation that strains judicial resources, these various "agents" and "officers" of the court deserve to receive absolute immunity for serving in the judicial process without the fear of retaliation in the form of lawsuits or grievances. *Id.*

4.02 Specific Types of Negligence

The following types of mental health negligence cases appear to be the most common:

1. Failure to take steps to prevent threats of imminent suicide;
2. Failure to take steps to prevent sexual relationships with patients by staff and other treating professionals;
3. Negligent placement and supervision of children;
4. Failure to warn or to protect third persons threatened by patients;
5. Failure to properly diagnose and treat a client;
6. Failure to report child abuse when mandatory;
7. Failure to obtain informed consent prior to treatment;
8. Unauthorized disclosure of confidential information;
9. Failure to develop and follow an appropriate treatment plan;
10. Failure to provide the mandatory disclosure statement required by C.R.S. § 12-245-216;
11. Failure to comply with the title use restrictions in C.R.S. § 12-245-218 (see section 6.01 of this book);
12. Engaging in the prohibited activities described in C.R.S. § 12-245-224 (see section 6.07 of this book);
13. Engaging in the unauthorized practices described in C.R.S. § 12-245-228 (*see* section 6.08 of this book);
14. Failure to undertake steps to properly supervise those under your professional direction;
15. Failure to follow the Rules and Regulations of the Mental Health Licensing Boards (*see* section 6.05 of this book);
16. Failure to maintain appropriate professional boundaries;
17. Failure to obtain a consultation or refer a case when it is beyond or outside a psychotherapist's area of expertise;

18. Failure to provide continuity of care (abandonment); and
19. Failure to terminate therapy when continuation of treatment is not needed.

4.03 A Word of Caution

The legal definition of the term "psychotherapy" has great significance in determining the standard of care owed by a therapist to a client. C.R.S. § 12-245-202(14) defines this term as follows:

> "Psychotherapy" means the treatment, diagnosis, testing, assessment, or counseling in a professional relationship to assist individuals or groups to alleviate mental disorders, understand unconscious or conscious motivation, resolve emotional, relationship, or attitudinal conflicts, or modify behaviors that interfere with effective emotional, social, or intellectual functioning. Psychotherapy follows a planned procedure of intervention that takes place on a regular basis, over a period of time, or in the cases of testing, assessment, and brief psychotherapy, psychotherapy can be a single intervention.

This definition emphasizes the fact that psychotherapy is a "planned procedure of intervention." Hence, the formulation of a treatment plan following the evaluation and diagnosis of a client is an integral aspect of the treatment process. The treatment plan should not only be formulated with care, but also reviewed on a regular basis in order to ensure that the plan is appropriate and properly implemented. Documentation of treatment planning and of treatment plan reviews is of utmost importance. A best practice for therapists is to formulate, review, and follow a treatment plan, which demonstrates a planned process of intervention that complies with the basic definition of "psychotherapy."

4.04 Duty to Warn and Protect

Statutory Duty

In 1986, the Colorado General Assembly enacted C.R.S. § 13-21-117, which outlines the conditions under which mental health providers have a duty to warn or protect specific persons from threats of physical violence made by a client.

The statute states that physicians, social workers, psychiatric nurses, psychologists, or other mental health professionals, as well as mental health hospitals, community and mental health centers or clinics, or institutions and their staff, shall not be liable for damages in any civil action for failure to predict, warn, or protect any person against a mental health patient's violent behavior, except when the patient has communicated to the mental health care provider a serious threat of imminent physical violence against a specific person or persons, including those identifiable by their association with a specific location or entity.

Under this statute, a psychotherapist must apply a two-part test to determine whether there is a duty to warn. First, the client must make a "serious threat of imminent physical violence," although the statute does not define what constitutes that type of threat. Therefore, the psychotherapist must bring to bear all professional judgment and discretion when determining whether such a threat has been made by a client.

The second part of the test concerns whether a threat has been made against a "specific person or persons, including those identifiable by their association with a specific location or entity." When the Aurora movie theater killings occurred in 2013, the Colorado legislature added the provision that the duty to warn and protect includes a warning to those individuals at a specific location, such as a mall, school, movie theater, health care facility, or other place that has been identified in a client's imminent threat to harm persons present. What individuals would you warn if a specific location has been threatened by a client who is dangerous to others? Examples of individuals to notify include law enforcement, the manager of the premises, the owner of the premises, security at the location, and anyone else in a position of authority at the location.

Prior to the enactment of this statute, the U.S. District Court for the District of Colorado decided *Brady v. Hopper*, 570 F. Supp. 1333 (D. Colo. 1983). In this case, the plaintiffs, who were all shot and seriously injured by John Hinckley in his attempt to assassinate President Reagan, brought an action against the perpetrator's psychiatrist for alleged negligence in examining, diagnosing, and treating John Hinckley. The plaintiffs also sought recovery for failure to warn others of the dangers Hinckley posed.

The psychiatrist moved to dismiss the case on the grounds that the patient had never made any threats against the President, or anyone else, and that further inquiry by the psychiatrist would have revealed only that the patient was obsessed with a certain actress and movie.

In interpreting Colorado law, and dismissing the action, the Federal District Court wrote:

> [A] therapist or others cannot be held liable for injuries inflicted upon third persons absent specific threats to a readily identifiable victim. . . . Unless a patient makes specific threats, the possibility that he may inflict injury on another is vague, speculative, and a matter of conjecture. However, once the patient verbalizes his

> intentions and directs his threats to identifiable victims, then the possibility of harm to third persons becomes foreseeable, and the therapist has a duty to protect those third persons from the threatened harm.

Brady, 570 F. Supp. at 1338. Although this case was decided prior to the enactment of the statute, it is helpful in defining and understanding the specificity requirement that there be readily identifiable victims.

The *Brady* case was appealed to the United States Court of Appeals for the Tenth Circuit, which affirmed the trial court's dismissal of the action. In doing so, the Tenth Circuit made it clear that generalized threats are insufficient to invoke the duty to warn, but that if the threats are specific and relate to specifically identifiable victims, the duty to warn arises, and a psychotherapist must take action to warn or protect the intended victims.

C.R.S. § 13-21-117 specifies how the duty to warn and protect must be discharged once the duty arises. Under the statute, the mental health care provider is required to make reasonable and timely efforts to notify any person or persons specifically threatened, notify an appropriate law enforcement agency, and take other appropriate action including, but not limited to, hospitalizing the patient, as discussed in sections 2.12 and 2.13 of this book. Pursuant to this statute, a therapist who has discharged the duty to warn and protect is entitled to immunity from suit or from a grievance.

C.R.S. § 13-21-117 does *not* apply to the following cases:

1. The negligent release of a mental health patient from a mental hospital or ward; or
2. The negligent failure to initiate involuntary 72-hour treatment and evaluation after a personal patient evaluation determining that the person appears to be mentally ill and, as a result of such mental illness, appears to be a danger to self or others.

Additional Colorado Case Law

In addition to *Brady v. Hopper*, there have been several other Colorado cases that have addressed the issue of a psychotherapist's duty to warn and protect others. In 1989, the Colorado Supreme Court handed down its ruling in *Perreira v. State*, 768 P.2d 1198 (Colo. 1989). In that case, the surviving spouse of a police officer who was killed by a mental patient brought a wrongful death action against the State Mental Hospital, the treating psychiatrist, and the State of Colorado. At trial, the jury rendered a verdict in favor of the spouse. The defendants appealed and the Colorado Court of Appeals reversed the trial court's decision. The

Colorado Supreme Court reversed the Court of Appeals and held that the psychiatrist had a duty to exercise due care in determining whether an involuntarily committed patient had a propensity for violence and presented an unreasonable risk of bodily harm to others upon release.

The *Perreira* case arose prior to the enactment of C.R.S. § 13-21-117. Hence, the statute was not interpreted or construed specifically in the case. However, when the Colorado Supreme Court made its ruling in 1989, it cited the statute and stated that it was instructive and helpful in terms of determining the duty of the psychiatrist in treating an involuntary outpatient.

The patient had been recently released from an involuntary commitment for short-term treatment. In its holding, the Colorado Supreme Court held that a staff psychiatrist had a legal duty to exercise due care in determining whether the patient had a propensity for violence, and if released from his involuntary commitment, would represent an unreasonable risk of serious harm to others, including a police officer in the position of Officer Perreira at the time of his death. The Colorado Supreme Court further held that if the psychiatrist knew or should have known, in accordance with the knowledge and skill ordinarily possessed by psychiatric practitioners under similar circumstances, that the patient had a *propensity for violence,* and thus, presented an unreasonable risk of serious bodily harm to others, then the psychiatrist was obligated to take reasonable precautions to protect members of the public from the danger created by a patient's release. These precautions included giving due consideration to extending the term of the patient's commitment and placing appropriate conditions and restrictions on the patient's release consistent with his needs and the safety of others.

In *Halverson v. Pikes Peak Family Counseling and Mental Health Center, Inc.,* 795 P.2d 1352 (Colo. App. 1990), the plaintiff alleged that while she was an inpatient at the defendant's crisis center, she was sexually assaulted by another patient who had a history of violent behavior. The plaintiff contended that the mental health center was negligent in failing to protect her and in failing to supervise and control the attacker after the defendants had noticed the attacker's violent propensity towards the plaintiff.

The trial judge granted the defendant's motion for dismissal for failure to state a claim. The plaintiff appealed and the Colorado Court of Appeals reversed the trial court's decision.

The defendants argued that C.R.S. § 13-21-117 provided immunity for their failure to warn or protect the plaintiff against potential violent behavior of the defendant. The plaintiff contended that the immunity conferred by C.R.S. § 13-21-117 was inapplicable to acts of *hospitalized* patients and that the statute was intended only to provide immunity for a health care provider's failure to protect or warn others against potential violent behavior of *outpatients,* over whom the provider maintained no control. The Colorado Court of Appeals specifically rejected the plaintiff's argument and held that the immunity provision of C.R.S. § 13-21-117 applied to both outpatient and inpatient mental health care providers. The case was reversed, however, on the grounds that the plaintiff had demonstrated that the violent patient had made a serious threat of imminent physical violence against the plaintiff. Thus, under the language of the statute, immunity would not apply.

Columbine and Virginia Tech: Zero Tolerance for Threats of Violence

After the Columbine tragedy in 1999, mental health professionals were reminded of their duty to warn and protect when a student makes a serious threat of imminent violence. After the Virginia Tech shootings in 2007, the entire profession reexamined procedures and laws designed to protect the public. While we must remain tolerant of individual differences, we have learned in the past that we cannot tolerate threats of violence.

In the home, when a man threatens to kill his partner, the police are called and he goes to jail. In an airport, if you make a comment about having a bomb, you go to jail. Try to tell the police that you are just joking! Ever since Columbine, if a student makes a threat of violence, it will be taken seriously. We have zero tolerance policies in our society for threats of domestic violence, for threats in schools, and for threats in airports, and for threats to national security.

After Virginia Tech, school administrators and even law enforcement officials looked to mental health professionals for an answer to the question: How do we prevent school violence from occurring? Although therapists are not mind readers and cannot know what a client is thinking, the words a client uses in making a threat of violence do indicate the individual's intent. When a person says, "I am going to kill myself," those words signify an imminent risk of harm. The same is true whenever a client says, "I am going to kill _____." Such a statement is chilling, and it justifies action to hospitalize the client due to the imminent danger that exists. Whenever a client says, "I am going to kill myself" or makes a threat to kill others, it must be handled with the same attitude of zero tolerance that applies to threats of violence in the home, at airports, at schools, and in the workplace.

When a client says, "I am thinking about killing myself," a thorough evaluation must be conducted, and if any question exists concerning whether hospitalization is necessary, a consult with another professional is warranted. A "safety contract" is never appropriate when a person meets the criteria for hospitalization; that is, when the individual has a mental disorder and is imminently dangerous to self or others.

Keep in mind that by hospitalizing an individual, you are potentially saving lives. The conventional wisdom that you will hear everywhere is: Err on the side of safety.

4.05 Invasion of Privacy

A psychotherapist has a duty of confidentiality with respect to communications made by a client in the course of treatment. A psychotherapist could face potential civil liability if such communications are disclosed without consent and are of such a nature as to be offensive and objectionable to a reasonable person of ordinary sensibilities. Given that most communications are of a highly personal nature, a disclosure by a psychotherapist would most likely be offensive and objectionable. Accordingly, civil liability for breach of privacy could be imposed on a psychotherapist who violated this duty of confidentiality.

4.06 Outrageous Conduct

Colorado law provides that a person who engages in extreme or outrageous conduct, recklessly, or with the intent of causing emotional distress may be found liable for the damages suffered as a result of such conduct.

Extreme and outrageous conduct is conduct that is so outrageous in character, and so extreme in degree, that a reasonable member of the community would regard the conduct as atrocious, beyond all possible bounds of decency, and utterly intolerable in a civilized community. Such outrageous conduct occurs when knowledge of all the facts by a reasonable member of the community would arouse that person's resentment against the defendant and lead that person to conclude that the conduct was extreme and outrageous.

A person intends to cause extreme emotional distress if that person engages in conduct for the purpose, in whole or in part, of causing severe emotional distress in another person, knowing that his or her conduct is substantially certain to have that result.

A person whose conduct causes severe emotional distress in another has acted recklessly if, at the time, that person knew, or because of other facts known to him or her, reasonably should have known there was a possibility that his or her conduct would cause severe emotional distress in another person.

Severe emotional distress consists of highly unpleasant mental reactions and is so extreme that no person of ordinary sensibilities could be expected to tolerate and endure it. The duration and intensity of the emotional distress are factors to be considered in determining its severity.

Under this theory of tort liability, a psychotherapist must at all times act in a manner that is forthright and professional.

Examples of outrageous conduct that readily come to mind include, but are not limited to:

1. Having sexual relations with a client; or
2. Financially defrauding a client.

4.07 Sexual Relations with a Client

C.R.S. § 18-3-405.5 provides for criminal penalties in the event of a sexual assault—that is, an intimate relationship or sexual contact with a client—by a psychotherapist with a client. The statute sets forth two types of sexual assault.

The first type is aggravated sexual assault on a client. This occurs when a psychotherapist knowingly inflicts sexual penetration or sexual intrusion on a victim who is a client of the therapist.

The second type of sexual assault is a class 1 misdemeanor and occurs when a psychotherapist knowingly subjects a client to *any* sexual contact. This statute specifically provides that consent by the client to the sexual penetration, intrusion, or contact shall not constitute a defense to such action.

The term "psychotherapist" is defined in C.R.S. § 18-3-405.5 to mean any person who performs or purports to perform psychotherapy, whether or not such person is licensed by the state pursuant to Title 12, C.R.S., or is certified by the state pursuant to Part 5 of Article l of Title 25, C.R.S.

Although the foregoing statute is criminal in nature, it may be used to establish the existence of a duty in a civil case for the purpose of establishing liability against a person who has violated the statute.

In *Ferguson v. People*, 824 P.2d 803 (Colo. 1992), the Colorado Supreme Court upheld the constitutionality of C.R.S. § 18-3-405.5. In that case, the defendant was charged with nine counts of aggravated sexual assault based on acts of sexual intercourse between the defendant and a client occurring between October 1988 and March 1989.

The charges against the defendant were tried to a jury, which returned guilty verdicts on four counts. Prior to sentencing, the defendant moved for a judgment of acquittal on the basis that C.R.S. § 18-3-405.5 violated his due process and equal protection rights under the Constitution. The district court, after determining that no fundamental constitutional right was affected by the statute, concluded that it was rationally related to legitimate governmental interests of protecting psychotherapy clients. The defendant was thereafter sentenced to concurrent two-year terms on the four convictions.

It has been forcefully stated that psychotherapist-client sex is the very antithesis of effective and responsible psychotherapy. When the therapist mishandles transference and becomes sexually involved with a client, medical authorities are unanimous in considering such conduct to be malpractice. The experts would agree that there are absolutely no circumstances that permit a psychiatrist to engage in sex with his or her patient.

4.08 Failure to Report Child Abuse

As discussed in Chapter 2, C.R.S. § 19-3-304 requires certain groups of persons who have reasonable cause to know or suspect that a child has been subjected to abuse and neglect, or who have observed a child being subjected to circumstances or conditions that would reasonably result in abuse or neglect, to immediately report such fact to the County Department of Social Services or local law enforcement agency. This statute provides that any person who willfully violates this provision commits a class 2 misdemeanor criminal offense and shall be civilly liable for damages proximately caused by it.

Please refer to Chapter 2, Part II for a detailed analysis of the requirements pertaining to this statute.

4.09 Insurance Fraud

Abuse of Health Insurance

In 1985, the Colorado General Assembly enacted C.R.S. § 18-13-119, which addressed the problem of abuse of health insurance by health care providers. In enacting the statute, the legislature specifically found that business practices that have the effect of eliminating the need for actual payment by the recipient of health care services of required co-payments and deductibles in health benefit plans interfered with contractual obligations entered into between the insured and insurer relating to such payments. Further, the legislature determined that such interference is not in the public interest when it is conducted as a regular business practice, because it has the effect of increasing health care costs by removing the incentive co-payments and deductibles created to make the consumer a cost-conscious consumer of health care services. The Colorado General Assembly also declared that advertising such practices by health care providers might aggravate the adverse financial and other impacts on recipients of health care. Accordingly, the General Assembly declared that such business practices were illegal and that the violation thereof or the advertising of such business practices would be grounds for disciplinary actions.

The statute provides that "abuse of health insurance" is a petty offense. The health care provider commits abuse of health insurance if the provider knowingly:

1. Accepts from any third-party payor as payment in full for services rendered the amount the third-party payor covers; or
2. Submits a fee to a third-party payor that is higher than the fee he has agreed to accept from the insured patient with the understanding of waiving the required deductible or co-payment.

The statute created the following exceptions:

1. Reimbursements made pursuant to Articles 4 and 15 of Title 26, C.R.S.;
2. Federal Medicare laws for inpatient hospitalization; and
3. Mental health services purchased in accordance with Part 2 of Article 1 of Title 27, C.R.S.

Health care services are exempt from the provisions of C.R.S. § 18-13-119 if they are provided in accordance with a contract or agreement between the employer and an employee or employees, and the contract includes as part of any employee's salary or employment benefits terms that authorize a practice that would otherwise be prohibited by this statute.

The waiver of any required deductible or co-payment for charitable purposes is exempt if:

1. The person who provides the health care determines that the services are necessary for the immediate health and welfare of the patient;
2. The waiver is made on a case-by-case basis and the person who provides the health care determines that payment of the deductible or co-payment would create a substantial hardship for the patient; and
3. The waiver is not a regular business practice of the person who provides the health care.

The statute also states that any person who provides health care and waives the deductible or co-payment for more than one-fourth of his or her patients during any calendar year, excluding patients covered by the exemptions cited above, or who advertises through newspapers, magazines, circulars, direct mail, directories, radio, television, or otherwise that he or she will accept from any third-party payor, as payment in full for services rendered, the amount the third-party payor covers, will be presumed to be engaged in waiving the deductible or co-payment as a regular business practice.

This statute was upheld in *Parrish v. Lamm,* 758 P.2d 1356 (Colo. 1988), in which the plaintiff sought a declaration that the statute was unconstitutional, on grounds that it regulated commercial speech in violation of the First Amendment to the U.S. Constitution. In upholding the constitutionality of this statute, the Colorado Supreme Court held that the legislature may regulate or ban entirely commercial speech related to illegal activity, since such speech does not rise to the level of a fundamental right.

Given the foregoing restrictions, a psychotherapist should review his or her billing practices to avoid the inadvertent abuse of insurance as described in this statute.

Other Forms of Insurance Fraud

There are other forms of insurance fraud that psychotherapists should avoid. These include, but are not limited to:

1. Billing for services that were not rendered.
2. Billing for work that was performed by another person.
3. Excessive billing or overcharging for services.
4. Miscoding of services rendered in order to qualify for insurance, e.g., coding marital counseling as treatment for anxiety.
5. Making a false representation in billing for insurance benefits.

C.R.S. § 10-1-128 addresses fraudulent insurance acts.

4.10 Billing Practices

I have received numerous inquiries concerning billing standards and billing practices from therapists across the country. The following are among the frequently asked questions, with answers.

Q. If I am a clinical supervisor and I am on insurance panels, can I bill for services provided by the supervisee, if she provides treatment to clients, but is not on the insurance panels?

A. No, the only person who can bill for treatment is the actual provider. The Colorado mental health boards' supervision rule provides that a clinical supervisor must ensure that bills accurately reflect who provided the treatment.

Q. Can I bill insurance companies for couples counseling or marital counseling, and if so, what CPT Code do I use?

A. Some health insurance plans do provide coverage for marital counseling or family therapy. The CPT Code for family therapy (conjoint) is 90837. You may also use the CPT Code 90838 for "Psychotherapy, 60 minutes with patient and/or family member when performed with an evaluation and management service." Because marital counseling is a type of therapy, you can also use some more general CPT Codes for psychotherapy, depending on the length of the session. If you have a question concerning whether an insurance plan provides benefits for couples counseling or will pay for marital counseling, check with the insurance representative. It may be that the clients will need to pay the old-fashioned way for treatment: out of their pockets.

Q. Can I bill insurance for telephone conferences with clients, either in emergencies where clients are in crisis or in a situation where a client cannot make it to my office due to weather conditions?

A. An excellent question. All of the CPT Codes referenced above are for "face-to-face" treatment. Therefore, if an intervention or session is done on the telephone, your bill should indicate that the place of service (POS) was the phone. Many insurance panels require that therapists be available to clients in the event of clinical emergencies. Therefore, those plans should pay for phone calls in emergencies.

Q. What are the general standards for billing?

A. Bills must be accurate, and any diagnostic code must reflect the client's presenting problem; the units of time billed must be accurate; and, of course, the provider whose name is on the bill must be the individual who provided treatment. Any misrepresentations of fact on a billing statement may be considered a "fraudulent insurance act" under Colorado law.

4.11 Responding to a Lawsuit

When a lawsuit is brought against a psychotherapist, the following procedures should be followed:

1. The date and manner in which the summons and complaint was received should be recorded.
2. Any malpractice insurance policy should be reviewed and the reporting procedures described in the policy should be followed. This will normally involve written notice to the carrier and forwarding a copy of the summons and complaint to the carrier. It is recommended that a telephone call be made to verbally report the lawsuit, and that the phone call be followed by a written confirmation of the report.

3. Correspondence with the malpractice carrier should be mailed certified mail, return receipt requested.
4. The substance of the lawsuit should not be discussed with anyone. Statements made by a party to a lawsuit are potentially admissible and may be used against that person at trial in a variety of damaging ways. Hence, the best rule is to refrain from any discussion.
5. Typically, a malpractice carrier has a duty to defend and satisfy any judgment that is entered, up to the amount of its policy limit for liability coverage. It will fulfill its obligation by obtaining an insurance defense attorney. He or she has been hired by the insurance company to defend the psychotherapist, but simultaneously this lawyer has duties to the insurance company that may not coincide with those of the psychotherapist. Hence, the psychotherapist should obtain separate counsel for the purpose of monitoring the litigation and ensuring that the defense counsel is fulfilling his or her duty to the psychotherapist.
6. If you carry no malpractice insurance, you should immediately obtain a trial attorney.

4.12 Malpractice Insurance

Professional liability insurance is highly recommended. Psychotherapists are particularly vulnerable, given the emotional and mental instability of their clientele. If the psychotherapist works for an agency or business entity, the psychotherapist should review the agency's insurance policy, determine the extent of coverage, and consider supplementing it with private insurance.

The amount of malpractice insurance should be the maximum amount that is affordable. In this day and age, a million-dollar policy is considered minimally adequate. A question arises as to the amount of the deductible. In this regard, business sense applies. The psychotherapist should realize that in the event a lawsuit is commenced, the deductible would have to be paid by the psychotherapist.

In a professional corporation, partnership, or any other association, malpractice insurance is required in order to avoid vicarious liability for the acts of the other partners. Tort law and agency law impose upon professionals who are in a partnership, or who practice in a professional corporation, joint and several liability for the acts of the other shareholders or partners. In lay terms, this means that all partners are liable, even if the tortious act is committed by only one of them. Hence, malpractice insurance is warranted.

Many insurance policies for therapists now have coverage of at least $5,000 for defense of a grievance. This is minimal coverage; professionals may wish to ask for a higher level of coverage in the insurance policy, in the event that they need to defend a licensing board complaint.

4.13 Malpractice Prevention

Psychotherapists should realize that malpractice claims can be prevented. To minimize malpractice, psychotherapists should maintain professional competence at all times. There is simply no substitute for knowledge and the proper exercise of that skill and care required of psychotherapists. Accordingly, it is recommended that psychotherapists subscribe to current professional journals and regularly attend continuing education programs. Additionally, psychotherapists should not accept a case beyond their competence level. Referring cases and jointly cooperating on cases are excellent ways to avoid getting in over your head. An important aspect of competence is knowing the law and your responsibilities. Accordingly, periodic review of the relevant mental health laws is warranted.

Often, malpractice occurs as a result of administrative oversight. Consequently, office management needs to be professional, and supervision needs to occur on a regular basis. Written policies and procedures for office management should be developed, distributed, and followed.

One area of disagreement between clients and psychotherapists is the matter of fees. Licensed professionals are required to provide each client with a disclosure statement that covers such matters as patient rights, fees, etc. All psychotherapists should consider using an engagement agreement or letter, which defines the psychotherapist-client relationship and carefully defines the expectations regarding compensation.

An important consideration in any malpractice case is the adequacy of client records, which document the services rendered and advice given. There is controversy in the field about what should and should not be documented. It is, however, highly recommended that the client's progress be adequately charted, and that all services and advice given be documented. This often is not a high priority for psychotherapists, but such oversight can have devastating results in litigation.

One major complaint levied against professionals is that they do not respond to phone calls in a timely manner. It is recommended that all phone calls be returned within 24 hours and that an adequate response system be developed. If a client feels cut off or abandoned by a professional, the first inclination is to obtain an attorney. This can be avoided by simply maintaining close contact.

All professionals, at times, have a tendency to procrastinate. In order to avoid this first step toward malpractice, psychotherapists should adopt an attitude of making a priority of doing those things they would like to avoid, rather than delaying.

From a statistical standpoint, the odds are that a psychotherapist will never be sued for malpractice. Therapists can decrease the prospect that they will be sued by adhering to some basic rules. Therapists who follow these rules will significantly decrease the chance of being sued.

1. **Know the legal standards that apply to your practice.** Therapists need to be thoroughly familiar with the laws that apply to them and to their practice. In general, these laws are contained in the Colorado Mental Health Act, which is contained in C.R.S. §§ 12-245-201, *et seq.* A copy of the mental health statutes can be obtained from the Department of Regulatory Agencies, and is normally furnished to therapists along with the database application or an application for licensure. The importance of knowing and understanding these laws is surpassed only by the importance of adhering to them. Many of the specific statutes with which therapists must comply are discussed in this book. The various provisions contained in the Colorado Mental Health Act constitute the legal standards that apply to the practice of psychotherapy. Compliance with all of the statutes is essential, but one statute has special import: C.R.S. § 12-245-224, which is discussed in section 6.07 of this book. This law, in particular, establishes specific standards to be followed and proscribes conduct that violates the basic principles of psychotherapy.
2. **Know the ethical standards for psychotherapists and follow them.** All of the major national professional associations have adopted codes of ethics for their members. These codes of ethics establish the ethical standards that guide psychotherapists in their practice. The codes of ethics adopted by organizations such as the National Association of Social Workers, the American Psychological Association, the American Association for Marriage & Family Therapy, and the American Counseling Association apply specifically not only to the organization's members, but also to other therapists who practice in a special discipline. For example, the AAMFT Code of Ethics establishes the ethical standards to be followed by therapists, both licensed and unlicensed, who practice marriage and family therapy.
3. **Stay current in the field.** Membership in a national professional association or its state affiliate provides numerous benefits. These include

opportunities to attend conferences, workshops, and seminars that focus on treatment standards, professional trends, updates on the law, and current information concerning regulatory changes. In addition, professional associations provide newsletters and publications to their members that keep them informed about changes in the field. Another important benefit of membership in professional associations is professional liability insurance at group rates.

4. **Practice with informed consent.** Adhere to the basic principles of informed consent in treating your clients. These principles are discussed in section 4.14 of this book. This process will enable you to establish a better relationship with your client, and enable your client to better understand treatment goals and your treatment plan. You can elevate your practice above the "generally accepted standards" by doing the following: (1) conduct a thorough evaluation of your client, and document in your records the information on which your assessment of the client is based; (2) identify for the client the presenting problem(s) and the specific behavioral goals to be achieved in therapy (*e.g.*, learn skills to control anger); (3) prepare a written treatment plan that identifies the probable length of treatment and method to be used to accomplish treatment goals (*e.g.*, 36 weeks of group counseling); and (4) review the treatment plan and document in your records the process of re-evaluating the client's problems, if your client is not progressing as anticipated. The federal model for informed consent requires the client to sign off on the treatment plan, to demonstrate that the client has been informed about the process involved in treatment. Keep in mind that your disclosure statement is your informed consent form, and let it inform the client as much as possible about matters that should be disclosed.

5. **Keep good records.** Your treatment records should serve two purposes: (1) to help your client by recording basic information concerning your client's history and clinical picture at the time of your treatment, so that subsequent therapists can profit from your experience with the client; and (2) to protect you in case questions arise years later concerning what treatment you provided and why you pursued a particular course of treatment. In addition to basic progress notes, take care to document in your records any statutory report that you are required to make, including information concerning any consultation regarding a client; a description of any treatment information disclosed, along with the authorization for disclosure of information; and documentation concerning any specific

problem(s) discussed in clinical supervision. In addition, all referrals need to be documented.

6. **Never sue a client.** Trying to collect a fee by suing a client raises many troubling questions. How can you sue the client without breaching confidentiality? Moreover, the client will typically claim that he or she did not pay because the treatment was no good. A counterclaim alleging malpractice is, too frequently, the response to such a suit.
7. **Do not allow clients to tape-record treatment sessions.** And if you record sessions for purposes of supervision, erase the tape after it has been used for that purpose. If a lawsuit should happen, and tapes of treatment sessions exist, your own words, taken out of context, can and will be used against you. Even if clients flatter you by saying that they want to listen to tapes of treatment sessions as homework, so that they can listen to your wise counsel and the reassuring tones of your voice, "Just say no."
8. **Maintain appropriate boundaries.** Identify ground rules for treatment that establish your role as therapist and help you to avoid problems (*e.g.*, I cannot accept gifts from clients; our clinic policy does not allow us to hug clients). Do not engage in bartering with clients. Do not give your client legal advice—that is not your role.
9. **Refer out when a client's problems are outside of your area of expertise.** And document in writing the fact that you made a referral anytime that is done.
10. **Do not take the law into your own hands.** Anytime you are required to make a statutory report involving a 72-hour hold, child abuse, or a duty to warn, report the information that you are required to disclose. Then let the caseworker or law enforcement officer whose role it is to investigate the matter conduct the investigation. As the therapist, it is your role, when necessary, to report certain information, but it is not your role to investigate cases, interview witnesses, confront alleged perpetrators, etc. So, do not take the law into your own hands by becoming the investigator.
11. **Maintain liability insurance.** This will enable you to aggressively defend any grievance before it becomes a lawsuit, and it will allow you, with the assistance of competent counsel, to aggressively defend any suit that may be filed. The insurance companies who write insurance policies for mental health practitioners typically hire attorneys who are excellent advocates in defending malpractice suits. In addition, a consulting expert will usually be retained to evaluate the standard-of-care issues and, hopefully, testify on your behalf. Of course, in addition to having an attorney retained by

your liability insurance carrier to defend you, you can also hire personal counsel to give you a second opinion or to consult with you, if needed.

4.14 Informed Consent

Treating Adults

The Colorado General Assembly has enacted a statute defining "consent" in C.R.S. § 27-10.5-102(5). This statute expresses a policy, when treating mentally ill or developmentally disabled persons, that informed consent should be given in writing, voluntarily, and should contain the following:

1. A fair explanation of the procedures to be followed, including an identification of those that are experimental;
2. A description of the attendant discomforts and risks;
3. A description of the benefits to be expected;
4. A disclosure of appropriate alternative procedures, together with an explanation of the respective benefits, discomforts, and risks; and
5. An offer to answer any inquiries concerning procedures. Wherever inherent risks in the implementation of a treatment plan exist, a psychotherapist should advise the client of those risks, and have the client sign an informed consent form, acknowledging the disclosures that have been made concerning the potential risks posed by the methods of treatment that will be employed.

Obtaining informed consent from psychotherapy clients is required by law and is an effective, proactive approach to malpractice prevention. It demonstrates that a psychotherapist is being careful in the formulation and implementation of a treatment plan and is being thoughtful of the client and the consequences that may occur as a result of treatment.

The mandatory disclosure form that must be given to clients at the initial therapy session requires that clients be informed of the right to receive information about the methods of therapy, the techniques used, the duration of therapy, and the fee structure (see section 6.02 of this book for more information on mandatory disclosures). Most psychotherapists have not undertaken the steps to develop a written summary of this information so that it can be made readily available. Surprisingly few therapists actually provide written information of the methods and techniques of therapy. The author highly recommends that a writing be prepared that summarizes this information and that the client be given a copy. In this way, the client's choice to participate in therapy can be based upon informed consent.

Informed Consent for Treatment of Children

Informed consent for treatment of children, in compliance with AAMFT Code of Ethics (2015) Principle 1.2, requires MFTs to engage in a careful process to obtain parental consent for treatment. When a child's parents are married, either parent can provide consent for the treatment of a child. When the parents are divorced, however, therapists need to ask during intake about the court's order regarding "decision-making authority," and comply with the order, obtaining consent for treatment from both parents when the court has awarded joint decision-making.

Informed Consent for Outpatient Treatment of 12-Year-Olds

Although the age of majority across the United States is 18 years, in Colorado an adolescent 12 years of age or older may, in certain circumstances, be authorized to consent to treatment with a licensed mental health professional, with an LPC candidate, a psychologist candidate, or a licensed school social worker, when the professional determines: (a) the minor is knowingly and voluntarily seeking mental health services; and (b) the provision of psychotherapy services is clinically indicated and necessary to the minor's well-being.

Notification to Parents of the Evaluation and Treatment of a 12-Year-Old

C.R.S. § 12-245-203.5 provides that the mental health professional may notify the 12-year-old's parents or legal guardian of the psychotherapy services with the minor's consent, unless notifying the parent or guardian would be inappropriate or would be detrimental to the minor's care and treatment. The professional may notify the child's parent or guardian without the child's consent, if, in the professional's opinion, the minor is unable to manage their own care and treatment. The mental health professional must engage the minor client in a discussion about the importance of involving and notifying the minor's parent or guardian, and shall encourage parental notification to help support the minor's care and treatment.

Mandatory Notification

Notification to the 12-year-old's parents is mandatory if the child is experiencing suicidal ideation or makes a threat to commit suicide, or if a 72-hour hold evaluation is ordered for the child.

Required Documentation

C.R.S. § 12-245-203.5 requires that the treating professional "shall fully document when the mental health professional attempts to contact or notify the minor's parent or legal guardian, and whether the attempt was successful or unsuccessful, or the reason why, in the mental health professional's opinion, it would be inappropriate to contact or notify the minor's parent or legal guardian." This documentation must be included in the minor's clinical record, along with a written statement signed by the minor indicating that the minor is voluntarily seeking psychotherapy services.

Services to the Minor Must Be Culturally Appropriate

These psychotherapy services must be provided in a culturally appropriate manner. Written and oral instruction, training for providers and staff, and the overall provision of services must be provided in a manner and format to support individuals with limited English proficiency or challenges with accessibility related to a disability and with respect for diverse backgrounds, including individuals with different cultural origins and individuals who are lesbian, gay, bisexual, or transgender.

Decision-Making Authority Granted by the Courts in Domestic Litigation

Across the United States, courts are currently awarding "decision-making authority" for the selection of children's medical doctors, mental health professionals, schools, etc., to either one parent who is awarded sole authority, or to both parents who are granted joint authority to select their children's treatment providers. Experience has shown that parents do not always understand this issue and may not provide accurate information when questions are asked regarding who has been awarded the authority by the court to provide consent for the treatment of children; therefore, therapists must ask for and obtain a copy of the Divorce Decree and Custody Order so they can determine who has been granted decision-making authority by the court. When this authority is conferred upon one parent, that is the only individual who can consent to treatment. When this authority has been granted to both parents jointly, then both parents must provide informed consent for treatment in compliance with Colorado law and ethical principles.

Foreseeably, problems do arise when therapists take one parent's word for the fact that they have the sole authority to provide informed consent for treatment, and do not request the court records. All too often, a therapist will receive a call or e-mail from an outraged parent, upset over the fact that the parents were awarded joint authority by the court to select medical and mental health professionals, but no one obtained his or her consent. Inevitably, the outraged parent demands that the therapist cease and desist from providing treatment to the child. A therapist in this situation may apologize for the mistake and offer to send an informed consent form to the parent, only to find that a complete lack of trust exists on the part of the outraged parent, who fears that if issues arise regarding custody or visitation, the therapist will be biased towards the parent who brought the child in for treatment. Whatever professional relationship has been established with a child is then destroyed, when the therapist who did not obtain joint consent for treatment must terminate the therapy process and refer out. When a conflict like this arises, demands by an outraged parent to terminate treatment for lack of consent are often accompanied by a threat that a complaint will be sent to the therapist's state licensing board.

Part of the informed consent process requires disclosure to the client or client representative concerning the limits on confidentiality in compliance with C.R.S. § 12-245-216 and ethical codes for mental health professionals. In a case where the parents are divorced and the mother has been given sole authority to consent to treatment for a child, does the child's father automatically have the right to receive information concerning the child's treatment? Yes. In Colorado both parents are entitled to information concerning their children's medical and mental health treatment unless a court has ruled otherwise. Of course, MFTs and other therapists trained in family systems generally want to include both parents in the treatment process, by providing information to the parents about the children's presenting problems and the parents' role in helping their children to overcome problems.

Pursuant to C.R.S. § 27-65-103, which gives adolescents 15 years of age or older the authority to consent to inpatient or outpatient treatment by a licensed mental health professional, parents still have the right to information concerning "services given" or the "services needed" by an adolescent, with or without the adolescent's consent. An adolescent who is competent to consent to treatment at age 15 owns the privilege, so that the adolescent, not the parents, has the right to authorize the release of confidential treatment information. When an adolescent is competent to consent to treatment, then he or she is also competent to "execute a waiver" or to provide written authorization for release of treatment information in compliance with C.R.S. §§ 27-65-102 and -103; and in compliance with C.R.S. § 12-245-202.5.

OBH Standards for Informed Consent

As stated in Section 6.20, the Behavioral Health Administration (BHA), formerly known as the Office of Behavioral Health (OBH), requires that informed consent provided to clients by clinicians at facilities regulated by the BHA include the following information:

The benefits of the proposed treatment: Treatment planning will focus on meeting the goals of treatment formulated for the client, based on the assessment of the client's needs. Treatment goals will include: (1) reducing any symptoms the client may be experiencing, such as anxiety, depression, emotional distress, or difficulty adjusting to situations the client is dealing with; (2) alleviating conditions that interfere with the client's functioning or enjoyment of life, such as relationship problems, substance abuse, or addiction to alcohol or habit-forming drugs; (3) improving the client's relationships with parents, children, other family members or co-workers; and (4) learning coping skills to assist the client to function better in employment situations; to control anger; to deal with past trauma, or to adjust to other difficult situations.

Alternative treatment modes and services: Counseling may take the form of group therapy or individual counseling. In some circumstances, residential treatment may be needed, or the client may need to be referred to a hospital for an evaluation and for inpatient treatment. Clients may receive referrals to doctors, their primary care physician, or other specialists who can assist them with problems.

The manner in which treatment will be administered: Depending on the treatment plan that is prepared, individual counseling may be scheduled once per week for an hour; or group therapy may be recommended for weekly 90-minute sessions. Any treatment will be conducted by behavioral health therapists who are licensed, certified, or registered by the State of Colorado.

Expected side effects from the treatment: On occasion, people in therapy who work on their problems and emotional difficulties can experience pain or distress as they recall past traumatic incidents, personal wrongs that have occurred, or their life's disappointments. Ideally, such side effects are overcome by the expected benefits of treatment.

Probable consequences of not receiving treatment: A failure to seek counseling in order to obtain the benefits discussed above can result in past problems or failures recurring. If individuals do not get the help they need, their emotional difficulties and distress may worsen, they may not improve relationship problems, and their ability to function and to enjoy life may continue to be impaired. Our potential is maximized by seeking help from a counselor when it is needed; and we may fail to reach our potential if we do not seek help.

4.15 Testifying in Divorce Litigation: Prevention of Foreseeable Risks

In Colorado and across the nation, the most frequent type of board complaint involving therapists arises from testimony in divorce and custody cases. Clients, or the parents of children receiving treatment from a therapist who are involved in bitterly contested custody battles, often consider the treating professional as an ally in the custody battle. These clients and their attorneys have unreasonable expectations concerning the role of a therapist who is providing treatment. They expect the therapist to make favorable recommendations to the court concerning parental responsibilities and parenting plans. However, that is not the proper role of a treatment professional. Such recommendations should only be made by custody evaluators, child and family investigators, guardians *ad litem*, or child representatives appointed by the court to conduct investigations and evaluations of parenting issues. Their recommendations can then be made to the court regarding the allocation of parental responsibilities and the implementation of parenting plans.

Therapists must comply with AAMFT Code of Ethics (2015) Principle 7.70, which states:

> To avoid a conflict of interest, marriage and family therapists who treat minors or adults involved in custody or visitation actions may not also perform forensic evaluations for custody, residence, or visitation of the minor. The marriage and family therapist who treats the minor may provide the court or mental health professional performing the evaluation with information about the minor from the marriage and family therapist's perspective.

For example, if a therapist is subpoenaed to court and is then asked by a client's attorney for recommendations concerning who should have custody of the parties' children or concerning whether it is appropriate for a parent to have parenting time with a child, the only appropriate response should be, "I have not conducted the evaluation necessary to provide an opinion on this issue, so I cannot answer the question."

However, problems arise when a client has unreasonable expectations concerning a therapist's role, and the client feels betrayed when the therapist does not support the client's position in the litigation. For example, if a child's mother does not want her estranged spouse to have any contact with their children, she may be outraged if the therapist expresses an opinion that fathers should have relationships with their children, and then pull the children out of treatment with the therapist. This is an all too frequent experience for therapists nationwide who have testified in court: their clinical relationship with clients is either damaged or destroyed as a result of testimony in court in a domestic case.

How can therapists avoid these risks? First, therapists should not agree to testify in court. Second, therapists should disclose to clients who are involved in custody battles at the outset of treatment that it is not the therapist's role to make recommendations to the court for purposes of domestic litigation, and that any courtroom testimony may damage the clinical relationship. The mandatory

Disclosure Statement is a vehicle by which an appropriate disclosure can be made. In it you can disclose:

> If you are involved in a divorce or custody litigation, you need to understand that my role as a therapist is not to make recommendations for the court concerning custody or parenting issues or to testify in court concerning opinions on issues involved in the litigation. By signing this disclosure statement, you agree not to call me as a witness in any such litigation. Experience has shown that testimony by therapists in domestic cases causes damage to the clinical relationship between a therapist and client. Only court-appointed experts, investigators, or evaluators can make recommendations to the court on disputed issues concerning parental responsibilities and parenting plans.

Such an agreement by a client is not enforceable if the client's attorney issues a subpoena to a therapist; however, these disclosures may correct any unrealistic expectations that clients might have.

To avoid the foreseeable risks that result from testimony in domestic litigation, therefore, therapists should not agree to testify in court and, if subpoenaed, should acknowledge their limitations as treating professionals who have not evaluated and ethically cannot evaluate issues to be decided by the court or make recommendations concerning them. And, of course, compliance with the AAMFT Code of Ethics is the best way to prevent such risks.

4.16 Maintaining Client Records

Each of the mental health boards has a specific rule requiring maintenance of client records and specific record-keeping entries for therapists. Therapists are encouraged to keep records that document the presenting problem that requires treatment on each date that the client is seen. Using "S.O.A.P." (Subjective, Objective, Assessment, Plan) notes, a therapist can: (1) document the presenting problem for each visit; (2) evaluate the therapist's assessment of that problem and plan for treating the client; (3) refer the client to another health care provider for evaluation or treatment; or (4) consult with another professional or seek supervision on a difficult clinical issue or ethical question. Keep in mind that every disclosure of treatment information must be documented, and a therapist must also document in the client's record each statutory report that is required, *e.g.*, a report concerning child abuse or neglect; a referral to a crisis unit of the client who requires a 72-hour hold; or a report made to law enforcement and to a potential victim, pursuant to C.R.S. § 13-21-117, when a therapist has a duty to warn and protect.

The Licensed Professional Counselor (LPC) Board Rule 4 C.C.R. 737-1 1.16 requires that the following essential record-keeping entries be made in the client's chart, and that the entire chart be maintained by an LPC for seven years after termination of treatment or the last client visit with an adult client: (1) identifying data, to include the client's name, sex, telephone number, date of birth, and address, as well as the name, address, and telephone number of the legal guardian of a child; (2) all contracts, release of information forms, and disclosure statements; (3) records of counseling including dates of service, session notes, test data, electronic data storage, and information concerning any disclosure of information made; (4) information concerning each report made pursuant to legal duties (*e.g.*, child abuse, duty to warn, 72-hour hold); and (5) a final closing statement. Note that records concerning treatment of a minor child must be kept for seven years commencing on the last day of treatment or on the client's eighteenth birthday, whichever comes first, but in no event must a minor's records be kept for more than twelve years.

Psychology Board Rule 3 C.C.R. 721-1 1.16 lists the essential record-keeping entries required to be prepared and maintained by a psychologist for seven years after termination of treatment or the last visit with a client who is an adult. Rule 1.16 also requires that the records of a minor be kept for the same period of time specified in the LPC Board's record-keeping rule.

Social Work Board Rule 4 C.C.R. 726-1 1.16 lists the required entries and requires that records of treatment for an adult client be maintained for seven years after termination of the treatment or the last client visit.

The Board of Licensed Marriage and Family Therapists Rule 4 C.C.R. 736-1 1.16 lists the entries that an LMFT must keep, and requires that records of treatment for an adult be maintained for seven years after termination of treatment or the last client visit. In compliance with the Rules of all of the Mental Health Boards, a minor's treatment records must be retained for seven years beginning on the last date of treatment or for seven years from the date when the minor reaches eighteen years of age, whichever comes later, but in no case must the records be kept for more than 12 years.

Records Disposition

The mental health boards' rules require that records be maintained and stored in a secure manner in order to ensure that only authorized persons have access to records and that confidentiality is protected. In the event of the therapist's death, disability, or the sale of a therapist's practice, the board rules also require that a professional executor be appointed to maintain mental health records for the period of time required. See Section 2.28 for additional information on a professional will.

Group Therapy Notes

Keep in mind that the standard of care for record-keeping in group therapy requires an individual note for each individual in the group. In general, the individual's group notes should not identify other members of the therapy group.

Informed Consent Issues Regarding Record-Keeping (in compliance with the NASW Code of Ethics and Social Work Board Rules)

Social workers who provide counseling to active duty military personnel, off base, are sensitive not only to the fact that treatment information is confidential and privileged, but also that it may be subject to a subpoena *duces tecum* seeking copies of the treatment records. Recent experience has shown that military tribunals, applying the Uniform Code of Military Justice, do not recognize the same privileges that Colorado law recognizes. Therefore, active duty military clients should give informed consent in your Disclosure Statement that their treatment records may be subpoenaed and subject to disclosure pursuant to a court order enforcing the subpoena.

The NASW Code of Ethics is instructive in this situation. Section 1.07, Privacy and Confidentiality, provides in part:

> (a) Social workers should respect clients' right to privacy. Social workers should not solicit private information from clients unless it is essential to providing services or conducting social work evaluation or research. Once private information is shared, standards of confidentiality apply.
>
> . . .
>
> (d) Social workers should inform clients, to the extent possible, about the disclosure of confidential information and the potential consequences, when feasible before the disclosure is made. This applies whether social workers disclose confidential information on the basis of a legal requirement or client consent.
>
> (e) Social workers should discuss with clients and other interested parties the nature of confidentiality and limitations of clients' right to confidentiality. Social workers should review with clients

> circumstances where confidential information may be requested and where disclosure of confidential information may be legally required. This discussion should occur as soon as possible in the social worker-client relationship and as needed throughout the course of the relationship.
>
> . . .
>
> (j) Social workers should protect the confidentiality of clients *during legal proceedings* to the extent permitted by law. When a court of law or other legally authorized body orders social workers to disclose confidential or privileged information without a client's consent and such disclosure could cause harm to the client, social workers should request that the court withdraw the order or limit the order as narrowly as possible or maintain the records under seal, unavailable for public inspection. [Emphasis added.]

How might an active duty military member be harmed by disclosure of treatment information? Information concerning the use of prescription medication, mental health problems, substance abuse, domestic violence, or marital infidelity can have serious consequences, from loss of a security clearance required for a service member to do his or her job, to the filing of charges in a court martial or involuntary discharge from the military. Thus, information in a social worker's notes or records that would be relatively innocuous to a civilian may be extremely harmful to an active duty military member, if disclosed.

The information a social worker keeps in a client's file is a matter of the therapist's professional judgment. However, in the process of taking notes and keeping records, you must adhere to the basic NASW Code of Ethics and the rules and regulations of the Colorado Board of Social Work Examiners. The NASW Code of Ethics Section 3.04, Client Records, provides:

> (a) Social workers should take reasonable steps to ensure that documentation in records is accurate and reflects the services provided.
>
> . . .
>
> (c) Social workers' documentation should protect clients' privacy to the extent that is possible and appropriate and *should include only information that is directly relevant to the delivery of services.* [Emphasis added.]

It is a matter of a social worker's professional judgment and discretion in taking notes to determine what information is "directly relevant to the delivery of services."

The Colorado Board of Social Work Examiners Rule 4 C.C.R. 726-1 1.16 requires that "every social worker shall create and shall maintain records" on each of his or her clients. The record entries that you must maintain include:

1. Identifying data, including the client's name;
2. Reason(s) for the professional services;
3. Dates of each contact with the client;
4. Information on each referral made and each consultation with another social worker or health care provider, including the date of the referral or consultation, the name of the person(s) to whom the client was referred, the name of the person with whom consultation was sought, the outcome of the referral, and the outcome of the consultation;
5. The name of any test(s) administered;
6. Information on each mandatory report made (e.g., report of suspected child abuse);
7. Fee information;
8. Any release of information;
9. The records must be prepared in a manner that allows any subsequent provider to reasonably conclude what occurred;
10. List the name of any test administered, each date on which the test was administered, and the name of the person administering the test; and
11. A final closing statement regarding fees billed and paid, after services have concluded.

Therefore, although you are required to keep records, each social worker, in taking notes, determines what information is relevant to the services being provided and protects clients' privacy by keeping irrelevant information out of records.

S.O.A.P. Notes

Therapists do not necessarily learn in graduate school the best method for taking notes during treatment sessions. An excellent method is illustrated by a case that I defended in which a psychologist was sued for allegedly violating the civil rights of a client who was an inmate in a correctional facility.

The client went to sick call one morning, telling the physician's assistant that he was waking up in the morning feeling weird, and that he was on "synthetic medication." The physician's assistant looked at his chart, saw that the individual was on psychotropic medications, and referred him to the psychologist for assessment of his problems.

When the client saw the psychologist, he told her, "I've been waking up mornings feeling weird. They've got me on synthetic medication, and I do not do well on synthetic meds." The psychologist noted these comments, reviewed the client's chart, and conducted a one-hour mental status evaluation. The chart indicated that this client had been diagnosed as Paranoid Schizophrenic and had been prescribed Prolixin, which he was taking daily, and which was also being injected every two weeks. The psychologist could also see that this client was current on his meds and had not missed his daily dose of Prolixin in over six months. During her mental status evaluation, she noted her client's demeanor, and also noted that he was responding to her questions appropriately — a significant fact since his diagnosis included delusional features.

The psychologist noted her observations of the client and her assessment of his presenting problem, the fact that he had a question concerning his medication. The psychologist then paged the doctor who was providing medication management to this client and discussed the situation with the doctor when she responded to the page. They discussed the fact that the client was showing no signs of an acute psychotic episode; that he was compensated; and that he was current on his medications and was rational, responding appropriately to questions. The doctor advised that she would meet with this client, and asked that he be scheduled to see her the following Monday so that she could ensure he was receiving the proper dosage of Prolixin.

The psychologist had been recording all of the information concerning her session with this client using the S.O.A.P. notes format. Her chart, containing the client's name and date, had the following notes:

S. "Wakes up in the mornings feeling weird; on synthetic meds."

O. Cheerful, compensated rational, current on meds.

A. Question concerning meds.

P. Contact M.D.; scheduled client to see M.D. on Monday.

That evening the client either slipped and fell from the balcony of his housing unit, or was thrown from it by another inmate. He was injured, and was airlifted to a hospital. He improved with treatment, incurred a staph infection, and died from it in the hospital. His family then initiated a lawsuit against the psychologist and the state, alleging that the client's civil rights had been violated. A consulting expert provided a report to the plaintiff's attorney, expressing the opinion that this client had been suicidal and should have been placed in administrative segregation to protect him from harming himself. (The expert's opinion was absurd, in view of the psychologist's session note!) The lawsuit was summarily dismissed, based upon the S.O.A.P. notes concerning this session.

In 50 words or less, this session note enabled the psychologist to paint an accurate clinical picture of her client's presentation at the time of this session. He was cheerful, not depressed; compensated, not decompensated; and rational, not delusional. This was not an acute psychotic episode by an individual who was noncompliant with his medications. The note enabled all of the essential information concerning the treatment session to be recorded. The client's **S**ubjective data, his presenting problem, is recorded, along with the psychologist's **O**bjective information concerning her observations of the client's demeanor and his mental state. The psychologist's **A**ssessment of the client was also recorded, as well as her **P**lan for follow-up care.

The S.O.A.P. note format, therefore, enables therapists to record information concerning their client's presenting problem on a particular day, thereby documenting the reason for the services provided. This is important in this era of managed health care, when insurance carriers and federal health care programs conduct utilization reviews to determine whether treatment on specific dates was reasonable and necessary. Such questions can be answered easily when S.O.A.P. notes have been taken.

This format answers the frequently asked question, "How extensive should my session notes be?" While note taking is a matter of a therapist's style to some degree, with some therapists being minimalists and others being more obsessive, this format enables therapists to maintain the essential data that should be recorded regarding a session.

4.17 Pastoral Counseling/Spiritual Counseling

The statute that defines the authority of the Colorado Department of Regulatory Agencies to license, regulate, and discipline mental health professionals limits the boards' jurisdiction. C.R.S. § 12-245-217(1) provides that:

> Any person engaged in the practice of religious ministry shall not be required to comply with the provisions of this article; except that such person shall not hold himself or herself out to the public by any title incorporating the terms "psychologist", "social worker", "licensed social worker", "LSW", "licensed clinical social worker", "clinical social worker", "LCSW", "licensed marriage and family therapist", "LMFT", "licensed professional counselor", "LPC", "addiction counselor", "licensed addiction counselor", "LAC",

"certified addiction counselor", or "CAC" unless that person has been licensed or certified pursuant to this article.

The right to religious freedom, guaranteed by the First Amendment to the U.S. Constitution, prohibits states from regulating the practice of a religion or from inhibiting religious freedom.

The mental health boards have all adopted rules that distinguish psychotherapy from spiritual counseling based on the practice of a religious ministry. The Colorado State Board of Unlicensed Psychotherapists Rule 4 C.C.R. 734-1 1.1 lists the following factors to be used by the Board in determining whether a person is engaged in the "practice of religious ministry" or in the practice of psychotherapy under the Board's jurisdiction:

1. Whether the client or guardian had received notice or reasonably understood that the therapy in question was part of a religious practice/ ministry.
2. Whether the client or guardian was seeking therapy from a religious entity to which the complainant belonged at any time.
3. Whether a written agreement or statement exists indicating the therapy in question was part of a religious practice/ministry.
4. Whether the therapy sessions were conducted in a house of worship or on property belonging to or controlled by a religious entity.
5. Whether the person conducting the therapy normally represented himself or herself as a religious official who was counseling as part of a religious ministry.
6. Whether therapy services were part of an ongoing relationship, formed because the provider is a spiritual counselor to the client.
7. Whether the provider of therapy holds a position of trust within a religious entity.
8. Whether the provider advertises therapy to the general public for a fee.
9. Whether the provider collects fees or expects/requires donations, offerings, tithes, or other compensation for therapy.
10. Whether the therapy provided is based on any religious orientation or viewpoint.
11. Whether the provider engaged in the practice of therapy is accountable or subject to any religious entity or person for misdeeds or acts of misconduct.
12. Whether the provider of therapy is a member of a religious entity holding tax-exempt status (*e.g.*, does the entity hold 501(c)(3) tax-exempt status?).

13. Whether the provider is trained in theology or any other field, area, or specialty related to the study of the religious or spiritual orientation.
14. Whether the provider has a declaration of religious mission or a statement identifying the religious views or belief of the entity or person.
15. Whether the provider of therapy services is recognized by consumers as a religious minister or spiritual healer.

Other factors in individual cases will also be considered by a board in determining whether it has jurisdiction over a minister, pastoral counselor, or other spiritual counselor.

C.R.S. § 13-90-107(1)(c) provides that a clergy member-, minister-, priest-, or rabbi-client privilege exists, and that a clergy member, minister, priest, or rabbi "shall not be examined without both his or her consent and also the consent of the person making the confidential communication as to any confidential communication made to him or her in his or her professional capacity in the course of discipline expected by the religious body to which he or she belongs." A "priest-penitent" privilege has long existed, which protects communications made by a penitent who confesses sins to a priest or other clergy member. If a church member admits wrongdoing or confesses sins to a minister, expecting absolution and expecting complete confidentiality for any admissions made, then a privilege exists which is inviolate.

C.R.S. § 19-3-304(2)(aa)(I) requires that a clergy member must report child abuse or neglect, but states that this requirement shall not apply to a person "who acquires reasonable cause to know or suspect that a child has been subjected to abuse or neglect during a communication about which the person may not be examined as a witness pursuant to section 13-90-107(1)(c), C.R.S., unless the person also acquires such reasonable cause from a source other than such a communication." This language is obviously confusing. What C.R.S. § 19-3-304 essentially provides is that if a church member confides or confesses that he or she has committed an act of child abuse in confidence to a clergy member, then a legal privilege exists protecting the confidentiality of these statements. If a clergy member has knowledge concerning suspected child abuse or neglect from his or her own observations or from statements made to the clergy member from a victim, then a duty exists to report the suspected child abuse or neglect.

Best Practice for a Pastoral Counselor

When ministers, priests, rabbis, or other clergy members engage in pastoral counseling as part of their religious ministry, it is prudent for the clergy member to provide a statement to the person being counseled that acknowledges that the counseling is being conducted as part of a religious ministry and that the clergy member is not providing psychotherapy or mental health counseling. Such a statement should be signed by the individual who is to receive counseling in order to avoid any confusion regarding the nature of the counseling being provided and to protect the clergy member in the event that the Department of Regulatory Agencies attempts to exercise jurisdiction over him or her. If a minister or pastoral counselor is licensed by one of the mental health boards, it is essential that the pastoral counselor not use his or her licensure status or honorific title such as "LPC," "LMFT," "LCSW," etc. on any written forms provided to the client or on any signs or office markings in the office where counseling occurs, unless the counselor is willing to submit to the jurisdiction of the mental health boards and to comply with all of the laws, regulations, and ethical standards applicable to psychotherapists.

4.18 Spiritual Counseling for Children

A program for spiritual guidance for children has been established by Dr. Jerome Berryman. Dr. Berryman has developed a Godly Play Program, which is discussed in depth on his website, www.godlyplay.org. Children learn about religion and religious beliefs, in part, by acting out Biblical stories and other scenes that involve moral principles.

Dr. Berryman's spiritual guidance for children does not constitute psychotherapy. Spiritual counselors for children who may have been trained in Dr. Berryman's approach may be identified for appropriate referrals through his website.

4.19 Legal Standards for Forensic Evaluations

Models for Forensic Evaluations

These include Social Security examinations, competency and sanity evaluations in criminal cases, independent medical evaluations or psychological evaluations for lawsuits, court-ordered psychological testing in domestic relations cases, and parental responsibility and parenting time evaluations in domestic cases.

Confidentiality and Privilege

The laws regarding confidentiality and privilege, which apply where health care providers have professional relationships with patients, do not apply to forensic evaluations. For example, C.R.S. § 12-245-220 contains an exception for competency and sanity evaluations, which are not deemed to be confidential, since these evaluations will be shared with the court and with attorneys in the case. Similarly, the subjects being evaluated by a forensic examiner are not required to give "informed consent" for the examination, since there is no treatment being provided. C.R.S. § 12-245-216, which mandates that informed consent for treatment be obtained by mental health professionals providing treatment to a client, contains an exception for court-ordered evaluations. Nevertheless, disclosures are appropriate for an individual being evaluated by a forensic examiner so that (1) the forensic examiner's role is clearly defined, and (2) it is understood that the forensic examiner will not be providing treatment to the person being evaluated.

Ethical Standards

American Psychological Association Ethical Principles regarding the conduct of forensic evaluations include the following:

> APA Ethics Code 2010
>
> *Ethical Principle 9.01 Bases for Assessments*
>
> (a) Psychologists base the opinions contained in their recommendations, reports, and diagnostic or evaluative statements, including forensic testimony, on information and techniques sufficient to substantiate their findings.
>
> (b) Except as noted in 9.01c, psychologists provide opinions of the psychological characteristics of individuals only after they have conducted an examination of the individuals adequate to support their statements or conclusions. When, despite reasonable efforts, such an examination is not practical, psychologists document the efforts they made and the result of those efforts, clarify the probable impact of their limited information on the reliability and the validity of their opinions and appropriately limit the nature and extent of their conclusions or recommendations.
>
> (c) When psychologists conduct a record review or provide consultation or supervision and an individual examination is not warranted or necessary for the opinion, psychologists explain this and the sources of information on which they based their conclusions and recommendations.
>
> *Ethical Principle 9.02 Use of Assessments*
>
> (a) Psychologists administer, adapt, score, interpret or use assessment techniques, interviews, tests or instruments in a manner

and for purposes that are appropriate in light of the research on or evidence of usefulness and proper application of the techniques.

(b) Psychologists use assessment instruments whose validity and reliability have been established for use with members of the population tested. When such validity or reliability has not been established, psychologists describe the strengths and limitations of test results and interpretation.

(c) Psychologists use assessment methods that are appropriate to an individual's language preference and competence, unless the use of an alternative language is relevant to the assessment issues.

Ethical Principle 9.03 Informed Consent in Assessments

(a) Psychologists obtain informed consent for assessments, evaluations or diagnostic services, as described in Standard 3.10, Informed Consent, except when (1) testing is mandated by law or governmental regulations; (2) informed consent is implied because testing is conducted as a routine educational, institutional or organizational activity (*e.g.*, when participants voluntarily agree to assessment when applying for a job); or (3) one purpose of the testing is to evaluate decisional capacity. Informed consent includes an explanation of the nature and purpose of the assessment, fees, involvement of third parties and limits of confidentiality and sufficient opportunity for the client/patient to ask questions and receive answers.

(b) Psychologists inform persons with questionable capacity to consent or for whom testing is mandated by law or government regulations about the nature and purpose of the proposed assessment services, using language that is reasonably understandable to the person being assessed.

. . .

Disclosures signed by the person to be evaluated concerning the forensic examiner's role and the use of the information being shared with the forensic examiner, as well as the report being prepared, are important in order to comply with these APA Ethical Principles. Form 5 in Appendix A is a Forensic Disclosure Form that contains appropriate disclosure regarding the forensic process.

Legal Standards

Pursuant to C.R.S. § 12-245-202(14), psychologists and other mental health professionals under Colorado law are engaging in the practice of psychotherapy when they are attempting to accomplish a psychotherapeutic objective *in a professional relationship with the client.* C.R.S. § 12-245-202(14) defines "psychotherapy" as:

> "Psychotherapy" means the treatment, diagnosis, testing, assessment, or counseling *in a professional relationship* to assist individuals or groups to alleviate mental disorders, understand unconscious or conscious motivation, resolve emotional, relationship, or attitudinal conflicts, or modify behaviors that interfere with effective emotional, social, or intellectual functioning. Psychotherapy follows a planned procedure of intervention that takes place on a regular basis, over a period of time, or in the cases of testing, assessment, and brief psychotherapy, psychotherapy can be a single intervention. [Emphasis added.]

The term "professional relationship" is significant and is defined as "an interaction that is deliberately planned or directed, or both, by the licensee, registrant, or certificate holder toward obtaining specific objectives," according to C.R.S. § 12-245-202(10).

Risk Management Principles

When an independent medical evaluation of a client is performed, the medical examiner does not have a duty to provide treatment to the person being examined. When there is no psychologist-patient relationship, there is no duty to (1) provide treatment to the person being examined, (2) make appropriate referrals for that individual, (3) make appropriate treatment recommendations concerning the individual, or (4) provide needed treatment to the individual. Where no professional relationship exists and no duty of care exists, the person being examined cannot sue for malpractice. Colorado courts have recognized a duty on the part of an independent examining physician not to harm the person being examined.

The forensic examiner has a duty to report any previously unreported child abuse or neglect, pursuant to C.R.S. § 13-90-107. That legal requirement should be disclosed to the person to be evaluated. Other disclosures that should be made to the individual being examined, in order to protect the forensic examiner from any kind of claim, include the forensic examiner's role and the fact that he or she is not providing treatment or establishing a relationship with the person being evaluated. The boundaries between the forensic examiner and the subject of the examination need to be clearly defined in appropriate disclosures.

An important consideration regarding the relationship of a forensic examiner to people being tested or evaluated concerns confidentiality and privilege. If a professional relationship exists between a treatment provider and the patient, then the medical records and treatment information are confidential and privileged, and cannot be disclosed without the consent of the patient pursuant to C.R.S. §§ 12-245-220 and 13-90-107(1)(g).

From a risk management perspective, establishing correct boundaries between the forensic examiner and the examinee assists the professional in defending any potential liability claim that may be made for alleged "breach of confidentiality" or "violation of privilege." In a forensic evaluation where no professional relationship exists, there is no duty of confidentiality or legal privilege preventing disclosure of the examiner's report to the court or agency that requested it.

Record-Keeping

Any records maintained by a forensic examiner should be kept locked, with access available only to authorized individuals on a need-to-know basis. The person evaluated is not necessarily entitled to a copy of any report or to the forensic examiner's file. Social Security Administration Regulations mandate that the forensic examiner share information only with the Social Security Administration:

> a. Request for Records: The subject of the evaluation and report, not being a client, does not have any right to receive copies of reports or other records, and should be informed of that fact in the Disclosures provided. If the court or other authority allows disclosure of the forensic examiner's report or other data, then such disclosure is permissible. Records should not be disclosed to anyone who does not have a 'need to know'.

Model Disclosures

In Appendix A, Form 5 is a form for use in forensic evaluations for the person to be evaluated. This form clearly establishes that no duty of confidentiality exists, explains how the examiner's report will be used, and makes it clear that no professional relationship or duty to provide care has been established.

The disclosures should divulge the fact that a forensic examiner will report any threat of imminent harm against a specific person and will also notify law enforcement of such a threat.

Reports

All reports should identify the basis for any opinions or conclusions stated and should disclose any limitations on the forensic examiner's ability to state conclusions or opinions. The examiner must, of course, remain objective in the entire process of a forensic evaluation. The report should state with specificity that the examiner has not assumed a duty to provide treatment, and is neither making treatment recommendations nor conducting an evaluation for purposes of treatment. The scope of the forensic examiner's role and the fact that no professional relationship has been established may be stated in the report. In formulating any conclusions or opinions, a professional must state any conclusions or opinions "to a reasonable degree of probability" in the professional's discipline or field.

4.20 College and University Counseling Programs: Best Practices

History is a great teacher. Experience has taught that foreseeable problems arise in certain situations brought by students to university counseling programs. For example, if a student reports that she has been sexually harassed by a professor or other university official, a therapist will inevitably be conflicted in attempting to treat the student in this situation. If a student presents to a campus counselor, needing treatment for trauma after being raped by a football player being recruited by the university, foreseeable problems will arise. If a student has been disciplined by a university for engaging in violent conduct, cheating, making threats of violence, or for stalking a student, and the student wants to seek counseling from a university counselor for the anxiety or depression caused by the discipline, inevitable conflicts for a counselor within the university will occur.

What are the foreseeable problems and conflicts associated with these scenarios? In these litigious times, students who feel wronged by a university employee, official, or program may find an attorney to sue the university. If a therapist at the university's counseling program has been providing services to the claimant, then that therapist will be the star witness for the client in the suit against the university. What a conflict will then ensue! The therapist will be torn between his or her therapeutic alliance with the client and loyalty to his or her employer, the university. Imagine being a therapist in a university counseling program and finding yourself cross-examined by the university's legal counsel, who is attempting to impeach your credibility, undermine your opinions, demonstrate that you are incompetent, and embarrass your client in any way possible. Enormous pressure is placed upon therapists in such situations, who may feel compromised regardless of what they do.

The practical solution for such problems is to avoid the situation. A student who has emotional problems allegedly caused by a university professor, employee, or program should be referred off campus. This prevents the therapist's ethical judgment from being questioned, impaired, or compromised. History has shown that attempting to handle such situations "in house" at campus counseling centers is ill-advised.

4.21 Best Practices for Therapeutic Supervised Parenting Time and Reintegration Therapy

In high conflict domestic relations and custody cases, courts often order that a parent be required to have "therapeutic supervised parenting time," in order to maintain the safety of a child or children when they have contact with the parent. Factors that may cause a court to require supervised parenting time include a history of drug or alcohol problems, allegations of child abuse, or other circumstances that impact a child's safety while in the parent's company. Therapeutic supervised parenting time is meant to be a process that will provide clinical services to the child who will be participating in the supervised parenting time process with a parent.

Legal Model for Therapeutic Supervised Parenting Time

Before beginning a therapeutic process whereby a clinician will be monitoring the time spent by a child in the company of a parent, obtain informed consent from the parent(s) or legal representative for the child who has authority to consent to treatment. If the supervised parenting time will involve a father, for example, then meet first with the child's mother in order to obtain appropriate history, intake information, and the factors that may have caused the court to order that parenting time be supervised. Discuss the clinical aspect of the supervised parenting time process, including the steps that will be taken to maintain the child's physical and emotional safety. No doubt, the primary purpose of the court-ordered process will be to improve the child's relationship with the parent, the child's comfort level in becoming better acquainted with the parent as they spend time together, and to provide psychoeducational information to the parent concerning the child's needs, the child's emotional safety, and basic parenting tips.

Because of conflicts that have arisen in the past, experience has shown that the child should be the identified client for the clinical aspect of supervised parenting time, so that the parent will be a collateral in the process, who receives feedback and psychoeducational information to better understand the child's needs and the ways in which the parent can improve his or her parenting practices.

After an initial meeting with the parent who may be providing consent for treatment for the child, but who will not be involved in the supervised parenting time, meet with the parent whose parenting time will be supervised. Establish a good legal and ethical boundary with that individual, informing the parent of the process and its ground rules. Disclose the fact that the parent will be a "collateral" in the child's treatment process, but will not be a counseling client. Prepare a statement concerning "Policies and Procedures," which will disclose the ground rules, logistics, and fact that statements made by the parent, as well as your observations of parent-child interactions, may be shared with the other parent, other professionals, or the court (with appropriate consent from the privilege holder for the child). Again, emphasize that a therapist-client relationship with the parent engaged in supervised parenting is *not* being established, only a therapist-client relationship with the child.

Meet with the child separately, on as many occasions as you may need, until the child is comfortable with the parenting time that will occur. Let the child provide input concerning the ground rules and procedures for the process, especially if the child has been a victim of abuse or neglect in the past committed by the parent whose parenting time is being supervised. Maintain good, thorough notes concerning your process to prepare the child for supervised interactions with the parent.

Maintaining Ethical Boundaries

Frequently, the judges who order therapeutic supervised parenting time invite the clinician who will be conducting that process to make recommendations to the court concerning when the parenting time process no longer needs to be supervised. Because the therapist will be conducting a therapeutic process, no *forensic* recommendations may be made to the court. If you need to frame concerns regarding a child's safety in having contact with the parent, then address clinical concerns and recommendations carefully, so that you are not committing a boundary violation by making a forensic recommendation to the court while serving in a clinical role.

Because of the fact that you will be providing therapeutic services to the child, designed to accomplish goals for your child client, ensure that you have consent in writing from the child's legal representative before providing any reports to the court or testimony in court regarding the process, the parent's compliance with your program rules, or progress made by the parent and child toward improving their relationship and the child's comfort level with the parent.

Legal Model for Reintegration Therapy

The same factors discussed above that cause judges to require parents and their children to engage in therapeutic supervised parenting time also cause judges to order "reintegration therapy." In addition, courts may order that a therapist assist in reuniting a child and parent when the parent has been absent for an extended period of time from the child's life.

After meeting with parents and the child, it may be an appropriate judgment on the part of the therapist to identify only the child as the client, and to identify the parent as a collateral in the reintegration treatment process. When the child is the client and the parent involved in reintegration therapy is a collateral, provide a written disclosure to the parent to inform the parent that no therapist-client relationship is being established with the parent, only with the child, and that the parent's statements and the therapist's observations concerning the parent's behaviors will not be confidential to the extent that they may be shared with the court, other professionals, and the other parent. Experience has shown that parents involved in their child's reintegration therapy can become contentious, adversarial, and non-compliant with the treatment process. In situations where no therapist-client relationship is being established with the parent, that individual cannot sue the therapist for malpractice, because of the fact that a therapist-client relationship is a requirement for filing a malpractice action.

Under appropriate circumstances, family therapy can be used in this treatment process, at the discretion of the therapist, in order to achieve the basic goals of creating a better relationship between the parent and child. However, a therapist must carefully assess the child's prior experience with the parent, the history of any child abuse, or other offensive conduct committed by the parent toward the child. If the assessment conducted by a therapist concludes that a child will probably be harmed by being required to have contact with the parent, then an appropriate clinical recommendation should be made indicating that it may not be safe for reintegration therapy to be initiated.

Ethical Considerations

Make certain that you receive informed consent in writing from the parent who has decision-making authority for the child, or from the child's legal representative, before commencing treatment. Obtain authorization in writing from the client or clients involved in the reintegration therapy process for any disclosure of treatment information. If this treatment is done as a family therapy process, in which both the child and parent(s) are clients, then informed consent from all of the members involved in family therapy must be obtained before writing reports to the court, and before testifying in court. Therapists should follow a clinical model for this treatment, and it may be necessary to obtain clinical supervision from someone who is familiar with reintegration therapy, its risks and procedures, before engaging in this type of treatment.

4.22 Medicaid Regulations

Many questions are being asked about Colorado law regarding the billing of Medicaid members, regardless of whether the member's health plan is administered by ValueOptions, BHI, or Colorado Access. Here are the answers to the questions being posed.

- Medicaid members cannot be billed for any service covered by Medicaid, regardless of whether the treatment provider has a contract to provide Medicaid services or not.
- If a treatment provider is not enrolled in the Colorado Medical Assistance Program as an authorized Medicaid fee-for-service provider, the therapist may not accept any payment from the Medicaid member for covered services.
- Payment may be collected from or billed to a Medicaid member only if the service rendered is not covered by Medicaid, such as couples counseling. To do so, Medicaid contractors are required to obtain a statement prior to the service, signed by the Medicaid member, acknowledging that the specific service being provided is not a Medicaid-covered benefit and agreeing to pay for the service.
- You may be able to obtain a "Single Case Agreement" with Medicaid if you are not a Medicaid contractor by arranging this agreement with a caseworker. Then, for that one case, you would be billing Medicaid as if you had a fee-for-service contract to provide Medicaid services.
- For additional questions regarding the proper billing of Medicaid-covered claims, call the Fiscal Agent at (800) 237-0757.
- For information about enrolling as a Medicaid contractor, contact Marceil Case, Provider Relations Manager: Marceil.Case@state.co.us.

Chapter 5: Restriction of Client Liberties

There are several legal proceedings that are intended to protect clients but result in the deprivation of their civil liberties. This chapter describes these proceedings so psychotherapists can be better equipped to serve the client who is involved in such proceedings.

5.01 Civil Protection Orders

A protection order (formerly called restraining orders) is a court order issued by the court for the purpose of preventing domestic violence. There are various types of protection orders:

1. A restraining order to prevent domestic abuse;
2. The automatic temporary injunction, which occurs upon the filing of a petition for dissolution of marriage or separation under C.R.S. § 14-10-107(4); and
3. A protection order to prevent emotional abuse of the elderly.

Violation of a protection order is a crime pursuant to C.R.S. § 18-6-803.5.

Prevention of Domestic Violence

"Domestic violence" is defined by C.R.S. § 18-6-800.3 as "an act or threatened act of violence upon a person with whom the actor is or has been involved in an intimate relationship" and it includes "any other crime against a person, or against property, including an animal . . . when used as a method of coercion, control, punishment, intimidation, or revenge directed against a person with whom the actor is or has been involved in an intimate relationship." Controlling a victim's finances, documents, or property in a way that makes the victim "more likely to return to an abuser due to fear of retaliation or inability to meet basic needs" is also a form of domestic violence.

A municipal court, county court, or district court may issue temporary and permanent protection orders to prevent domestic abuse. C.R.S. § 13-14-105. Such temporary or permanent orders may include a provision:

1. Restraining a party from threatening, molesting, or injuring any other party or the minor children of either of the parties;
2. Restraining a party from contacting any other party or the minor child of either of the parties;

3. Excluding a party from the family home or from the home of the other party upon a showing that physical or emotional harm would otherwise result;
4. Awarding temporary care and control of any minor children of either party involved for a period of not more than one year;
5. Determining parenting time rights for the other party;
6. Restraining a party (for up to one year) from ceasing to make payments for mortgage or rent, insurance, utilities or related services, transportation, medical care, or child care when the defendant has a prior existing duty or legal obligation; or
7. Restraining a party (for up to one year) from transferring, encumbering, concealing, or in any way disposing of personal effects or real property, except in the usual course of business or for the necessities of life.

In order to obtain a temporary protection order to prevent domestic abuse, a party must file a verified complaint alleging that the other party has committed acts constituting domestic abuse. The court, after hearing evidence and being fully satisfied that sufficient cause exists, may issue a temporary protection order to prevent domestic abuse and issue a citation directed to the other party demanding that the defendant appear before the court at a specific time and date to show cause, if any, why such temporary protection order should not be made permanent. Such temporary protection order may be issued only if the issuing judge finds that a danger to self or others exists to the life or health of one or more persons.

A copy of the complaint, together with a copy of the temporary protection order and a copy of the citation, must be served upon the defendant. The citation must inform the defendant that if the defendant fails to appear in court in accordance with the terms of the citation, a bench warrant may be issued for the arrest of the defendant.

Any person against whom a protection order is issued that excludes such person from a shared residence, may return to such shared residence one time to obtain sufficient undisputed personal effects as are necessary for such person to maintain a normal standard of living during any period prior to a hearing concerning such order. Such person is permitted to return to such shared residence *only if* such person is accompanied at all times by a peace officer.

On the date of the hearing, the judge will examine the record and the evidence and, if he or she believes that the defendant has committed acts constituting domestic abuse to the plaintiff or a minor child and if not restrained and enjoined will continue to commit such acts constituting domestic abuse, the judge may order that the temporary protection order be made permanent or order a permanent protection order with different provisions than the temporary protection order. The judge will inform the defendant that the violation of the protection order will constitute contempt of court and subject the defendant to such punishment as may be provided by law.

The foregoing procedure requires affirmative action by the party seeking the protection order. In particular, the party seeking the order must obtain the appropriate paperwork, file it with the county court, and take the appropriate steps to have the paperwork properly served upon the defendant.

Frequently, psychotherapists will find themselves in a situation where they must provide emotional support for their client who is a victim of such abuse. In such cases, referral to a competent attorney should be considered as a means of relieving the anxiety and burden on the victim. If finances are a consideration, the procedure can be accomplished by a person of average abilities and competence without the assistance of an attorney.

Emergency Protection Orders

Colorado law recognizes that there are circumstances that make it impossible to follow the protection order procedure. For example, there are times when the courts are closed for judicial business and an emergency order is needed. In such circumstances, a peace officer who has reasonable grounds to believe that an adult is in immediate and present danger of domestic abuse, based upon an allegation of a recent incident of actual domestic abuse or threat of domestic abuse, may telephone the on-call judge and request the issuance of a written or verbal emergency protection order. These emergency protection orders may include a provision:

1. Restraining a party from threatening, molesting, or injuring any other party or minor children of either of the parties;
2. Excluding a party from the family home or from the home of another party upon a showing that physical or emotional harm would otherwise result; and
3. Awarding temporary care and control of any minor children of a party involved.

The emergency protective order will expire not later than the close of judicial business on the next day of judicial business following the day of issue, unless otherwise continued by the court. The court may continue any emergency protection order only if the plaintiff has filed a complaint or protection order to prevent domestic abuse, and the judge is unable to set a hearing on a plaintiff's request for a temporary protection order on the day the complaint is filed.

A verbal emergency protection order may be issued only if the issuing judge finds that a danger to self or others exists to the life or health of one or more persons. Such an order must be reduced to writing and signed by the peace officer and must include a statement of the grounds for the order asserted by the officer.

The role of the psychotherapist with respect to an emergency protection order is much more limited than in those instances where a protection order to prevent domestic abuse is sought. Since the emergency protection order is initiated by a peace officer, the opportunity for a psychotherapist to become involved is limited. However, when a psychotherapist believes that a client may be the victim of domestic abuse, the psychotherapist should explain the availability of a protection order. In many cases, knowledge of the availability of this procedure may be comforting to a client.

Divorce Injunction

Upon filing a petition for dissolution of marriage or legal separation by a party, and upon personal service of the petition and summons on the other party, an automatic temporary injunction is in effect against both parties, which:

1. Restrains both parties from transferring, encumbering, concealing, or in any way disposing of, without the consent of the other party or an order of the court, any marital property, except in the usual course of business or for the necessities of life, and requires each party to notify the other party of any proposed extraordinary expenditures and to account to the court for all extraordinary expenditures made after the injunction is in effect;
2. Enjoins both parties from molesting or disturbing the peace of the other party; and
3. Restrains both parties from moving the minor child or children of the parties, if any, from the state without the consent of the other party or an order of the court.

This automatic temporary injunction can be modified or supplemented if either party petitions the court for a more definite or specific temporary order based upon the belief that irreparable injury would result to the moving party if no order were issued. The party may request that the court:

1. Restrain any party from transferring, encumbering, concealing, or in any way disposing of any property, except in the usual course of business or for the necessities of life, and, if so restrained, require him or her to notify

the moving party of any proposed extraordinary expenditures made after the order is issued;

2. Enjoin a party from molesting or disturbing the peace of the other party or of any child; and
3. Exclude a party from the family home or from the home of the other party upon a showing that physical or emotional harm would otherwise result.

Such a temporary injunction may be obtained without notice to the other party. However, the party to whom the temporary injunction is directed may appear before the court and move for dissolution or modification of the temporary injunction.

C.R.S. § 18-6-803.5 provides that whenever a police officer has probable cause to believe a protection order that prohibits "contacting, harassing, injuring, intimidating, molesting, threatening, or touching any protected person or protected animal, or from entering or remaining on premises, or from coming within a specified distance of a protected person or protected animal or premises or any other provision to protect the protected person or protected animal from imminent danger to life or health" was served on the restrained person and violated, it is the duty of the police officer to arrest or obtain an arrest warrant for said violator.

When a client consents, a psychotherapist may be asked to testify at the temporary orders hearing and to render opinions as to the effects of any emotional abuse inflicted upon a victim.

Summary

Psychotherapists should recognize that the temporary protection orders described above are effective only to the extent that the party to whom they are directed complies with them. Although the court will undertake appropriate steps to punish a violation of its protection order, the nature of domestic violence limits the overall effectiveness of such orders. Accordingly, a psychotherapist should counsel that such orders do not stop bullets, nor do they, in all cases, stop the violence. Hence, temporary residence at a safe-house or shelter should be considered. One should not rely solely upon protection orders for safety.

5.02 Involuntary Mental Health Commitments

C.R.S. §§ 27-65-101, *et seq.*, provide limitations and standards for the care and treatment of the mentally ill. The statutes were enacted by the General Assembly in order to:

1. Secure for each person who may be mentally ill such care and treatment as will be suited to the needs of the person and ensure that such care and treatment are skillfully and humanely administered with full respect for the person's dignity and personal integrity.
2. Deprive a person of his or her liberty for purposes of treatment or care only when less restrictive alternatives are unavailable and only when his or her safety or the safety of others is endangered.
3. Provide the fullest possible measure of privacy, dignity, and other rights to persons undergoing care and treatment for mental illness.
4. Encourage the use of voluntary rather than coercive measures to secure treatment and care for mental illness.
5. Provide appropriate information to family members concerning the location and fact of admission of mentally ill persons to inpatient or residential care and treatment.
6. Encourage the appropriate participation of family members in the care and treatment of a mentally ill person and, when appropriate, provide information to family members in order to facilitate such participation.

Statutory Standard for Determining Whether an Individual is "Dangerous to Self or Others"

The standard for 72-hour holds and for hospitalization of clients, which is "evidence-based," uses the term "danger to self or others." C.R.S. § 27-65-102(4.5) defines a person who is a "danger to self or others" as follows:

> (a) With respect to an individual, that the individual poses a substantial risk of physical harm to himself or herself as manifested by evidence of recent threats of or attempts at suicide or serious bodily harm to himself or herself; or
>
> (b) With respect to other persons, that the individual poses a substantial risk of physical harm to another person or persons, as manifested by evidence of recent homicidal or other violent behavior by the person in question, or by evidence that others are placed in a reasonable fear of violent behavior and serious physical harm to them, as evidenced by a recent overt act, attempt, or threat to do serious physical harm by the person in question.

Definition of "Gravely Disabled"

The definition of the term "gravely disabled," contained in C.R.S. § 27-65-102(17), is

> a condition in which a person, as a result of a mental health disorder, is incapable of making informed decisions about or providing for the person's essential needs without significant supervision and assistance from other people. As a result of being incapable of making these informed decisions, a person who is gravely disabled is at risk of substantial bodily harm, dangerous worsening of any concomitant serious physical illness, significant psychiatric deterioration, or mismanagement of the person's essential needs that could result in substantial bodily harm. A person of any age may be 'gravely disabled', but such term does not include a person whose decision-making capabilities are limited solely by the person's developmental disability.

As set forth in Section 27-65-106, a 72-hour hold may be sought for a person who is gravely disabled under this definition.

Emergency 72-Hour Hold

C.R.S. § 27-65-106 sets forth two emergency procedures by which a person appearing to be mentally ill may be taken into custody and confined for a 72-hour evaluation and treatment. Under C.R.S. § 27-65-105, a person may be held for a 72-hour evaluation when he or she appears to be mentally ill (and as a result, a danger to self or others) or gravely disabled. Mental retardation, however, is insufficient to either justify or exclude a finding of mental illness within the provisions of this article.

C.R.S. § 27-65-105(1)(a) provides that a peace officer, a medical doctor or psychologist, a registered professional nurse, a licensed marriage and family therapist, a licensed professional counselor, or a licensed clinical social worker may temporarily commit a mentally ill person into custody, or cause such person to be taken into custody and placed in a facility of the Department of Human Services for a 72-hour treatment and evaluation. In order for an intervening professional to initiate a 72-hour hold, the following conditions must be present:

1. The person must appear to be mentally ill, meaning that he or she suffers a substantial disorder of cognitive, volitional, or emotional processes that grossly impairs judgment or capacity to recognize reality and control behavior.

2. As a result of such mental illness, the person appears to be a danger to others, or to himself or herself, or appears to be gravely disabled.
3. The intervening professional must have *probable cause* to believe that there is in fact an appearance of mental illness or that the person is a danger to self or others or is gravely disabled.

A Form M-1 is included in Appendix A at Form 4. A Form M-1 may be signed by a licensed mental health professional or by a peace officer when probable cause exists to detain a client for a 72-hour hold.

A 72-hour hold may also be ordered by the court when an affidavit sworn to or affirmed before a judge contains sufficient facts to establish that the person appears to be mentally ill and, as a result of such mental illness, appears to be a danger to others or to himself or herself, or appears to be gravely disabled. The court may then order the person described in the affidavit to be taken into custody, transported to a 72-hour hold facility, and placed on hold for a 72-hour evaluation at the designated facility.

Any person taken into custody for a 72-hour hold must not be detained in a jail, lockup, or other place used for the confinement of persons charged with or convicted of penal offenses.

Court-Ordered Evaluations

C.R.S. § 27-65-106 provides that any person alleged to be mentally ill, who, as a result of mental illness, is a danger to others or to himself or herself, or is gravely disabled, may be ordered to submit to an evaluation of his or her condition. Such an order may be issued when any individual petitions the court in the county where the mentally ill person resides or is physically present and alleges that the person appears to be mentally ill and, as a result of such mental illness, appears to be a danger to others or to himself or herself, or appears to be gravely disabled, and requests that an evaluation of the person's condition be made.

The petition for a court-ordered evaluation must contain the following:

1. The name and address of the petitioner and his or her interest in the case.
2. The name of the person for whom the evaluation is sought (who will be designated as the respondent) and, if known to the petitioner, the address, age, sex, marital status, and occupation of the respondent.
3. Allegations of fact indicating that the respondent may have a mental illness and, as a result of the mental illness, may be a danger to others or to himself or herself, or gravely disabled and showing reasonable grounds to warrant an evaluation.

4. The name and address of every person known or believed by the petitioner to be legally responsible for the care, support, and maintenance of the respondent, if available.
5. The name, address, and telephone number of the attorney, if any, who has most recently represented the respondent. If there is no attorney, there will be a statement as to whether, to the best knowledge of the petitioner, the respondent meets the criteria established by the legal aid agency operating in the county or city and county to represent a client.

Upon receipt of a petition containing the above requirements, the court must designate a facility approved by the Commissioner of the Behavioral Health Administration (BHA), or an Emergency Medical Services (EMS) facility, to provide screening of the respondent to determine whether there is probable cause to believe the allegations.

In May 2022 the General Assembly adopted HB 22-1256, which modifies the procedures for involuntary mental health commitments. The sections of HB 22-1256 have effective dates of July 1, 2023 or July 1, 2024, and require the following:

1. The facility where the person is transported is required to submit an application, in writing, stating the circumstances and specific facts under which the person's condition was called to the attention of a certified peace officer or emergency medical services provider, and a copy of that application must be provided to the respondent;
2. The bill requires an intervening professional to screen the person immediately or within eight hours after the person's arrival at the facility to determine if the person meets the criteria for an emergency mental health hold, and the person has the right not to be detained more than 14 hours for the screening;
3. The person being transported has the right to be informed regarding the purpose for the transport and other rights that must be explained prior to transporting the individual, including the right not to be transported for more than six hours;
4. A certified peace officer is authorized to transport a person to an EMS facility for screening, even if a warrant has been issued for the person's arrest, if the certified peace officer believes it is in the best interest of the person to do so;
5. An intervening professional or certified peace officer is authorized to initiate an emergency mental health hold at the time of screening the respondent;

6. A certified peace officer may authorize a secure transportation provider to take a respondent into protective custody and transport the person to an EMS facility or designated facility for an emergency mental health hold;
7. The Commissioner of the BHA may require a standardized form to be used in the emergency mental health evaluation;
8. The EMS facility must immediately notify the BHA if a person is evaluated and the evaluating professional determines that the person continues to meet the criteria for an emergence mental health hold and the facility cannot locate appropriate placement;
9. Following the screening, the facility or professional person shall file a report with the court, which must include a recommendation regarding whether there is probable cause to believe that the respondent has a mental disorder and is a danger to self or others and whether the respondent will voluntarily receive evaluation or treatment;
10. If the evaluation concludes that the respondent does not meet criteria for an emergency mental health hold, then the facility is required to discharge the respondent, to provide the respondent with a copy of the discharge instructions, and encourage the person to designate a family member, friend, or lay person to participate in discharge planning; and
11. When a respondent is certified for short-term or long-term care and treatment, the individual is entitled to an attorney, regardless of income.

Long-Term Care and Treatment

C.R.S. § 27-65-109 provides that whenever a respondent has received short-term treatment for five consecutive months, the professional person in charge of the evaluation and treatment may file a petition with the court for long-term care and treatment under the following conditions:

1. The professional staff member providing short-term treatment has analyzed the respondent's condition and has found that the respondent has a mental illness and, as a result of the mental illness, is a danger to others or to himself or herself, or is gravely disabled.
2. The respondent has been advised of the availability of, but has not accepted, voluntary treatment. If reasonable grounds exist to believe that the respondent will not remain in a voluntary treatment program, his or her acceptance of voluntary treatment shall not preclude an order pursuant to C.R.S. § 27-65-109.

3. The facility that will provide long-term care and treatment has been designated or approved by the Commissioner of the BHA to provide such care and treatment.

Every petition for long-term care and treatment must include a request for a hearing before the court prior to the expiration of six months from the date of original certification. A copy of the petition must be delivered personally to the respondent and mailed to his or her attorney of record. Within 10 days after receipt of the petition, the respondent or his or her attorney may request a jury trial.

The court or jury will determine whether the foregoing conditions have been met and whether the respondent is mentally ill and, as a result, is a danger to others or to himself or herself, or is gravely disabled. The court will thereupon issue an order of long-term care and treatment not to exceed six months, or discharge the respondent for whom the long-term care and treatment was sought, or enter any other appropriate order, subject to available appropriations.

Any order for long-term care and treatment must grant custody of the respondent to the Department of Human Services for placement with an agency or facility. When a petition contains a request that a specific legal disability be imposed or that a specific legal right be deprived, the court may order the disability imposed or the right deprived if it or a jury has determined that the respondent is mentally ill or gravely disabled and that, by reason thereof, the person is unable to competently exercise the right or perform the function for which the disability is sought to be imposed.

An original order of long-term care and treatment expires upon the date it specifies, unless further extended. If an extension is sought, the professional in charge of the evaluation and treatment must certify to the court at least 30 days prior to the expiration date of the order that an extension of such order is necessary for the care and treatment of the respondent. A copy of the certification must be delivered to the respondent and mailed to his or her attorney of record. At least 20 days before the expiration of the order, the court must give written notice to the respondent and his or her attorney that a hearing on the extension may be had before the court or a jury upon written request to the court within 10 days after receipt of the notice. If no hearing is requested within such time, the court may proceed. However, if a hearing is timely requested, it must be held before the expiration date of the order in force. If the court or jury finds that the mental illness continues and, as a result, the respondent is a danger to others or to himself or herself, or is gravely disabled, the court must issue an extension of the order. Any extension must be for a period of not more than six months, but there may be as many extensions as the court orders.

Termination and Escape

Certifications for short-term treatment, extended certification, or an order for long-term care and treatment, or any extensions thereof, must terminate as soon as, in the opinion of the professional person in charge of treatment of the respondent, the respondent has received sufficient benefit from such treatment for him or her to leave. Whenever this occurs, the professional person in charge of providing treatment must notify the court in writing within five days of the termination. The professional person may also prescribe day care, night care, or any other similar mode of treatment prior to termination.

Before termination, an escaped respondent may be returned to the facility by order of the court without a hearing, or by the superintendent or director of such facility without order of court.

Right to Treatment

C.R.S. § 27-65-116 provides that any person receiving evaluation or treatment is entitled to medical and psychiatric care and treatment that is suited to meet his or her individual needs, delivered in such a way as to keep him or her in the least restrictive environment and to include the opportunity for participation of family members in his or her program of care and treatment when appropriate.

Patient's Rights

C.R.S. § 27-65-119 sets forth the following rights for persons receiving evaluation, care, or mental health treatment:

1. To receive and send sealed correspondence, without such correspondence being opened, delayed, held, or censored.
2. To have access to letter-writing materials, including postage, and to have staff members of the facility assist him or her if he or she is unable to write, prepare, and mail correspondence.
3. To have ready access to telephones, both to make and to receive calls in privacy.
4. To have frequent and convenient opportunities to meet with visitors and to see his or her attorney, clergy, or physician at any time.
5. To wear his or her own clothes, keep and use his or her personal possessions, and keep and be allowed to spend reasonable sums of his or her own money.
6. To receive a written copy of all of his or her rights.

The person's rights may be denied for good cause only by the professional person providing treatment. Denial of any right, however, shall in all cases be entered into the person's treatment record and made available, upon request, to the person or his or her attorney. No person admitted to a facility shall be fingerprinted unless required by other provisions of law. A person may be photographed upon admission for identification and administrative purposes of the facility. However, such photographs shall be confidential and shall not be released by the facility, except pursuant to a court order.

In addition to the foregoing, C.R.S. § 27-65-120 provides that any person receiving evaluation, care, or treatment shall be given the opportunity to exercise his or her right to register and to vote in primary and general elections. The agency or facility providing evaluation, care, or treatment shall assist such persons, upon their request, in obtaining voter registration forms and applications for absentee ballots.

Federal Law Concerning Patients' Rights

The federal statute that guarantees rights to patients in a federal mental health program or facility is 42 U.S.C. § 9501. This statute ensures for mental health patients the following rights:

1. The right to appropriate treatment and services in a setting that is supportive of the person's personal liberty, under conditions that restrict liberty only to the extent necessary, considering the individual's treatment needs.
2. The right to an individualized written treatment plan, which is to be developed promptly. A patient has the right to treatment based on this plan, the right to periodic review of treatment, and the right to appropriate revision of the plan, including a description of mental health services that may be needed after the individual is discharged from the mental health program or facility.
3. The right to ongoing participation, in a manner appropriate to the individual's capabilities, *in the planning of the mental health services* that will be provided. In this regard, a patient has the right to be provided with a reasonable explanation, in terms appropriate to the individual's condition, of the following:
   a. The person's general mental condition;
   b. The objectives of treatment;
   c. The nature of the treatment, and any significant adverse effects of it;

   d. The reasons why a particular treatment is considered appropriate;
   e. The reasons why access to certain visitors may not be appropriate; and
   f. Any appropriate alternative treatments, services, and mental health providers that are available.

4. The right *not* to receive a course of treatment pursuant to the treatment plan unless the person has given voluntary, informed consent in writing. This does not apply to emergency treatment or to a situation where a person has been committed by a court to a treatment program or a facility.
5. The right not to participate in experimentation in the absence of voluntary informed consent in writing, and the right to appropriate protection in connection with such participation, including the right to a reasonable explanation of the procedure to be followed, the benefits to be expected, the relative advantages of alternative treatments, and the potential discomfort and risks, as well as the right and opportunity to revoke such consent.
6. The right to freedom from restraint or seclusion, other than as a course of treatment or during an emergency, if such restraint or seclusion is ordered and documented in writing by a mental health professional.
7. The right to a humane treatment environment that affords reasonable protection from harm and appropriate privacy with regard to personal needs.
8. The right to confidentiality.
9. The right to access, upon request, to such person's mental health records, except that a patient may be refused access to information that was provided by a third party under assurances that it would remain confidential. In addition, a patient may be refused access to information if a mental health professional determines, in writing, that access would be detrimental to the patient's health.
10. The right, in a residential or inpatient setting, to converse with others privately, to have convenient and reasonable access to the telephone and mail, and to see visitors during regularly scheduled hours, except that a patient may be refused access to visitors if a mental health professional determines that it may be detrimental to the patient.
11. The right to be informed of these rights at the time of admission and periodically thereafter in terms appropriate to the individual's condition.

12. The right to assert grievances with respect to infringement of these rights, including the right to have grievances considered in a fair, timely, and impartial grievance procedure established by the program or facility.
13. The right to a qualified advocate, as well as the right of access to any available rights protection services within the program or facility and within the state mental health system, for the purpose of receiving assistance in understanding, exercising, and protecting these rights.
14. The right to exercise these rights without reprisal in any form.
15. The right to an appropriate referral to other providers of mental health services upon discharge from inpatient treatment.

Confidentiality of Records

C.R.S. § 27-65-121 and C.R.S. § 27-65-122 set forth detailed procedures for the maintenance of records and the release of information to third parties. See section 2.16 of this book for a discussion of such requirements.

Imposition of Legal Disability and Deprivation of Legal Rights

C.R.S. § 27-65-127 sets forth the procedures that must be followed by any interested person desiring to obtain a determination as to the imposition of a legal disability or the deprivation of a legal right for any person who has a mental illness and is a danger to himself or herself or others, or is gravely disabled or insane. Such interested person may petition the court for a specific finding as to such disability or deprivation of a legal right. The petition must set forth the disability to be imposed or the legal right to be deprived and the reasons therefor. The court may impose disability or may deprive a person of a legal right only upon finding that the respondent has a mental illness and is a danger to himself or herself or others, or is gravely disabled or insane, and that the requested disability or deprivation is both necessary and desirable.

No legal disability may be imposed, nor a legal right be deprived, for a period of more than six months without a review hearing by the court at the end of six months, at which time the findings previously entered by the court may be reaffirmed to justify continuance of the disability or deprivation.

Whenever any proceedings are instituted for the imposition of a legal disability or deprivation of a legal right, the court must appoint (1) an attorney to represent the respondent, and (2) other professional persons to assist the respondent in the preparation of his or her case. Upon demand, the respondent shall have the right to a trial on all issues by a jury of six. The burden of proof is upon the person seeking imposition of disability or deprivation of a legal right, and such must be proven by clear and convincing evidence.

5.03 Care and Treatment of a Minor

The provision of mental health services to a minor (one who is under the age of 18) raises various legal issues. These include: (1) whether the minor may consent to treatment, or whether parental consent is required for treatment; (2) whether the minor, or his or her parents, must be provided with the disclosure statement and must sign it; (3) whether, in treating a minor, the duty of confidentiality prevents a psychotherapist from disclosing confidential communications with the client's parents; (4) whether a minor may consent to inpatient mental health treatment; (5) whether the minor, or his or her parents, will be obligated to pay for treatment expenses; and (6) whether the due process rights of a minor who is subject to a 72-hour hold or who is receiving treatment under a court-ordered certification vary in any way from the due process rights of an adult.

C.R.S. § 27-65-103 provides that a minor who is 15 years of age or older "may consent to receive mental health services to be rendered by a facility or by a professional person." A "'facility' means a public hospital or a licensed private hospital, clinic, . . . or residential child care facility that provides treatment for persons with mental health disorders." C.R.S. § 27-65-102(7). A "professional person," from whom a 15-year-old may consent to receive mental health services, is a "person licensed to practice medicine in this state" or a licensed psychologist. C.R.S. § 27-65-102(17).

Regarding the issue of confidentiality, C.R.S. § 27-65-103(2) provides: "The professional person . . . rendering mental health services to a minor may, with or without the consent of the minor, advise the parent or legal guardian of the minor of the services given or needed."

Note that C.R.S. § 27-65-103(2) only authorizes disclosure by the therapist of the fact that services are needed or are being given.

A 12-year-old is now authorized to consent to outpatient treatment without parental consent when a licensed mental health professional determines that the child is voluntarily seeking treatment and that counseling services are clinically indicated. C.R.S. § 12-245-203.5. The details regarding informed consent for a 12-year-old, documentation required, and information for parents are discussed in Section 4.14.

With regard to the due process rights of a minor who is the subject of a voluntary commitment, C.R.S. § 27-65-103(5) provides that the need for continuing hospitalization of all minors who are voluntary patients shall be formally reviewed at least every two months. This review shall be conducted by an independent professional person, who is not a member of the minor's treatment team. The independent professional person shall determine whether the minor continues to meet the criteria for hospitalization.

In circumstances where a minor does not consent to mental health treatment, consent for treatment must be reviewed within 10 days by an independent professional person; and if the respondent does not meet criteria for a mental health hold, then the individual must be discharged. If the minor is to be held, then the minor must be informed of the right to retain an attorney, and the minor's parent or guardian must be notified. In general, if a minor has voluntarily consented to mental health treatment, the minor should give consent to the release of any records or information concerning treatment. On the other hand, if parental consent was necessary in order to provide mental health services to the minor, then authorization from the parent or guardian must be obtained for release of confidential information.

In Colorado, a parent or legal guardian is obligated to provide support for minor children up to the age of their majority (age 18) or up to the time when they become emancipated. Accordingly, it is the parent's obligation to pay for any mental health services provided to a minor.

The Child Mental Health Treatment Act

In 1999, the Colorado General Assembly enacted the Child Mental Health Treatment Act. The public policy supporting this enactment states that "it is desirable to assist children with mental health needs and such children's families . . . [and] to make mental health services more available to families who want treatment for their children." The legislative declaration contained in C.R.S. § 27-67-102 provides that in many situations, an action in dependency or neglect under the Children's Code is neither appropriate nor warranted in circumstances where "the parents are loving, caring parents who have become increasingly frustrated in their attempts to navigate the various governmental systems including child welfare, mental health, law enforcement, juvenile justice, education, and youth corrections in an attempt to find help for their children."

5.04 Treatment of Alcoholics

Emergency Commitment

C.R.S. § 27-81-111 provides that when any person is under the influence of or incapacitated by substances and clearly dangerous to the health and safety of himself or herself or others, such person shall be taken into protective custody by law enforcement authorities or an emergency service patrol, acting with probable cause, and placed in an approved treatment facility. If no such facilities are available, such person may be detained in an emergency medical facility or jail, but only for so long as necessary to prevent injury to himself or herself or others or to prevent a breach of the peace. A taking into protective custody under this statute is not an arrest, and no entry or other record is made to indicate that the person has been arrested or charged with a crime.

Under C.R.S. § 27-81-111, a law enforcement officer, emergency service patrolman, physician, spouse, guardian, relative of the person to be committed, or any other responsible person may make a written application for emergency commitment to the administrator of an approved treatment facility. The application must state the circumstances requiring the emergency commitment, including the applicant's personal observations and the specific statements of others, if any, upon which he or she relies in making the application. A copy of the application must be furnished to the person to be committed.

If the approved treatment facility administrator or his or her authorized designee approves the application, the person shall be committed, evaluated, and treated for a period not to exceed five days. The person will be brought to the facility by a peace officer, the emergency service patrol, or any interested person. If necessary, the court may be contacted to issue an order to the police or sheriff's department to transport the person to the facility.

If the approved treatment facility administrator or his or her authorized designee determines that the application fails to sustain the grounds for emergency commitment, the commitment request will be refused and the person detained will be immediately released, and the person shall be encouraged to seek voluntary treatment if appropriate.

When the administrator determines that the grounds for commitment no longer exist, he or she must discharge the person committed. No person committed under this statute may be detained in any treatment facility for more than five days, except that a person may be detained for longer than five days at the approved treatment facility if, in that period of time, a petition for involuntary commitment has been filed pursuant to C.R.S. § 27-81-112. A person may not be detained longer than 10 days after the date of filing of the petition for involuntary commitment.

Whenever a person is involuntarily detained pursuant to C.R.S. § 27-81-111, he or she must immediately be advised by the facility administrator or his or her authorized designee, both orally and in writing, of his or her right to challenge such detention by application to the courts for a writ of *habeas corpus*, to be represented by counsel at every stage of any proceedings relating to his or her commitment and recommitment, and to have counsel appointed by the court or provided by the court if he or she wants the assistance of counsel and is unable to obtain counsel.

Involuntary Commitment of Alcoholics

C.R.S. § 27-81-112 provides that a person may be committed to the custody of an approved treatment facility upon the petition of a spouse, guardian, relative, physician, an advanced practice nurse, the administrator in charge of any approved treatment facility, or any other responsible person. The petition must allege that the person has a substance use disorder and that he or she has threatened, attempted to inflict, or inflicted physical harm on himself or herself or on another, and that unless committed, he or she is likely to inflict physical harm on himself or herself or on another, or that he or she is incapacitated by substances. A refusal to undergo treatment does not constitute evidence of lack of judgment as to the need for treatment. The petition must be accompanied by a certificate of a licensed physician who has examined the person within two days before submission of the petition, unless that person whose commitment is sought has refused to submit to a medical examination, in which case the fact of refusal must be alleged in the petition. The certificate must set forth the physician's findings in support of the allegations of the petition.

The petition for commitment will not be accepted unless there is documentation of the refusal by the person to be committed to accessible and affordable voluntary treatment. Such documentation may include, but shall not be limited to, a physician's statements, an advanced practice nurse's statements, notations in the person's medical or law enforcement records, or witnesses' statements.

Upon the filing of the petition, the court will fix a date for a hearing no later than 10 days after the date the petition was filed. A copy of the petition and of the notice of the hearing will be personally served on the petitioner, the person whose commitment is sought, and one of his or her parents or his or her legal guardian if he or she is a minor. Additionally, a copy of the petition and notice of hearing must be mailed: (1) to the Office of Behavioral Health; (2) to counsel for the person whose commitment is sought; (3) to the administrator in charge of the approved treatment facility to which the person may have been committed for emergency treatment; and (4) to any other person the court believes advisable.

At the hearing, the court will hear all relevant testimony, including, if possible, the testimony of at least one licensed physician who has examined the person whose commitment is sought. The person must be present unless the court believes that his or her presence is likely to be injurious to him or her. In this event, the court will appoint a guardian *ad litem* to represent him or her throughout the proceeding. If the person has refused to be examined by a licensed physician, he or she will be given an opportunity to be examined by a court-appointed licensed physician. If he or she refuses and there is sufficient evidence to believe that the allegations of the petition are true or if the court believes that more medical evidence is necessary, the court may commit the person to a licensed hospital for a period of not more than five days for a diagnostic examination. In such event, the court will schedule a further hearing for final determination of commitment, in no event later than five days after the first hearing.

If, after hearing all relevant evidence, the court finds that grounds for involuntary commitment have been established by clear and convincing proof, it must make an order of commitment to the Office of Behavior Health. The Office has the right to delegate physical custody of the person to an appropriate approved treatment facility. The court may not order commitment of a person unless it determines that the Office is able to provide adequate and appropriate treatment.

Upon commitment of a person to the Office of Behavioral Health by the court, the court may issue an order to the sheriff to transport the person committed to the facility designated by the Office.

A person committed as provided in C.R.S. § 27-81-112 will remain in the custody of the Office for treatment for a period of up to 90 days unless sooner discharged. At the end of the 90-day period, he or she must be discharged automatically unless the Office, before expiration of the period, obtains a court order for his or her recommitment for a further period of 90 days unless sooner discharged.

A person recommitted who has not been discharged by the Office before the end of the 90-day period must be discharged at the expiration of that period unless the Office, before expiration of the period, obtains another court order. Only two recommitment orders are permitted.

Upon the filing of a petition for recommitment, the court will fix a date for hearing no later than 10 days after the date the petition was filed, and the court will proceed with a hearing.

A person committed to the custody of the Office of Behavioral Health must be discharged at any time before the end of the period for which he or she has been committed if either of the following conditions is met:

1. In case of a person with a substance use disorder committed on the grounds that he or she is likely to inflict physical harm upon another, that he or she no longer has an alcoholic condition that requires treatment or the likelihood no longer exists; or

2. In case of a person with a substance use disorder committed on the grounds of the need for treatment and/or incapacity, that the incapacity no longer exists, further treatment will not be likely to bring about significant improvement in the person's condition, or treatment is no longer appropriate.

The court must inform the person whose commitment or recommitment is sought of his or her right to contest the application, to be represented by counsel at every level of any proceedings relating to his or her commitment and recommitment, and to have counsel appointed by the court or provided by the court if he or she wants the assistance of counsel and is unable to obtain counsel. If the court believes that the person needs the assistance of counsel, the court must appoint counsel for him or her regardless of his or her wishes. The person whose commitment or recommitment is sought must be informed of his or her right to be examined by a licensed physician of his or her choice. If the person is unable to obtain a licensed physician and requests examination by a physician, the court will employ a licensed physician.

Patients in any approved treatment facility must be granted opportunities for continuing visitation and communication with their families and friends consistent with an effective treatment program. Patients shall be permitted to consult with counsel at any time. Neither mail nor other communication to or from a patient in any approved treatment facility may be intercepted, read, or censored.

5.05 Care and Treatment of the Developmentally Disabled

C.R.S. §§ 25.5-10-201, *et seq.*, set forth in general terms provisions for the care and treatment of the developmentally disabled. Developmental disability means a disability that is manifested before the person reaches 22 years of age. It constitutes a substantial handicap of the affected individual and is attributable to mental retardation or related conditions that include cerebral palsy, epilepsy, autism, or other neurological conditions when such conditions result in impairment of general intellectual functioning or adaptive behavior similar to that of mentally retarded persons.

In C.R.S. § 25.5-10-201, the rights of the developmentally disabled are identified in a compassionate legislative declaration, which promotes community support for developmentally disabled persons to "ensure the fullest measure of privacy, dignity, rights, and privileges" for developmentally disabled persons.

Limitation on Liability of Developmental Disability Service Providers

C.R.S. § 13-21-117.5 limits the liability of developmental disability service providers. The law provides that neither developmentally disabled individuals nor their family members may file a lawsuit against a service provider, unless the claimant has pursued "dispute resolution or other applicable intervention . . . within one year after the date of the discovery of the injury or grievance . . . ."

A claimant's submission of proof that a dispute resolution request has been filed and no action was taken by the Department of Human Services within 90 days "shall be a jurisdictional prerequisite to any action" brought by the claimant. Therefore, whenever a developmental disability service provider receives a letter from an attorney threatening a suit or forwarding a complaint, that provider should immediately respond by agreeing that the matter be submitted for dispute resolution pursuant to C.R.S. § 13-21-117.5.

Another provision of the same statute states that a provider of services "shall not be liable for damages in any civil action for failure to warn or protect any person against the violent, assaultive, disorderly, or harassing behavior of a person with a developmental disability, nor shall any such provider be held civilly liable for failure to predict or prevent such behavior," except where a "serious and credible threat of imminent physical violence and serious bodily injury against a specific person or persons" has been made by a person with a developmental disability.

If there is a duty to warn of such a threat, that duty shall be discharged "by the provider making reasonable and timely efforts to notify any person or persons specifically threatened." If the person threatened with imminent physical violence is a person with a developmental disability under a provider's care, "the provider shall take reasonable action to protect such person from serious bodily injury until the threat can reasonably be deemed to have abated."

Imposition of Legal Disability

C.R.S. § 25.5-10-216 sets forth the conditions under which a legal disability may be imposed or a legal right removed from a person with developmental disabilities. Under C.R.S. § 25.5-10-216, any interested person may petition the court to impose a legal disability or to remove a legal right that affects the rights of the disabled person to contract, determine a place of abode or provisions of care and treatment, operate a motor vehicle, or other similar rights.

Prior to granting the petition, the court must find that the person subject to the petition has been determined to be a person with developmental disabilities and that the requested disability or removal is both necessary and desirable in order to implement the individual habilitation plan developed for the person with developmental disabilities under the supervision of a developmental disabilities professional.

If a petition seeks to impose a disability or remove a legal right related to the selection of a place of abode, the court must also find that, based on the recent overt actions or omissions of the person subject to the petition, and because of his or her developmental disability, without the removal of said right, such person poses a probable threat of serious physical harm to himself or herself or others, or is unable to care for his or her own needs to the extent that his or her own life or safety is seriously threatened, and that the place of abode requested in the petition is the least restrictive residential setting appropriate for the individual needs of the person with developmental disabilities.

Within six months after legal disability has been imposed or a legal right has been removed, the court shall hold a hearing to review its order and either reaffirm the findings and continue the legal disability or removal, or remove the legal disability or restore the legal rights to the person subject to the petition.

When a petition is filed, the court shall appoint an attorney to represent the person subject to the petition. Such person may retain his or her own counsel at any time. Additionally, the court, at the request of an indigent respondent, shall appoint one or more developmental disabilities professionals of the respondent's choice to assist the respondent in the preparation of his or her case. The fees for both the attorney and the developmental disabilities professionals shall be paid for by the court for all indigent respondents.

The burden of proof is upon the party seeking imposition of a disability or removal of a legal right, and the standard of proof is by clear and convincing evidence.

Rights of the Developmentally Disabled

Pursuant to C.R.S. § 25.5-10-218, developmentally disabled persons have the same legal rights and responsibilities guaranteed to all other individuals under the federal and state constitutions and laws. Other statutes confer the following rights on developmentally disabled persons:

1. The right to have an individualized plan developed jointly by professional persons, the person receiving the services, and such person's parent or guardian (C.R.S. § 25.5-10-219);
2. The right to receive appropriate dental and medical care and treatment for any physical ailments and for the prevention of any illness or disability (C.R.S. § 25.5-10-220);

3. The right to be free from unnecessary or excessive medication (C.R.S. § 25.5-10-220(4));
4. The right to humane care and treatment (C.R.S. § 25.5-10-221);
5. The right to be free from physical restraint except when absolutely necessary to protect the person receiving services from injury to himself or herself or to prevent injury to others, and only if alternative techniques have failed and such restraint imposes the least possible restriction consistent with its purposes (C.R.S. § 25.5-10-221(8));
6. The right to fair employment practices (C.R.S. § 25.5-10-224);
7. The right to religious belief, practices, and worship (C.R.S. § 25.5-10-222);
8. The right to communicate freely and privately with persons of his or her own choosing (C.R.S. § 25.5-10-223(1));
9. The right to receive and send sealed, unopened packages and correspondence without incoming or outgoing packages or correspondence being opened, delayed, held, or censored by any person (C.R.S. §§ 25.5-10-223(2) and (3));
10. The right to reasonable access to telephones, both to make and receive calls in privacy (C.R.S. § 25.5-10-223(4));
11. The right to reasonable and frequent opportunities to meet with visitors (C.R.S. § 25.5-10-223(4));
12. The right to suitable opportunities for the resident's interaction with persons of their choice (C.R.S. § 25.5-10-223(5));
13. Sterilization rights (C.R.S. § 25.5-10-231);
14. The right to vote in all primary and general elections and to assistance in registering to vote, obtaining applications for absentee ballots, and obtaining absentee ballots (C.R.S. § 25.5-10-225);
15. The right to possession and use of his or her own clothing and personal effects, including the right to receive reasonable amounts of his or her own money or funds held in trust (C.R.S. § 25.5-10-227);
16. The right to establish committees to hear the views and represent the interests of all persons served by an agency serving developmentally disabled persons and to attempt to influence the policies of the agency to the extent that they influence provision of services (C.R.S. § 25.5-10-228);
17. The right to read or have explained any rules or regulations adopted by an approved service agency pertaining to such person's activities (C.R.S. § 25.5-10-229); and

18. The right to be free from discrimination (C.R.S. § 25.5-10-230).

Limitations on Sterilization

C.R.S. § 25.5-10-231 provides that any person with developmental disabilities who is over the age of 18 years and who has given informed consent may be sterilized if all the following conditions are met:

1. The lawful parent or legal guardian of the person with developmental disabilities has consented to the procedure.
2. A psychiatrist or psychologist, who consults with and interviews the person with developmental disabilities, consents to the procedure.
3. A person who works in the field of developmental disabilities who is knowledgeable in it, and who consults with and interviews the person with developmental disabilities, consents to the procedure.

In no event shall a person with developmental disabilities who is competent and has not given consent be sterilized.

Any person with developmental disabilities, or the parent, legal guardian, or custodian of said person may, pursuant to C.R.S. § 25.5-10-232, file a petition with the court for sterilization. The only issue before the court will be the capacity to give consent for voluntary sterilization. The court will set a hearing to determine the person's competency to give such consent. If the person is incompetent to give consent, the court may order sterilization. C.R.S. § 25.5-10-233. The person with developmental disabilities must be represented by counsel at the hearing, and provided with the opportunity to present testimony and cross-examine witnesses.

5.06 Criminal Insanity

Colorado's criminal statutes recognize the defense of not guilty by reason of insanity. The current test of insanity is set forth in C.R.S. § 16-8-101.5(1) as follows:

> (a) A person who is so diseased or defective in mind at the time of the commission of the act as to be incapable of distinguishing right from wrong with respect to that act is not accountable; except that care should be taken not to confuse such mental disease or defect with moral obliquity, mental depravity, or passion growing out of anger, revenge, hatred, or other motives and kindred evil conditions, for, when the act is induced by any of these causes, the person is accountable to the law; or
>
> (b) A person who suffered from a condition of mind caused by mental disease or defect that prevented the person from forming a

culpable mental state that is an essential element of the crime charged. . . .

In January 1992, the Colorado Supreme Court decided the case of *People v. Serravo*, 823 P.2d 128 (Colo. 1992). In this case, the jury found the defendant not guilty by reason of insanity in connection with the stabbing of his wife. The defendant contended that God directed him to establish a sports complex in Denver and that this godly mission required him to sever his relationship with his wife, who opposed his efforts. The defendant terminated his relationship with his wife by stabbing her in the back.

The prosecution appealed the acquittal of the defendant and asked the appellate courts to clarify the meaning of the phrase "right from wrong" and to decide from whose viewpoint "right" and "wrong" should be considered, *i.e.*, that of the individual, society generally, or society as expressed by positive law. The defendant contended that right and wrong should be defined by his own personal reference and understanding of right and wrong, while the prosecution argued that right and wrong should be defined by reference to legal right and wrong.

The Colorado Supreme Court rejected both approaches and held that right and wrong refers to a cognitive inability to distinguish right from wrong under existing societal standards of morality rather than under a purely subjective and personal standard of morality.

In deciding the case, the court noted that the use of the prosecution's proposed definition (*i.e.*, knowledge that an act was illegal rather than knowledge that it was immoral) would result in the acquittal of a person who knew that his or her actions were profoundly immoral but did not know that they were prohibited by law. The court determined that such a person should be considered sane, and therefore held accountable for his or her criminal act. Conversely, the court noted that the prosecution's proposed definition would result in the conviction of a person who knew that his or her actions were prohibited by law but did not have any comprehension of the immoral nature of the acts. In the court's opinion, such a person should not be held criminally accountable. Accordingly, it held that right and wrong should always be measured by a societal standard of morality.

Temporary Insanity

Unique legal issues have arisen when defendants have contended that they were temporarily insane for reasons beyond their control. For example, in *People v. Low*, 732 P.2d 622 (Colo. 1987), a defendant offered evidence that he had ingested a large quantity of cold medication, which rendered him temporarily incapable of distinguishing right from wrong. The trial court allowed the evidence and found the defendant temporarily insane.

On appeal, the Colorado Supreme Court ruled that the trial court erred, because temporary insanity is not a mental state recognized under Colorado law. The court held that the defendant should have been required to plead and prove that his insanity was caused by an ongoing mental disease or defect.

Procedural Matters

When a defense of not guilty by reason of insanity is entered, the defendant seeks to avoid legal responsibility on the grounds of his or her insanity. Once the plea has been entered, the trial court orders a sanity examination pursuant to C.R.S. § 16-8-105(1) or 16-8-105.5. Upon receipt by the court of the sanity examination report, the matter is set for trial on the issue of whether the defendant was sane at the time the offense was committed. There is a presumption of sanity, and the defendant carries the burden of introducing evidence of insanity. Once the evidence is introduced, the prosecution then bears the burden to prove that the defendant was sane beyond a reasonable doubt. In such hearings, expert opinions from psychiatrists and psychologists are inevitable. However, evidence of the defendant's sanity or insanity is not limited to experts, since C.R.S. § 16-8-109 allows a lay person to render an opinion as to a defendant's insanity, provided the lay witness had sufficient opportunity to observe the person whose sanity is at issue.

If the defendant is found sane, the case proceeds to trial on the merits. If, on the other hand, the defendant is found not guilty by reason of insanity, the defendant is committed to the custody of the Executive Director of the Department of Human Services until he or she is deemed eligible for release. This commitment is for the purpose of treatment and not punishment.

C.R.S. § 16-8-120(3) sets forth the current test for releasing a defendant who has been found not guilty by reason of insanity and committed. The statute provides that the defendant may be released if the defendant has no abnormal mental condition that would be likely to cause him or her to be dangerous either to himself or herself or to the community in the reasonably foreseeable future, and if he or she is capable of distinguishing right from wrong and has substantial capacity to conform his or her conduct to the requirements of the law.

This issue is determined at a hearing, which may be brought by the court, the prosecutor, or the defendant. The burden of proof is on the defendant to show his or her sanity by a preponderance of the evidence. If the jury or court finds the defendant eligible for release, the trial court has the power to place certain conditions on the release. If such conditions are imposed by the court, the

Department of Human Services retains jurisdiction to monitor compliance with the conditions imposed by the court, and to report periodically to the District Attorney concerning the defendant's status. The trial court is also required by C.R.S. § 16-8-115(3) to review the status of the conditionally released defendant every 12 months.

A conditional release may be revoked pursuant to C.R.S. § 16-8-115.5. This generally occurs when someone has reason to believe that the defendant has violated a condition of the release and reports it to the appropriate authority. When the state has probable cause to believe that a conditional release should be revoked, the prosecutor may apply for a warrant to take the defendant into custody or proceed by way of a summons. Once the defendant is in custody, a petition for revocation of the conditional release must be filed within 10 days. Thereafter, the defendant is entitled to a preliminary hearing. If no probable cause for revocation is found at this temporary hearing, the defendant will be released. However, the finding that probable cause does exist will result in a temporary revocation and commitment of the defendant, pending a final hearing, which must be held within 35 days.

At the final hearing, the prosecution has the burden to prove by a preponderance of the evidence that the defendant has become ineligible to remain on conditional release. This does not mean that the court has to find that the defendant is dangerous, but only that there has been a violation of the terms or conditions of the conditional release. If the defendant is found ineligible to remain on conditional release, the court will recommit the defendant. If the prosecution fails to fulfill its burden of proof, the defendant is released on the same or modified conditions.

5.07 The Colorado Red Flag Law

The Colorado Red Flag Law, C.R.S. §§ 13-4.5-101, *et seq.*, which was passed as HB 19-1177 in 2019, authorizes courts to issue Extreme Risk Protection Orders requiring an individual to surrender any firearms in the person's possession or control, or issuing a search warrant for law enforcement officials to search for firearms that the individual may possess. This statute allows an Extreme Risk Protection Order to be issued when the court finds that a person poses "significant risk of causing personal injury to self or others in the near future by having in his or her custody or control a firearm or by purchasing, possessing, or receiving a firearm."

This law has implications for mental health professionals who may be asked to write a report to the court when a client poses such a risk and meets the criteria for a 72-hour hold for evaluation and treatment, or is asked to evaluate a person who may pose a significant risk to self or others in the near future. Evidence that the court may consider in deciding whether to issue an Extreme Risk Protection Order against a respondent includes: (a) a recent act or credible threat of violence by the respondent against self or others, whether or not such violence or credible threat involves a firearm; (b) a pattern of acts or credible threats of violence by the respondent within the past year against self or others; (c) a history of use of or a threat to use unlawful physical force against another person or the respondent's history of stalking another person; (d) evidence of the abuse of controlled substances or alcohol by the respondent: and (e) the respondent's ownership, access to, or intent to possess a firearm.

A 72-hour hold for evaluation and treatment of the respondent shall be considered by the court before issuing an Extreme Risk Protection Order. If the court determines that the respondent meets the standard for an involuntary hold, then the court shall order mental health treatment and evaluation pursuant to C.R.S. § 27-65-106 in addition to issuing an Extreme Risk Protection Order. When such an order is issued, it shall be served on the respondent along with a notice that includes "referrals to appropriate resources, including domestic violence, behavioral health and counseling resources."

Immunity: This Act provides that no "criminal or civil liability" is imposed on "any person or entity for acts or omissions made in good faith related to obtaining an Extreme Risk Protection Order." This law does not mandate a report to law enforcement against a client, unless the client poses a significant risk of injury to self and others, and meets the criteria for a 72-hour hold as a result. So, if a therapist is served with a subpoena to testify against a client at a hearing on an Extreme Risk Protection Order, the therapist needs client consent to testify in court or to share information regarding the client, unless the client is a danger to self or others and meets the criteria for a hospital hold that the court is authorized to order, as stated above.

Chapter 6: Licensing Considerations

6.01 Licensed Professionals

The Colorado General Assembly has declared that in order to safeguard the public health and safety of the people, and in order to protect the people of this state against the unauthorized, unqualified, and improper application of psychotherapy, psychology, clinical social work, marriage and family therapy, professional counseling, and school psychology, it is necessary that certain regulatory agencies be established. To fulfill this declaration of public policy, Title 12, Article 43, of the Colorado Revised Statutes was enacted in 1988 and has been amended in subsequent years. In 2019, Article 43 was renumbered and revised as Article 245.

The Colorado General Assembly has created categories for those who are seeking licensure as Psychologists, Licensed Marriage and Family Therapists, or Licensed Professional Counselors, and who have begun the process of completing the required supervised hours of therapy for licensure. The categories are Psychologist Candidate, Marriage and Family Therapist Candidate, and Licensed Professional Counselor Candidate. To qualify as a candidate, an individual should apply to DORA for this status, after a clinical supervisor has been obtained. Note that in the form Disclosure Statement in Appendix A (Form 2), those who are candidates for licensure can disclose this fact to potential clients.

In 2016, the Colorado General Assembly adopted a statute that clarifies the regulation of therapists who are Psychologist candidates, Marriage and Family Therapist (MFT) candidates, or Licensed Professional Counselor (LPC) candidates. The new law provides that the Psychology Board will regulate Psychologist candidates; the MFT Board will regulate MFT candidates; and LPC candidates will be regulated by the LPC Board.

Definitions

Title 12, Article 245, governs the following persons:

1. A "psychologist" is defined as a person who practices psychotherapy and who is a licensed psychologist pursuant to the provisions of Article 245.
2. "Psychology" is defined as the observation, description, evaluation, interpretation, treatment, or modification of behavior, cognitions, or emotions by the application of psychological, behavioral, and physical

principles, methods, or procedures, for the purpose of preventing or eliminating symptomatic, maladaptive, or undesired behavior, cognitions, or emotions and of enhancing interpersonal relationships, work and life adjustment, personal effectiveness, behavioral health, and mental health.

3. "Licensed social worker, licensed independent social worker, or licensed clinical social worker" means a social work practitioner licensed by the state pursuant to the Mental Health Act.
4. "Social work practice" means the professional application of social work theory and methods by a graduate with a master's degree in social work, a doctoral degree in social work, or a bachelor's degree in social work from an accredited social work program, for the purpose of prevention, assessment, diagnosis, and intervention with individual, family, group, organizational, and societal problems, including alcohol and substance abuse and domestic violence, based on the promotion of biopsychosocial developmental processes, person-in environment transactions, and empowerment of the client system. Social work theory and methods are based on known accepted principles that are taught in professional schools of social work in colleges or universities accredited by the Council on Social Work Education.
5. A "marriage and family therapist" is defined as a person who practices psychotherapy and who is a marriage and family therapist licensed pursuant to Article 245.
6. "Marriage and family therapy" means the rendering of professional marriage and family therapy services to individuals, couples, and families, singly or in groups, whether such services are offered directly to the general public or through organizations, either public or private, for a monetary fee. Marriage and family therapy utilizes established principles that recognize the interrelated nature of individual problems and dysfunctions to assess, understand, diagnose, and treat emotional and mental problems, alcohol and substance abuse, and domestic violence, and to modify intrapersonal and interpersonal dysfunction.
7. A "licensed professional counselor" is defined as a person who practices psychotherapy and who is a professional counselor licensed pursuant to the provisions of Article 245. See Section 6.19 regarding the Interstate Licensed Professional Counselor Compact, SB 22-077, adopted by the Colorado General Assembly in 2022 as C.R.S. §§ 24-60-4301 and -4302, which provides for LPC's to become "privileged to practice."

8. "Professional Counseling" means those activities that assist the person receiving counseling in developing and understanding personal, emotional, social, educational, and vocational development; alcohol and substance abuse; and domestic violence; and in planning and effecting actions to increase functioning or gain control of his or her behavior in such areas. Such activities include, but are not limited to, skill-building in communications, decision-making, problem solving, clarifying values, promoting adaptation to loss and other life changes, developing social skills, restructuring cognitive patterns, defining educational and career goals, and facilitating adjustment to personal crises and conflicts. It includes testing and assessment, and individual and group counseling. Professional counseling follows a planned procedure of intervention that takes place on a regular basis, over a period of time; or, in the cases of testing, assessment, and brief professional counseling, it can be a single intervention.
9. "Unlicensed psychotherapist" means any person whose primary practice is psychotherapy or who holds himself or herself out to the public as being able to practice psychotherapy for compensation and who is not licensed under this Article to practice psychotherapy. "Unlicensed psychotherapist" also means a person who is a certified or licensed school psychologist, licensed pursuant to C.R.S. § 22-60.5-210, who is practicing outside of a school setting.
10. "Psychotherapy" is defined in C.R.S. § 12-245-202(14) as:

    > [T]he treatment, diagnosis, testing, assessment, or counseling in a professional relationship to assist individuals or groups to alleviate behavioral and mental health disorders, understand unconscious or conscious motivation, resolve emotional, relationship, or attitudinal conflicts, or modify behaviors that interfere with effective emotional, social, or intellectual functioning. Psychotherapy follows a planned procedure of intervention that takes place on a regular basis, over a period of time, or in the cases of testing, assessment, and brief psychotherapy, psychotherapy can be a single intervention.

11. An "Addiction Counselor" is defined as follows. A "Licensed Addiction Counselor" is a person licensed by the State Board of Addiction Counselor Examiners to provide professional behavioral health disorder treatment, according to C.R.S. § 12-245-801; a "Certified Addiction Counselor" means

an individual who has a certificate issued by the State Board of Addiction Counselor Examiners authorizing the individual to practice addiction counseling commensurate with his or her certification level and scope of practice.

Title Use Restrictions

A person who is licensed pursuant to Title 12, Article 245 is subject to certain defined duties and enjoys certain privileges.

Pursuant to C.R.S. § 12-245-218, the following titles are limited to those who have been licensed or registered: "Licensed clinical social worker," "clinical social worker," "LCSW," "licensed social worker," "LSW," "marriage and family therapist," "LMFT," "professional counselor," "LPC," "psychologist," "psychologist candidate," "psychology," or "psychological." No other persons shall hold themselves out to the public by any title or description of services using those terms, unless authorized to do so by virtue of their licensure or their having registered as a social worker.

A person who is not licensed under Title 12, Article 245, but whose primary practice is psychotherapy or who holds himself or herself out to the public as being able to practice psychotherapy for compensation, is considered to be a registered psychotherapist. These individuals are subject to the provisions of Title 12, Article 245 and therefore must abide by the requirements set forth therein.

Database Registration Requirement

C.R.S. § 12-245-703 requires the Board of Unlicensed Psychotherapists to maintain a database of all unlicensed persons practicing psychotherapy in Colorado. Each registered psychotherapist is required to report to the State Board of Registered Psychotherapists such therapist's name, current address, educational qualifications, disclosure statements, therapeutic orientation or methodology, and years of experience in each specialty area for inclusion in the database. At the time of recording of the above information, the psychotherapist must indicate whether he or she has been convicted of or entered a plea of guilty or a plea of nolo contendere to any felony or misdemeanor. Each psychotherapist is required to update the above information.

Effective July 1, 1998, no unlicensed person may practice psychotherapy if such person is not included in the database required to be maintained by the State Board of Unlicensed Psychotherapists. Any person who violates this provision commits a class 2 misdemeanor. A subsequent violation is a class 6 felony. Notwithstanding the reporting requirements, no unlicensed psychotherapist may use the term "regulated," "certified," "clinical," "state registered," "state-approved," or any other term, abbreviation, or symbol that would falsely give the impression that the psychotherapist or the service that is being provided is recommended or approved by the state, based solely on inclusion in the database.

Pursuant to C.R.S. § 12-245-217, an employee of a community mental health center is not required to comply with the database registration provision unless, as an unlicensed psychotherapist, such a person is practicing psychotherapy outside the scope of his or her employment as an employee of a community mental health center.

Effective August 31, 2020, the 2020 Sunset Review law provided that no new unlicensed psychotherapists could be registered in Colorado. Those registrants who had already been granted the ability to practice as unlicensed psychotherapists prior to August 31, 2020, were "grandfathered in" as therapists who could practice in Colorado. However all other therapists were required to be licensed in order to practice.

Scope of the Mental Health Act

Pursuant to C.R.S. § 12-245-217, the State of Colorado mental health boards do not regulate the following persons:

1. Any person engaged in the practice of religious ministry, so long as that person does not hold himself or herself out to the public by any title incorporating the terms "psychologist," "social worker," "licensed social worker," "LSW," "licensed clinical social worker," "clinical social worker," "LCSW," "licensed marriage and family therapist," "LMFT," "licensed professional counselor," "LPC," "addiction counselor," "licensed addiction counselor," "LAC," "certified addiction counselor," or "CAC";
2. Any person who is engaged in the practice of employment or rehabilitation counseling performed in the private and public sectors; except that Title 12, Article 245 does apply to employment or rehabilitation counselors practicing psychotherapy in the field of mental health;
3. Employees of the Department of Social Services, employees of county departments of social services, or personnel under the direct supervision and control of the Department of Social Services or any county department of social services for work undertaken as part of their employment;
4. The provisions of C.R.S. § 12-245-703 (regarding database registration) shall not apply to employees of community mental health centers or clinics as those centers are defined by § 27-66-101, but such persons practicing

outside the scope of employment as employees of a community mental health center or clinic shall be subject to the provisions of § 12-245-703;

5. Certified school psychologists licensed pursuant to C.R.S. § 22-60.5-210, and persons who are not licensed under Article 245 for work undertaken as part of their employment with public schools;
6. Mediators resolving judicial disputes under Part 3 of Title 13, Article 22;
7. A professional coach, including a life coach, executive coach, personal coach, or business coach, who has had coach-specific training and who serves clients exclusively as a coach, so long as the professional coach does not engage in the practice of psychotherapy or addiction counseling; and
8. A person who resides in another state and who is currently licensed or certified as a psychologist, marriage and family therapist, clinical social worker, professional counselor, or addiction counselor in that state to the extent that the licensed or certified person performs activities or services in this state, if the activities and services are:
   (a) Performed within the scope of the person's license or certification;
   (b) Do not exceed 20 days per year in this state;
   (c) Are not otherwise in violation of this article; and
   (d) Disclosed to the public that the person is not licensed or certified in this state.

6.02 Mandatory Disclosure of Information

C.R.S. § 12-245-216 states that every unlicensed psychotherapist, licensee, or registrant must provide a written disclosure statement containing the following information to each client during the initial client contact:

1. The name, business address, and business phone number of the licensee, registrant, or certificate holder.
2. An explanation of the levels of regulation applicable to mental health professionals under this article and the differences between licensure, registration, and certification, including the educational, experience, and training requirements applicable to the particular level of regulation.
3. A listing of any degrees, credentials, certifications, registrations, and licenses held or completed by the licensee, registrant, or certificate holder, including the education, experience, and training the licensee, registrant, or certificate holder was required to satisfy in order to complete the degree, credential, certification, registration, or license.

4. A statement indicating that the practice of both licensed and unlicensed persons in the field of psychotherapy is regulated by the [Division of Professions and Occupations], and an address and telephone number for the board that regulates the licensee, registrant, or certificate holder.
5. A statement indicating that:

   a. In a professional relationship, sexual intimacy is never appropriate and should be reported to the board that licenses, registers, or certifies the licensee, registrant, or certificate holder;

   b. The client is entitled to receive information about the methods of therapy, the techniques used, the duration of therapy, if known, and the fee structure;

   c. The client may seek a second opinion from another therapist or may terminate therapy at any time;

   d. The information provided by the client during therapy sessions is legally confidential, except as provided in C.R.S. § 12-245-220, and except for certain legal exceptions that will be identified by the licensee, registrant, or certificate holder should any such situation arise during therapy;

   e. If the mental health professional is an unlicensed psychotherapist, a statement indicating that a registered psychotherapist is a psychotherapist listed in the State's database and is authorized by law to practice psychotherapy in Colorado but is not licensed by the State and is not required to satisfy any standardized educational or testing requirements to obtain a registration from the State; and

   f. A client's records may not be maintained after seven years pursuant to C.R.S. § 12-245-226(1)(a)(II)(A), when the client is an adult.

6. In compliance with HB 17-1011, signed into law by the governor on July 30, 2017, therapists are also mandated to disclose the provider's Client Record Retention Policy. The record retention policy needs to be consistent with the appropriate board's Record-keeping Rule, Rule 1.16. For adults, records must be kept for seven years after the end of treatment or the last session with a client. For minors, treatment records must be retained for seven years from the last date of treatment or for seven years from the date when the minor reaches 18 years of age, whichever comes later; but in no event is a therapist required to keep these records for longer than 12 years. The form Disclosure Statement in Appendix A contains this new mandated disclosure.

7. The Surprise Billing Disclosure Form, Form 2a in Appendix A, is the latest mandated disclosure required by DORA. This disclosure can be incorporated into a therapist's Client Disclosure Statement, or can be used as a separate form, in the same format that it was in when DORA emailed it to all licensees in March 2020.
8. All of the Mental Health Boards have adopted or are in the process of adopting a Rule requiring that all mental health therapists must give their clients a Disclosure regarding any conviction or discipline that the therapist has received based on sexual misconduct in compliance with C.R.S. § 12-30-115. The prospective client must sign the Disclosure, "acknowledging receipt and agreeing to treatment with the licensee." The Board Rules include a model Disclosure form for this purpose.

Unless the client, parent, or guardian is unable to write, or refuses or objects, the client, parent, or guardian shall sign the disclosure form *not later than the second visit* with the psychotherapist. You must then give the client a copy of the disclosure statement. If a client or the client's legal representative refuses to sign the disclosure statement, thereby refusing to consent to treatment, the therapist must honor the client's exercise of the right to refuse treatment.

The statute provides that if the client is a minor age 15 or older who is consenting to mental health services pursuant to C.R.S. § 27-65-103, disclosure shall be made to the minor. If the client is a child whose parent or legal guardian is consenting to mental health services, disclosure shall be made to the parent or legal guardian.

In residential, institutional, or other settings where psychotherapy may be provided by multiple providers, disclosure shall be made by the primary therapist. The institution shall also provide a statement to the patient concerning the regulation of psychotherapy and the client's right to see information on methods of therapy, the right to seek a second opinion, the inappropriateness of sexual intimacy, and the legal confidentiality of communications.

The statute does not require any disclosure of information in the following circumstances:

1. In an emergency;
2. Pursuant to a court order or involuntary procedures pursuant to C.R.S. §§ 27-65-105 to 27-65-109;
3. Where the sole purpose of the professional relationship is for forensic evaluation;

4. When the client is in the physical custody of either the Department of Corrections or the Department of Human Services and such department has developed an alternative program to provide similar information to such client and such program has been established through rule or regulation;
5. When the client is incapable of understanding such disclosure and has no guardian to whom disclosure can be made; or
6. By a person licensed or certified pursuant to this article or by a registered psychotherapist practicing in a hospital that is licensed or certified under C.R.S. § 25-1.5-103(1)(a).

If the client has no written language or is unable to read, the statute requires that an oral explanation shall accompany the written copy.

As a matter of good practice, all psychotherapists should prepare a disclosure statement fulfilling the requirements of C.R.S. § 12-245-216, have it reviewed by competent legal counsel, give a copy of it to the client, and get a signed copy of it from the client, acknowledging receipt of the disclosure statement at the time of the initial client contact.

According to C.R.S. § 12-245-228, it is unlawful for any person to violate C.R.S. § 12-245-216 by failing to provide to the client the required disclosure statement and to obtain the client's signature acknowledging receipt. A violation of C.R.S. § 12-245-228 subjects a person to penalties pursuant to C.R.S. § 12-20-407. In addition, C.R.S. § 12-245-228 provides that the civil penalties for a violation of C.R.S. § 12-245-216 include recovery of the amount of any fees paid for services by the psychotherapist, and also "[d]amages for injury or death occurring as a result of the services may be recovered . . . without any showing of negligence." *Id.*

Psychotherapists who are supervised by a licensed professional must include in their disclosure statement the name and address of the supervisor and an explanation that the client's case will be discussed with the supervisor. Whenever there is a change in the supervisory relationship, a disclosure statement must be given including the new supervisor's information.

Because of the confusion surrounding the exceptions to confidentiality, it is highly recommended that disclosure statements specifically list the possible instances where confidentiality may not apply. The use of an informed consent document that contains the client's waiver of confidentiality in those specific instances (addressed in Chapter 2, Part II) is highly recommended. A form disclosure statement is contained in Appendix A at Form 2. This form may be modified for specific areas of practice, adding appropriate disclosures as needed.

6.03 Non-Disclosure of Confidential Communications

C.R.S. § 12-245-220 provides that a psychotherapist shall not disclose, without the consent of the client, any confidential communications made by the client to the psychotherapist, or the advice given thereon, in the course of professional employment; nor shall a psychotherapist's employee or associate, whether clerical or professional, disclose any knowledge of said communications acquired in such capacity; nor shall any person who has participated in any therapy conducted under the supervision of a licensee or unlicensed psychotherapist, including, but not limited to, group therapy sessions, disclose any knowledge gained during the course of such therapy without the consent of the person to whom the knowledge relates.

This duty of confidentiality does not apply when:

1. A client or the heirs, executors, or administrators of a client file suit or a complaint against a psychotherapist on any cause of action arising out of the care or treatment of such client.
2. A mental health practitioner was in consultation with a physician, registered professional nurse, licensee, registrant, or registered psychotherapist against whom a complaint was filed, based on the case out of which the suit or complaint arises.
3. A review of services of a psychotherapist is conducted by one of the following groups:

   a. A board or a person or group authorized by such board to make an investigation;

   b. The governing board of a hospital where the psychotherapist practices or the medical staff of such hospital if the medical staff operates pursuant to written bylaws; or

   c. A professional review committee established pursuant to C.R.S. § 12-245-212(1) if said person has signed a release authorizing such review.
4. When a therapist makes a report to a school district or to law enforcement regarding a significant threat made by a client against a school or the occupants of a school, or when a therapist reports the behaviors of a client that in the therapist's judgment create a significant threat to the health or safety of students, teachers, administrators, or other school personnel. For more information regarding this exception to confidentiality, see section 2.02.
5. This statute does not prohibit any other disclosures required by law.

6. C.R.S. § 12-245-220 provides that the duty of non-disclosure and confidentiality does not apply to any delinquency or criminal proceeding, except as provided in C.R.S. § 13-90-107, the statute pertaining to privilege.

For a more detailed discussion of confidentiality, see Chapter 2.

6.04 Grievance Procedures and Statute of Limitations on Board Complaints

If a licensee, registrant, or registered psychotherapist has violated any of the provisions of C.R.S. § 12-245-224, the board that licenses, registers, or regulates such psychotherapist may (1) deny, revoke, or suspend any license, registration, or listing of any unlicensed psychotherapist; (2) issue a letter of admonition; (3) issue a confidential letter of concern; (4) place a psychotherapist on probation; or (5) apply for an injunction pursuant to C.R.S. § 12-245-230 to enjoin a therapist from practicing psychotherapy.

Typical types of grievances that are submitted by clients against psychotherapists concern the same types of complaints that lead to litigation. These include:

1. Failure to conform to generally accepted treatment practices;
2. Treating outside a therapist's area of expertise;
3. Failure to refer a client to a specialist or to another therapist when a client is not making progress in therapy;
4. Failure to comply with C.R.S. § 12-245-216, which requires that each client receive a disclosure statement at the time of the initial visit;
5. Boundary violations; and
6. Breach of confidentiality.

When a complaint is submitted by a client or other person to a mental health regulatory board, the psychotherapist named in the complaint is required to respond to it; disciplinary action can be taken against a therapist for failing to respond to the complaint. Then, in most cases, the board investigates the complaint. If probable cause exists to believe that a violation of state laws or regulations pertaining to the practice of psychotherapy has occurred, then the case is referred to the Attorney General's office for prosecution. Those cases involving violations that are less serious in nature may be resolved by the issuance of a letter of admonition. When no probable cause exists to establish a violation of legal or ethical standards, then the complaint is dismissed, and the matter remains confidential.

Where a violation occurs that does not disqualify a psychotherapist from maintaining a license, the board generally issues a letter of admonition or places the licensee on probation for a period of two to three years, with the imposition of various conditions. The conditions include: (1) having the psychotherapist submit to a mental health evaluation; (2) requiring practice monitoring, which usually means a weekly monitoring of cases by a practice monitor; and (3) requiring additional training or education in specific areas of ethics or practice.

In the grievance process, the Assistant Attorney General handling a complaint will generally make an offer of discipline, which is designed to resolve the grievance proceeding if the therapist agrees to accept the discipline imposed. If no such agreement is made, then the case proceeds to a hearing before an administrative law judge (ALJ), who issues findings of fact and a determination concerning whether a disciplinary violation has occurred. Regardless of the decision entered by the ALJ, the board itself has the right to reject the ALJ's determination and substitute its own decision in the case.

Statute of Limitations

For several years, Reo N. Leslie, Jr., D.Min, LPC, LMFT, CAC III, worked with the Colorado General Assembly to establish a statute of limitations on licensing board complaints. Rep. Melton was the sponsor of HB 17-1011, which was enacted into law and signed by the governor. This law provides that any complaint to one of the mental health boards relating to "maintenance of records of a client eighteen years of age or older" must be submitted to the board "within seven years after the person discovered or reasonably should have discovered the misconduct." This new law further provides that a therapist "shall notify a client that the client's records may not be maintained after the seven-year period for filing a complaint." This provision further states: "The required notice must be provided to the client in writing no later than one hundred eighty days after the end of the client's treatment. The notice may be included with the licensee's disclosures pursuant to section 12-245-216(1) or sent to the client's last-known mailing address."

This provision establishing a seven-year statute of limitations on record-keeping complaints further provides: "The board must either take disciplinary action on the complaint or dismiss the complaint no later than two years after the date the complaint or notice was filed with the board." According to the specific terms of the bill signed by the governor, this seven-year period of limitations "does not apply to the filing of a complaint . . . with the board for any other violation of this article 245, including the acts described in section 12-245-224 or 12-245-228." Therefore, this statute of limitations only applies to a complaint related to maintenance of treatment records of a client who is 18 years of age or older.

6.05 Rules of the Mental Health Boards

The mental health regulatory boards have adopted rules for the regulation of the psychotherapists or addiction counselors under their jurisdiction. Every psychotherapist should, as a matter of good practice, obtain a copy of the most current rules and know their requirements. A number of the rules pertain to procedural matters regarding the handling of a grievance against a licensed or unlicensed professional. There are several rules, however, that require greater familiarity. These rules are discussed below.

Rule 4 C.C.R. 734-1 1.4—Declaratory Orders (C.R.S. § 24-4-105(11))

The Board of Unlicensed Psychotherapists has adopted Rule 4 C.C.R. 734-1 1.4, which provides that anyone may petition the Board for a ruling (declaratory order) "to terminate a controversy or to remove uncertainty as to the applicability to the petitioner of any statutory provision or of any Board Rule or Order." This means, in practical terms, that a therapist could request a ruling from the Board concerning any duty to report suspected child abuse, for example, where the professional's duty is unclear under the attendant facts and circumstances. This Rule contains specific procedures that must be followed in requesting a ruling.

Rule 4 C.C.R. 734-1 1.5—Mandatory Disclosure Statement

Rule 4 C.C.R. 734-1 1.5 of the Board of Unlicensed Psychotherapists clarifies the requirements of the mandatory disclosure of information required under C.R.S. § 12-245-216. Section 6.02 of this chapter sets forth the important aspects of this Rule.

LPC Board Rule 4 C.C.R. 737-1 1.7—Supervision of Mental Health Practitioners and Other Supervisory Relationships

The Board of Licensed Professional Counselor Examiners has promulgated Rule 4 C.C.R. 737-1 1.7, which was intended to establish a legal minimum standard that protects the public from harm, educates the public as to the minimum standards for supervision, promotes the professional growth of both supervisor and supervisee, and mandates new credentials for clinical supervisors effective September 1, 2021.

Definitions

Rule 4 C.C.R. 737-1 1.7(B) sets forth the following definitions:

1. **"Clinical supervision"** occurs when there is close, ongoing review and direction of a supervisee's clinical practice.

2. **"Consultation"** describes a voluntary relationship between professionals of relative equal expertise or status, wherein the consultant offers his or her best advice or information on an individual case or problem for use by the consultee as he or she deems appropriate in his or her professional judgment.
3. **"Administrative supervisor"** is the person who bears responsibility for the non-clinical functioning of an employee, such as performance appraisals, personnel decisions, etc. The administrative supervisor may be held accountable for misconduct by a psychotherapist when he or she knew or should have known of a violation of generally accepted standards of practice or any prohibited activity, and when he or she had responsibility for corrective administrative action and failed to act.
4. **"Modes of supervision"** include but are not limited to individual, group, telephone, electronic mail, audio-visual, process recording, direct observation, telecommunication (teleconferencing, fax, videotapes), and hospital round supervision. The appropriate modality of supervision shall be determined by the training, education, and experience of the supervisee and the treatment setting (*i.e.*, urban/rural or the availability of resources), and at all times based on community standards and client needs. The level of supervision provided, including whether every case is directly supervised and whether the supervisor meets with the client, is determined by the education, training, and experience of the supervisee, the specific needs of the clients being served, and the professional judgment of the supervisor. Nothing in this rule should be assumed to abridge the rights of the client to a reasonable standard of care.

Specific Duties

Rule 4 C.C.R. 737-1 1.7(C) imposes upon supervisors a number of detailed responsibilities. Specifically, the rule requires that all supervisors oversee their supervisees by:

> (1) Monitoring the supervisee's activities to assure s/he is providing services that meets (sic) generally accepted standards of practice.
>
> (2) Verifying that it is the practice of any supervisee to provide the mandatory disclosure form as required pursuant to C.R.S. § 12-245-216.
>
> (3) If appropriate, verifying that clients are informed as to any changes in the supervisory relationship.

(4) Giving an adequate termination of supervision notice to the supervisee.

(5) Keeping records that document supervision that meet the generally accepted standards of practice.

(6) Assisting the supervisee in becoming aware of and adhering to all legal, ethical, and professional responsibilities.

(7) Assuring that no inappropriate relationships exist between the supervisor and supervisee, and supervisor and client.

(8) Assuring the supervisee meets any licensing, certification or registration requirements prior to engaging in any psychotherapy.

(9) Assisting to assure that the supervisee is in compliance with the Mental Health Practice Act.

(10) Verifying and assuring the supervisee is in compliance with any existing restricted licensure, certification or registration status or probation.

As a practice guide, those psychotherapists who may have assumed positions of supervision should develop and incorporate a checklist of the foregoing duties in order to ensure that their duties as supervisor have been fulfilled. A supervisor should note that the failure to reasonably perform any of the foregoing supervisory responsibilities could subject such person to a malpractice claim.

Supervisor Qualifications

LPC Board Rule 4 C.C.R. 737-1 1.7(D) requires:

(1) The supervisor shall have sufficient knowledge of legal, ethical, and professional standards relevant to the clients being served.

(2) The supervisor shall have clinical experience and competence adequate to perform and direct the services provided by the supervisee.

(3) Effective September 1, 2021, professional counselors engaged in the clinical supervision of mental health professionals must meet the following additional criteria:

a. Three years or 3,000 hours of post-graduate clinical experience as a counselor AND

b. Successful completion of ONE of the following:

(1) A minimum of a two credit-hour graduate course on clinical supervision from a CACREP accredited or equivalent program; OR

(2) A minimum of six clock hours of clinical supervision training that includes all of the following content areas:

(a) Role and functions of clinical supervisors;

(b) Models and methods of clinical supervision;

(c) Supervisory relationship issue;

(d) Cultural issues in clinical supervision;

(e) Group supervision;

(f) Legal and ethical issues in clinical supervision; and

(g) Evaluation of supervisee competency; OR

(3) Approved Clinical Supervisor (ACS) certification from the Center for Credentialing and Education (CCE); OR

(4) A doctorate in Counselor Education and Supervision from a CACREP accredited or equivalent program or other counseling doctorates that have a supervision component.

c. Three professional development hours, as set forth in Rule 1.18, per renewal period specific to clinical supervision.

6.06 Standards for Clinical Supervision

Clinical supervision in Colorado is conducted pursuant to licensing board rules. For example, Psychology Board Rule 3 C.C.R. 721-1 1.7 defines clinical supervision and sets forth the supervisor's duties. This rule states that it is the supervisor's duty to "[assist] the supervisee in becoming aware of and adhering to all legal, ethical, and professional responsibilities," and, in general, to direct the supervisee's clinical practice to ensure that the therapist "is providing services that meet generally accepted standards." This is an awesome undertaking on the part of supervisors, and provides an enormous contribution to the profession through the training that is given and the experience imparted to the supervisee.

A supervisor's failure to comply with the duties set forth in the Board's supervision rules could impose liability on the supervisor, if he or she knew or should have known of the fact that treatment was being provided that did not comply with clinical or ethical standards. I have often advised clinical supervisors to include a provision in a written contract with supervisees that the supervisee will comply with the applicable ethical code (*e.g.*, the NASW or AAMFT Code of

Ethics). In addition, the clinical supervision contract should provide that the supervisee will (1) maintain a policy of liability insurance with a minimum of $1,000,000 in coverage, and (2) provide the supervisor with a Certificate of Insurance. See the Clinical Supervision Contract in Appendix A at Form 7.

When the professional relationship between a clinical supervisor and the supervisee has ended, that fact should be confirmed in writing so that no claim can be made that the supervisor remains responsible for monitoring and directing the supervisee's practice.

The situation that most often leads to a malpractice suit is a critical incident where a client commits suicide or kills another person. Therefore, supervisors should be most vigilant in consulting with a supervisee in cases where a client may be dangerous to self or others. In addition, supervisors should keep thorough notes concerning all individual and group clinical supervision sessions, and should especially keep thorough records concerning consultations regarding whether a client is suicidal or dangerous to others.

Keep in mind that supervisors must maintain accurate records concerning the number of hours of clinical supervision when the supervisee is seeking licensure, since the supervisor will be required to certify to the appropriate licensing board the number of hours of clinical supervision with the supervisee.

Requirements for Clinical Supervisors

Clinical supervisors must ensure that their supervisees provide disclosure statements to clients identifying the clinical supervisor and his or her role. The purpose for this practice is twofold: (1) to disclose the fact that treatment information will be shared with the supervisor in clinical supervision; and (2) to identify any conflictual dual relationship that may exist between the client and the clinical supervisor.

For example, when the therapist is going through the disclosure statement with the client during the first treatment session and mentions the clinical supervisor's name, the client may say, "Oh, I know her; she is my psychology professor." Or, a client might inform the therapist that the clinical supervisor is a close friend, a relative, or is otherwise engaged in a relationship with the client that creates a conflictual dual relationship between the supervisor and the client. Any prior relationship that would impair the supervisor's judgment in directing the treatment process creates a prohibited dual relationship.

Clinical supervisors must keep records of the supervision. C.R.S. § 12-245-224(1)(n) prohibits the failure "to render adequate professional supervision of persons practicing pursuant to this article under such person's supervision."

Record-keeping practices vary widely among supervisors. Experience has demonstrated, however, that the licensing boards expect clinical supervisors to maintain their own notes concerning each case discussed in supervision, notes concerning each issue on which the supervisor was consulted, and detailed records concerning the amount of face-to-face supervision or group supervision conducted by the supervisor.

Each supervisor must use his or her professional judgment to determine whether to maintain a copy of each client file for purposes of clinical supervision. At a minimum, supervisors should maintain thorough notes concerning directions they give to supervisees concerning specific clients' cases, as well as notes concerning each consultation with supervisees on difficult issues encountered in treatment. For risk-management purposes, supervisors should maintain copies of any records or notes from the client file concerning mandatory reports made by the supervisee of suspected child abuse or neglect, a duty to warn and protect, or situations concerning threats of suicide or harm to others.

Each clinical supervisor should have a list of resources and reference materials that supervisees are required to have and to consult. Such resources include:

- *The Legal Guide for Practicing Psychotherapy in Colorado;*
- A copy of the Colorado mental health statutes;
- The board rules for the licensing board to which the supervisee is applying for licensure;
- A copy of the code of ethics for the professional association that is most applicable to the supervisee's practice; and
- A copy of the supervision contract. A contract for clinical supervision is contained in Appendix A as Form 7.

Each supervisor must have a contract for clinical supervision, which discusses the fees and policies for the supervision. The contract should set forth specifically all ground rules and expectations for the supervision process. As stated in the previous section, the supervision contract should require the supervisee to maintain professional liability insurance at all times and to provide a copy of the current Certificate of Insurance to the supervisor.

In the rare instances when a supervisor learns of a client's dissatisfaction with the therapist, indicated by the filing of a grievance or the submission of correspondence threatening a lawsuit, the clinical supervisor should direct the therapist to put his or her malpractice insurer on notice of the potential claim. The supervisor should do the same, providing notice to the therapist's insurance carrier of the potential liability claim. If a client commits suicide, it would also be prudent at that time to put insurers on notice of the situation in the event that a lawsuit is filed.

The Supervision Rules for Psychotherapists and Psychologists impose upon the supervisor the duty to ensure that billing records are accurate. It is never appropriate for a clinical supervisor to submit a bill for a treatment session that was actually conducted by the therapist and not by the supervisor; to do so constitutes billing fraud.

The duties of a clinical supervisor encompass all aspects of treatment, requiring the supervisor to ensure that:

- Assessments are done thoroughly and accurately;
- Disclosure statements are signed by every client;
- Record-keeping practices adhere to legal and ethical standards;
- Adequate session notes are being kept;
- Appropriate treatment plans are formulated to meet the clients' goals of treatment;
- The therapist is aware of all ethical standards;
- The therapist is charting any disclosure of treatment information; and
- Appropriate billing records are being maintained.

Clinical supervisors should meet with the therapists whom they are supervising so that each therapist receives (at a minimum) one hour of supervision for every 20 hours of treatment. If audio recordings or videotapes of treatment sessions are made so that the supervisor can see or hear treatment sessions, the supervisor must ensure that the tapes are erased or recorded over when they are no longer needed for supervisory purposes.

Clinical Supervision and Consultations: Confidentiality

In preparation for an ethics seminar on clinical supervision, my co-presenter and I researched state laws and ethics codes regarding the confidentiality of information obtained in clinical supervision by a supervisor. The generally accepted standard, established by ethical codes and practices nationwide, is that clinical supervision is a confidential process, the same as the counseling done by a supervisee with a client. Some states have exceptions to this rule, established by their state licensing board rules, but in general the supervision process is as confidential as mental health treatment itself. The Colorado mental health boards' supervision rule does not contain any special exceptions to the confidentiality of this treatment process.

The AAMFT Code of Ethics (2015) Principle 4.7 provides that clinical supervision is confidential and confidences may not be disclosed except by written waiver.

Imagine informing your clinical supervisor of action you had taken to save a client's life by calling the police for a welfare check, and having the supervisor inform you: "What you did constitutes a breach of confidentiality. You did not have consent to call the police. I am required to file a complaint against you." The supervision process is intended to be confidential, just as treatment is required to be confidential, in order to encourage disclosures and discussion. Clinical supervision is part of the treatment process. The same exceptions to confidentiality that apply in a counseling relationship also apply in clinical supervision: reporting of child abuse and neglect, compliance with the *Tarasoff* duty, initiation of a 72-hour hold, etc. Colorado law, C.R.S. § 12-245-226(9), prohibits a board complaint containing confidential treatment information from being submitted, unless the client consents.

Consider another hypothetical. A therapist comes to you for peer consultation and advises you of a situation where a client is experiencing suicidal ideation, but does not have a plan. The client had phoned the therapist to cancel a treatment session, and spoke with slurred speech. The client is on painkillers for chronic pain problems. The therapist informs you that she contacted the police for a welfare check on the client, who was not at home when the police arrived. In this situation would it be proper for you, as consultant, to say, "You breached confidentiality when you called the police and sent them to the client's home, so I must file a grievance against you"? Because consultations are a form of supervision according to the licensing boards' supervision rule, they, too, are confidential.

If clinical supervision were not a confidential process, supervisees would not be encouraged to ask questions about difficult situations involved in their practice or to discuss problems that arise in counseling. Confidentiality in the clinical supervision process serves an important purpose, just as it does in a counseling relationship.

Clinical Supervision Contract

Clinical supervisors need to have a Clinical Supervision Contract containing the following agreements and provisions:

1. A statement concerning the compensation to be paid to the clinical supervisor for conducting the clinical supervision;
2. An agreement that the supervisee will maintain professional liability insurance, and will provide a Certificate of Insurance to the supervisor;

3. An agreement that the supervisee will comply with the Colorado Mental Health Act and the licensing board rules;
4. An agreement that the supervisee will comply with the code of ethics for a professional association; for example, American Association for Marriage and Family Therapy (AAMFT), National Association of Social Workers (NASW), American Mental Health Counselors Association (AMHCA), American Psychological Association (APA), or American Counseling Association (ACA);
5. An agreement that the supervisee will obtain informed consent from clients for treatment, and will have the client or client's legal representative sign a Client Disclosure Statement;
6. A provision that the supervisee will obtain informed consent from clients to consult with the therapist's clinical supervisor;
7. A provision in the contract that the supervisor-supervisee relationship is confidential;
8. An agreement regarding the frequency with which supervision will occur; *e.g.*, one hour of supervision for every 20 hours of treatment by the supervisee;
9. A statement regarding any specific procedures required to comply with licensing board regulations regarding the requirements for licensure;
10. A statement that the supervisor's duties will be to consult with the supervisee, to direct the treatment process, and to assist the supervisee in complying with all legal and ethical standards;
11. An agreement that both supervisor and supervisee will keep records concerning the dates when clinical supervision was provided, and the length of time spent in supervision;
12. An agreement that both the supervisor and supervisee will maintain notes regarding the cases and issues discussed in clinical supervision;
13. An agreement that the supervisee will maintain in the client's chart all essential records required in compliance with the licensing board's record-keeping rule; and
14. An agreement that the supervisee's bills for treatment of clients will accurately represent the treatment that was provided and the length of time spent in treatment, and will accurately state the identity of the individual who provided clinical services to the client.

It is essential for clinical supervisors to know and follow the licensing board's supervision rule. This rule provides that it is the duty of the supervisor to direct the therapy given by the supervisee to the client. This rule also requires clinical supervisors to ensure that billing records are accurate, so the supervisor needs to review the supervisee's billing practices and records, and also to provide training in the use of Health Care Financing Administration (HCFA) forms, as well as the use of CPT Codes, for the time when the supervisee is licensed and able to do insurance billing.

A copy of the Clinical Supervision Contract, which can be used by supervisors, is contained in Appendix A at Form 7.

6.07 Prohibited Activities

Pursuant to C.R.S. § 12-245-224, a person practicing psychotherapy under Title 12, Article 245, is in violation of the law if he or she:

1. Has been convicted of a felony or has pled guilty or *nolo contendere* to a felony; or has received a deferred sentence to a felony charge.
2. Has violated or attempted to violate, directly or indirectly, or assisted or abetted the violation of, or conspired to violate any provision or term of Article 245 or rule promulgated pursuant to the article or any order of a board established pursuant to the article.
3. Has used advertising that is misleading, deceptive, or false.
4. Has committed abuse of health insurance pursuant to C.R.S. § 18-13-119.
5. Has advertised through newspapers, magazines, circulars, direct mail directories, radio, television, or otherwise that he or she will perform any act prohibited by C.R.S. § 18-13-119.
6. Habitually or excessively uses or abuses alcohol, a habit-forming drug, or a controlled substance, as defined in C.R.S. § 18-18-102(5).
7. Fails to notify the board that regulates his or her profession of a physical illness; a physical condition; or a behavioral, mental health, or substance use disorder that affects the person's ability to treat clients with reasonable skill and safety, or that may endanger the health or safety of persons under his or her care; fails to act within the limitations created by a physical or mental illness or condition that renders the person unable to treat clients with reasonable skill and safety or that may endanger the health or safety of persons under his or her care; or fails to comply with the limitations agreed to under a confidential agreement pursuant to C.R.S. § 12-245-223.

8. Has acted or failed to act in a manner that does not meet the generally accepted standards of the professional discipline under which the person practices. Generally accepted standards may include, at the board's discretion, the standards of practice generally recognized by state and national associations of practitioners in the field of the person's professional discipline.
9. Has performed services outside of his or her area of training, experience, or competence.
10. Has maintained relationships with clients that are likely to impair his or her professional judgment or increase the risk of client exploitation, such as treating employees, supervisees, close colleagues, or relatives.
11. Has exercised undue influence on a client, including the promotion of the sale of services, goods, property, or drugs in such a manner as to exploit the client for the financial gain of the practitioner or third party.
12. Has failed to terminate a relationship with a client when it was reasonably clear that the client was not benefiting from the relationship and was not likely to gain such benefit in the future.
13. Has failed to obtain a consultation or perform a referral when such failure is not consistent with generally accepted standards of care.
14. Has failed to render adequate professional supervision for persons practicing psychotherapy under his or her supervision, according to the generally accepted standards of care.
15. Has accepted commissions or rebates or other forms of remuneration for referring clients to other professional persons.
16. Has failed to comply with any of the requirements pertaining to mandatory disclosure of information.
17. Has offered or given commissions, rebates, or other forms of remuneration for the referral of clients (although a licensee, certified school psychologist, or registered psychotherapist may pay an independent advertising or marketing agent compensation for advertising or marketing services rendered on his or her behalf by such agent, including compensation that is paid for the results of performance of such services on a per-patient basis).
18. Has engaged in sexual contact, sexual intrusion, or sexual penetration with a client during the period of time in which a therapeutic relationship exists or for up to two years after the period in which such a relationship exists.

19. Has resorted to fraud, misrepresentation, or deception in applying for or in securing licensure or taking any examination provided for in this article.
20. Has engaged in any of the following activities and practices: Repeated ordering or performing of demonstrably unnecessary laboratory tests or studies without clinical justification for the tests or studies; the administration, without clinical justification, of treatment that is demonstrably unnecessary; or ordering or performing any service or treatment that is contrary to the generally accepted standards of the person's practice and is without clinical justification.
21. Has falsified or repeatedly made incorrect essential entries or repeatedly failed to make essential entries on patient records.
22. Has used or recommended rebirthing or any therapy technique that may be considered similar to rebirthing as a therapeutic technique. "Rebirthing" means the re-enactment of the birthing process through therapy techniques that involve any restraint that creates a situation in which a patient may suffer physical injury or death.
23. Has committed a fraudulent insurance act in violation of C.R.S. § 10-1-128.
24. Has sold or fraudulently obtained or furnished a license, certification, or registration to practice as a social worker, marriage and family therapist, professional counselor, psychologist, or addiction counselor or has aided and abetted such conduct.
25. Has failed to respond in the manner required by the board to a complaint filed with or by the board against the licensee, registrant, or certificate holder.

6.08 Unauthorized Practice

C.R.S. § 12-245-228 states that it is unlawful for any person to practice or offer or attempt to practice "as a psychologist, social worker, marriage and family therapist, licensed professional counselor, psychotherapist, or addiction counselor without an active license, registration, or certification issued under [Article 245]."

Any person who violates this provision is subject to penalties pursuant to C.R.S. § 12-20-407.

The statute also provides that when a client has been the recipient of services that are prohibited by this article, his or her personal representative is entitled to recover the amount of any fee paid for the services. Damages for any injury or death occurring as a result of the services may be recovered without any showing of negligence.

6.09 Professional Service Corporations

C.R.S. § 12-245-213 provides that licensees, registrants, or certificate holders may form professional service corporations for the practice of psychology, social work, marriage and family therapy, professional counseling, psychotherapy, or addiction counseling under the "Colorado Business Corporation Act," if the corporations meet the following requirements:

1. The name of the corporation must contain the words "professional company," "professional corporation," or the abbreviations.
2. The corporation may be organized with any other person, and any other person may own shares, if the professional practice is performed under the supervision of a licensee and the licensee remains individually responsible for its professional acts and conduct.
3. Lay directors and officers must not exercise any authority whatsoever over professional matters.
4. The articles of incorporation provide, and all shareholders of the corporation agree, that either all shareholders of the corporation shall be jointly and severally liable for all acts, errors, and omissions of the employees of the corporation or that all shareholders of the corporation shall be jointly and severally liable for all acts, errors, and omissions of the employees of the corporation, except during periods of time when the corporation shall maintain, in good standing, professional liability insurance that meets the following standards: (a) the insurance insures the corporation against liability imposed upon the corporation by law for damages resulting from any claim made against the corporation arising out of the performance of professional services for others by those officers and employees who are licensed to practice or who are certified school psychologists or by those who provide professional services under supervision; (b) the insurance policy insures the corporation against liability imposed upon it by law for damages arising out of the acts, errors, and omissions of all nonprofessional employees; (c) the insurance is in an amount for each claim of at least $100,000, multiplied by the number of persons licensed, registered, or certified to practice who are employed by the corporation. The policy may provide for an aggregate maximum limit of liability per year for all claims of $300,000, also multiplied by the number of licensees, registrants, or certificate holders employed by the corporation, but no corporation is required to carry insurance in excess of $300,000 for each claim with an aggregate maximum limit of liability for all claims during the year of $900,000.

6.10 Psychiatrists

A psychiatrist is not subject to the provisions of C.R.S. §§ 12-245-101, *et seq.* However, the provisions of the Colorado Medical Practice Act, as embodied in C.R.S. §§ 12-240-101, *et seq.*, govern the conduct of psychiatrists. Additionally, the Colorado State Board of Medical Examiners promulgates specific rules that apply to all physicians.

C.R.S. § 12-240-121 defines unprofessional conduct for physicians as follows:

1. Resorting to fraud, misrepresentation, or deception in applying for or securing a license, or in taking the examination.
2. Resorting to fraud, misrepresentation, or deception in applying for professional liability coverage or privileges at a hospital.
3. Conviction of an offense involving moral turpitude or a felony.
4. Administering, dispensing, or prescribing any habit-forming drug or any controlled substance other than in the course of legitimate professional practice.
5. Any conviction of violation of any federal or state law regulating the possession, distribution, or use of any controlled substance.
6. Habitual intemperance or excessive use of any habit-forming drug or any controlled substance.
7. The aiding or abetting, in the practice of medicine, of any person not licensed to practice medicine as defined under this article or of any person whose license to practice medicine is suspended.
8. Practicing medicine as the partner, agent, or employee of, or in joint venture with, any person who does not hold a license to practice medicine within this state, or practicing medicine as an employee of, or in joint venture with, any corporation other than a professional service corporation for the practice of medicine. Any licensee holding a license to practice medicine in this state may accept employment from any person to examine and treat the employees of such person.
9. Violating, or attempting to violate, directly or indirectly, or assisting in or abetting the violation of or conspiring to violate, any provision or term of C.R.S. §§ 12-240-101, *et seq.*
10. Exhibiting such physical or mental disability as to render the licensee unable to perform medical services with reasonable skill and with safety to the patient.
11. Advertising in a way that is misleading, deceptive, or false.

12. Engaging in a sexual act with a patient during the course of patient care or within six months following the termination of the professional relationship with the patient.
13. Refusing, as an attending physician, to comply with the terms of a declaration executed by a patient, and failure of the attending physician to transfer care of said patient to another physician.
14. Violation or abuse of health insurance.
15. Advertising through newspapers, magazines, circulars, direct mail, directories, radio, television, or otherwise that the licensee will perform any act prohibited by C.R.S. § 18-13-119(3).
16. Any act or omission that fails to meet generally accepted standards of medical practice.
17. Violation of any valid Board order or any rule or regulation promulgated by the Board in conformance with law.
18. Dispensing, injecting, or prescribing an anabolic steroid as defined in C.R.S. § 18-18-102(3), for the purpose of hormonal manipulation that is intended to increase muscle mass, strength, or weight without a medical necessity to do so or for the intended purpose of improving performance in any form of exercise, sport, or game.
19. Dispensing or injecting an anabolic steroid as defined in C.R.S. § 18-18-102(3), unless such anabolic steroid is dispensed from a pharmacy prescription drug outlet pursuant to a prescription order or is dispensed by any practitioner in the course of his or her professional practice.
20. Prescribing, distributing, or giving to a family member or to oneself except on an emergency basis any controlled substance as defined in C.R.S. § 18-18-204.
21. Failing to report to the Board any adverse action taken against the licensee by another licensing agency in another state or country, etc.
22. Failing to report to the Board the surrender of a license to practice medicine in another state or jurisdiction.
23. Failing to accurately answer the questionnaire accompanying the renewal form required pursuant to C.R.S. § 12-240-130(2).
24. Engaging in any of the following activities and practices: (a) willful and repeated ordering or performance, without clinical justification, of demonstrably unnecessary laboratory tests or studies; (b) the administration, without clinical justification, of treatment which is

demonstrably unnecessary; (c) the failure to obtain consultations or perform referrals when failing to do so is not consistent with the standard of care for the profession; or (d) ordering or performing, without clinical justification, any service, x-ray, or treatment which is contrary to recognized standards of the practice of medicine.

25. Falsifying or repeatedly making incorrect essential entries or repeatedly failing to make essential entries on patient records.
26. Committing a fraudulent insurance act in violation of C.R.S. § 10-1-128.
27. Failure to establish and maintain financial responsibility, as required by C.R.S. § 13-64-301.
28. Failing to respond in an honest, materially responsive, and timely manner to a complaint issued pursuant to C.R.S. § 12-240-125(4).
29. Any act or omission in the practice of telemedicine that fails to meet generally accepted standards of medical practice.
30. Entering into or continuing in a mentorship relationship with an advanced practice nurse pursuant to C.R.S. §§ 12-240-108 and 12-255-112(4) that fails to meet generally accepted standards of medical practice.
31. Failing to comply with medical marijuana requirements of § 14 of article XVIII of the state constitution, C.R.S. § 25-1.5-106, or the rules promulgated by the state health agency pursuant to C.R.S. § 25-1.5-106(3).
32. Engaging in conversion therapy with a patient who is under 18 years of age.
33. Any suspension of a license pursuant to C.R.S. § 24-4-104(4) where the board finds the crime is a continuing threat to patient safety.
34. Any conviction of an offense under C.R.S. § 18-13-131.

C.R.S. § 12-240-138 provides that persons licensed to practice medicine may form professional service corporations for the practice of medicine under the Colorado Business Corporation Act, if such corporations are organized and operated in accordance with the following provisions:

1. The name of the corporation must contain the words "professional company," "professional corporation," or abbreviations thereof.
2. The corporation must be organized solely for purposes of conducting the practice of medicine by persons licensed to practice medicine in the State of Colorado.
3. All shareholders of the corporation must be persons licensed to practice medicine in the State of Colorado, and who at all times own their shares in

their own right. They must be individuals who, except for illness, accident, time spent in the armed services, on vacation, and on leaves of absence not to exceed one year, are actively engaged in the practice of medicine in the offices of the corporation.

4. The articles of incorporation must provide that any shareholder who ceases to be or for any reason is ineligible to be a shareholder will dispose of all of his or her shares forthwith, either to the corporation, or to any person who is licensed to practice medicine in the State of Colorado and who, except for illness, accident, time spent in the armed services, on vacation, and on leaves of absence not to exceed one year, is actively engaged in the practice of medicine in the offices of the corporation.
5. The president must be a shareholder and a director and, to the extent possible, all other directors and officers must be persons who are licensed to practice medicine in the State of Colorado, and who, at all times, own their shares in their own right and who, except for illness, accident, time spent in the armed services, on vacation, and on leaves of absence not to exceed one year, are actively engaged in the practice of medicine in the offices of the corporation. The directors and officers must not exercise any authority whatsoever over professional matters.
6. The articles of incorporation must provide, and all shareholders of the corporation must agree, that all shareholders shall be jointly and severally liable for all acts, errors, and omissions of the employees of the corporation or that all shareholders of the corporation will be jointly and severally liable for all acts, errors, and omissions of the employees of the corporation except during periods of time when each person, licensed to practice medicine in the State of Colorado, who is a shareholder or any employee of the corporation, has a professional liability policy insuring himself or herself and all employees who are not licensed to practice medicine who act at his or her direction in the amount of $50,000 for each claim and an aggregate top limit of liability per year for all claims of $150,000, or the corporation maintains in good standing professional liability insurance which meets the following minimum standards:

    a. The insurance insures the corporation against liability imposed upon the corporation by law for damages resulting from any claim made against the corporation arising out of the performance of professional services for others by those officers and employees of the corporation who are licensed to practice medicine.

b. Such policies insure the corporation against liability imposed upon it by law for damages arising out of the acts, errors, and omissions of all non-professional employees.

c. The insurance is in an amount for each claim of at least $50,000, multiplied by the number of persons licensed to practice medicine employed by the corporation. The policy may provide for an aggregate top limit of liability per year for all claims of $150,000, also multiplied by the number of persons licensed to practice medicine employed by the corporation, but no firm is required to carry insurance in excess of $300,000 for each claim with an aggregate top limit of liability for claims during the year of $900,000.

6.11 Addiction Counselors

In 2011, the Colorado General Assembly established a board to regulate certified and licensed addiction counselors: the State Board of Addiction Counselor Examiners. Like the other mental health boards, this Board is comprised of seven members, four of whom must be certified or licensed addiction counselors. This Board certifies, licenses, regulates, and disciplines all certified and licensed addiction counselors.

Requirements for Licensure as an Addiction Counselor

Pursuant to C.R.S. § 12-245-804, the requirements to be licensed as an addiction counselor include the following:

a. The applicant must be at least 21 years of age;

b. The applicant may not be in violation of any provision of the Mental Health Act or in violation of any rules promulgated by the Addiction Counselor Board;

c. The applicant must hold a master's or doctorate degree in the behavioral health sciences from an accredited school, college, or university or an equivalent program as determined by the Board;

d. The applicant must demonstrate professional competence by passing a national exam demonstrating special knowledge and skills in behavioral health disorders counseling, approved by the Board of Addiction Counselor Examiners;

e. The applicant must demonstrate professional competence by passing a jurisprudence examination administered by the Division of Registrations;

f. The applicant must meet the requirements for a Certificate of Addiction Counseling, Level III;

g. The applicant must have completed the number of hours of addiction-specific training, specified by the Board by rule, including training in evidence-based treatment approaches, clinical supervision, ethics, and co-occurring disorders; and

h. The applicant must have completed at least 5,000 hours of clinically supervised work experience.

Certified Addiction Counselors

The statute establishing the Addiction Counselor Board has provided that an applicant for certification as an addiction counselor shall be certified if the individual files an application and submits evidence to the Board that he or she:

a. Is at least 18 years of age;

b. Is not in violation of any provision of the Mental Health Act or of any rules promulgated by the Addiction Counselor Board or by the State Board of Human Services; and

c. Has met the requirements for certification at a particular certification level, specified in rules adopted by the Behavioral Health Administration (BHA).

Addiction Counseling by Other Mental Health Professionals

The regulatory and licensure statutes adopted by the Colorado General Assembly in 2011 do not prohibit other psychotherapists or other professionals licensed under Colorado law from rendering services within their scope of practice as set forth in the statutes regulating their professional practices, so long as they do not represent themselves to be certified or licensed addiction counselors.

6.12 Psychiatric Technicians

The Colorado General Assembly has declared that in order to safeguard life, health, property, and the public welfare of the people of the State of Colorado, and to protect the people against unauthorized, unqualified, and improper application of interpersonal psychiatric nursing relationships, it is necessary that a proper regulatory authority be established for licensing and reviewing persons who practice as psychiatric technicians.

C.R.S. § 12-295-103(4) defines "practice as a psychiatric technician" to mean:

> [T]he performance for compensation of selected acts requiring interpersonal and technical skills and includes the administering of

selected treatments and selected medications prescribed by a licensed physician or dentist, in the care of and in the observation and recognition of symptoms and reactions of a patient with a behavioral or mental health disorder or an intellectual and developmental disability under the direction of a licensed physician and the supervision of a registered professional nurse. The selected acts in the care of a patient with a behavioral or mental health disorder or an intellectual and developmental disability must not require the substantial specialized skill, judgment, and knowledge required in professional nursing.

C.R.S. § 12-295-111 has given the State Board of Nursing the power: (1) to revoke, suspend, withhold, or refuse to renew any license to practice as a psychiatric technician; (2) to place a licensee on probation; or (3) to issue a letter of admonition to a licensee upon proof that any such person has committed any of the following acts:

1. Has procured or attempted to procure a license by fraud, deceit, misrepresentation, misleading omission, or material misstatement of fact;
2. Has been convicted of a felony or any crime that would be a violation of Title 12, Article 295;
3. Has willfully or negligently acted in a manner inconsistent with the health or safety of persons under his or her care;
4. Has had a license to practice as a psychiatric technician or any other health care occupation suspended or revoked in any jurisdiction;
5. Has violated any provision of Title 12, Article 295 or has aided or knowingly permitted any person to violate any provision of the statute;
6. Has negligently or willfully practiced as a psychiatric technician in a manner that fails to meet generally accepted standards of practice;
7. Has negligently or willfully violated any order, rule, or regulation of the Board pertaining to practice or licensure as a psychiatric technician;
8. Has falsified or in a negligent manner made incorrect entries or failed to make essential entries on patient records;
9. Is addicted to or dependent on alcohol or habit-forming drugs, is a habitual user of a controlled substance or other drugs having similar effects, or is diverting controlled substances, except that the Board has the discretion not to discipline the licensee if he or she is participating in good faith in a program approved by the Board designed to end such addiction or dependency;

10. Has a physical or mental disability that renders him or her unable to practice as a psychiatric technician with reasonable skill and safety to the patients and that may endanger the health or safety of persons under his or her care;
11. Has violated the confidentiality of information concerning any patient;
12. Has engaged in any conduct that would constitute a crime, and that conduct relates to such person's employment as a psychiatric technician;
13. Willfully fails to respond in a materially factual and timely manner to a complaint issued pursuant to C.R.S. § 12-255-116.5(3);
14. Fraudulently obtains, sells, transfers, or furnishes any psychiatric technician diploma, license, renewal of license, or record, or aids or abets another in such activity;
15. Advertises, represents, or holds himself or herself out in any manner as a psychiatric technician or practices as a psychiatric technician without having a license to practice as a psychiatric technician issued under this article;
16. Uses in connection with his or her name any designation tending to imply that he or she is a licensed psychiatric technician without having a license issued under this article; or
17. Practices as a psychiatric technician during the time his or her license is suspended or revoked.

C.R.S. § 12-295-118 states that penalties may be imposed pursuant to C.R.S. § 12-20-407 for any person to practice or offer or attempt to practice as a psychiatric technician without an active license to practice in that capacity. Further, a person commits a class 6 felony "for the second or any subsequent offense."

6.13 Michael Skolnik Medical Transparency Act of 2010

In 2010, the Colorado General Assembly extended the provisions of the Michael Skolnik Medical Transparency Act so that its requirements apply to all mental health professionals and to other healthcare professionals, as well. This statute, C.R.S. § 24-34-110, states that the people of Colorado need to be fully informed about the past practices of healthcare professionals in order to "provide transparency to the public regarding the competency of persons engaged in the practice of certain health care professions" so that informed decisions can be made when choosing a healthcare provider. This statute was effective July 1, 2011, and it applies to each applicant for a new license or for renewal of an existing license, as well as to persons who are registered with the Database of Registered

Psychotherapists. All such applicants are required to provide the following information to the Director of the Division of Registrations at the Colorado Department of Regulatory Agencies (DORA):

1. The applicant's full name, including any known aliases; the current address where the applicant's practice is located; and the applicant's education and training related to his or her profession.
2. Information pertaining to any license, certification, or registration to practice the applicant's profession, issued during the preceding 10 years, including any "public disciplinary action taken" against the applicant by the state board or agency that licenses or regulates the professional, as well as any agreement or stipulation entered into between the applicant and a state regulatory authority, "whereby the applicant agrees to temporarily cease or restrict his or her practice," or any board order "restricting or suspending the applicant's license, certification, or registration."
3. Healthcare professionals must report "[a]ny final action of an employer that results in the applicant's loss of employment where the grounds for termination constitute a violation of the laws governing the applicant's practice."
4. Any "criminal conviction or plea arrangement" resulting from the commission of "a felony or crime of moral turpitude in any jurisdiction at any time after the person has been issued a license, certification, or registration to practice his or her health care profession in any state or country."
5. "Any final judgment against, settlement entered into by, or arbitration award paid on behalf of the applicant on or after September 1, 1990, for malpractice."
6. Any refusal by an insurer of professional liability insurance to issue a policy to the applicant due to past claims experience.
7. An applicant may submit information regarding awards or recognitions he or she has received or charity care he or she has provided that is related to the professional's practice.

This statute further requires that doctors, therapists, and other professionals to whom the statute applies "shall report any updated information" to the Director of Registrations within 30 days after the date of the action being reported, in order to ensure that the information provided to the public is as accurate as possible.

Penalty

For failure to comply with the Michael Skolnik Medical Transparency Act, the Director may impose an administrative fine "not to exceed five thousand dollars" against a person who fails to comply with this section. In addition, the Director of Registrations "shall notify the applicable state board that regulates the profession[al] when the director imposes a fine," and the professional's regulatory or licensing board may also take disciplinary action. This statute specifically provides that the failure of a professional to comply with the statute "constitutes unprofessional conduct or grounds for discipline" by the board or agency that regulates the professional.

Healthcare Professions Profile Program

The Colorado Department of Regulatory Agencies, Division of Occupations and Professions, which is implementing the Michael Skolnik Medical Transparency Act, is establishing a "profile system" that will contain a profile of each professional containing the information that the individual is required to report to DORA. Until each professional applying for a license or for renewal of a license or a registration has provided the information required by this statute, no license, registration, or renewal will be issued by DORA. The Division of Occupations and Professions will then post the professionals' profiles on its website, containing the information needed by the people of Colorado, so that consumers can be fully informed when choosing a healthcare provider.

Constitutional Issues

Informed consumers and informed healthcare professionals alike may question why other licensed professionals and those who are fiduciaries, entrusted with investing money or with the authority to engage in financial transactions, are not required to make similar disclosures. Does the Michael Skolnik Medical Transparency Act violate equal protection of the law because it only applies to healthcare professionals and not to other professionals for whom integrity, honesty, and compliance with the law are vitally important? Does this statute violate the provisions of the Colorado Constitution and the U.S. Constitution, which prohibit *ex post facto* laws and which generally require statutes to be prospective in their application? This is a legitimate issue that will be determined by courts, if the issue is ever raised in an attack on this statute.

6.14 Statutory Requirement for Continuing Professional Development

The Colorado Mental Health Act requires continuing professional development on the part of LMFTs, LCSWs, LPCs, and Certified Addiction Counselors. C.R.S. § 12-245-307 requires psychologists to obtain 40 hours of professional development activities every two years. The Board of Psychologist Examiners' website has information concerning the procedures for developing a professional development plan, and explains what activities a psychologist may perform in order to receive credit for compliance with this requirement.

Requirement for Professional Development

During each renewal cycle for licensure or registration with the Division of Registrations database, each therapist must complete 40 Professional Development Hours (PDH). One PDH is defined as one hour of active learning. DORA has adopted a phased process for Continuing Professional Development (CPD), which consists of the following steps:

Step 1. Reflective Practice. The first step is to identify learning opportunities. DORA will have an online Professional Practice Rubric, which will identify any knowledge areas that a therapist may want to address. For example, for licensed clinical social workers, the Social Work Board has identified seven "competency dimensions" common to all social work practice settings. These seven dimensions are: practice skills, communication and critical thinking, values and ethics, cultural competence, professional relationship skills, professional identity skills, and professional knowledge.

Step 2. SMART Goals. After having identified the areas of competency that a therapist wishes to pursue, the therapist then sets learning goals following the SMART principle, adopted by DORA: Specific, Measurable, Achievable, Relevant, and Timed. DORA provides on its website a worksheet to assist therapists in formulating goals.

Step 3. Learning Plan. Each therapist then develops a Learning Plan, which can be completed online through the DORA CPD Portal. The purpose of the Learning Plan is to help each therapist achieve his or her individual goals.

Step 4. Action. To implement the Learning Plan, therapists can adopt a Professional Development Activity (PDA) as part of the therapist's strategy for accomplishing the Learning Plan and the SMART Goals formulated. Activities that may be part of the Learning Plan include volunteer service, consultation, supervision, presenting, course work, publication, and independent learning.

Step 5. Documentation. Documentation enables therapists to track their progress and document the number of hours in which they are engaged in PDAs. Each therapist will maintain his or her own documentation of the learning process. DORA will audit selected therapists, who will be asked to provide their documentation of PDAs.

Step 6. Evaluation. Each therapist will self-evaluate his or her learning accomplishments as he or she meets goals that have been set. In the evaluation, a therapist will identify the outcome of PDAs, describing how learning will impact the therapist's practice. DORA will provide a self-evaluation form to assist in this process.

Deadlines for Continuing Professional Development

The Colorado General Assembly mandated that the Continuing Professional Development Program begin on January 1, 2011. In order to assist therapists in the CPD process, DORA set up websites to inform therapists about the requirements for licensure and compliance with both the statutes and DORA's regulations. Information about the CPD process can be found at https://www.colorado.gov/pacific/dora/Mental_Health_CPD; the Professional Development Rubric is online at https://www.colorado.gov/pacific/dora/Mental_Health_CPD_Forms.

6.15 Technology in Counseling: Teletherapy, Electronic Supervision, and Use of Social Media

Several states have enacted laws that prohibit therapists who are licensed out-of-state from providing counseling service to clients in-state. New York, California, Ohio, North Carolina, Idaho, Alaska, and New Jersey have adopted such laws. A therapist in Colorado whose client relocates temporarily to another state or moves out-of-state should be able to provide continuity of care by continuing to provide services to the client until that individual can establish a professional relationship with a new therapist, so long as the services provided out-of-state do not exceed 30 days. There is a caveat, however: A client who is in crisis cannot be assessed by telephone or through an internet interaction.

Standards have not yet evolved that would allow an assessment of a client in crisis through the use of videoconferencing.

The primary risk for therapists concerns the use of chatrooms, blogs, or websites where clients and others can post comments. The confidentiality of clients may be breached inadvertently, and clients or members of the public may post comments, believing that they will receive an immediate response if they are in crisis. It is impossible to monitor such sites on a 24/7 basis, and the liability that could exist is a significant risk and burden for therapists. Blogs by healthcare providers in which they discuss their stories or their own past mental health problems or addictions can create the risk that the professionals have shared too much information that clients can access, which may lead to potential embarrassment when clients begin asking questions about therapists' own histories. The experience of both therapists and medical doctors has shown that treatment providers are horrified when they learn that clients have been able to access photos of them in bathing suits, or have been able to access photos of their children and other family members on Facebook.

Experience has also demonstrated that allowing clients to e-mail therapists with questions about clinical issues can create difficulties. In a recent disciplinary matter, a licensing board sanctioned a therapist for sending "too many e-mails" to her borderline client, who had initiated over 700 e-mails to the therapist in an 18-month period. Therefore, it is recommended that therapists adopt an e-mail policy, disclosed to clients during the intake process, in which e-mails are only used for logistical purposes to schedule appointments. Therapists need to disclose to clients that if they are in crisis, they should call 911 or go to the nearest hospital emergency room, rather than sending an e-mail or text message to their therapist regarding the situation. Establish a written policy concerning the use of e-mails that can be communicated to clients and strictly enforced.

Clients do use the internet to shop for therapists or to Google their therapist. Although this may seem invasive, it is a standard practice among consumers today. Is it appropriate for therapists to Google their clients? What should therapists do when they read a client's blog or website and learn that a client may have problems or issues that have not been shared in therapy? In general, young people in particular will try on internet personas, and they need to have the freedom to do so. Therapists generally allow clients to exercise such freedom without being confronted by a therapist with material that has been found online. Allow clients, therefore, in general, to disclose in treatment the presenting problem(s) for which the individual wants to seek counseling.

The Colorado General Assembly has enacted the Psychology Interjurisdictional Compact Act (PICA), which is intended to adopt interstate procedures for the practice of teletherapy or "telepsychology." C.R.S. §§ 24-60-3901, *et seq*. The State Board of Psychologist Examiners and DORA are currently authorized to adopt rules and regulations that will implement teletherapy practices for Colorado psychologists, consistent with the provisions of the PICA. C.R.S. § 12-245-308.

DORA'S Teletherapy Policy

In 2011, the State Mental Health Boards all adopted Policy 30-1, which applies to all therapists in the State of Colorado. This policy provides that mental health professionals have the discretion to determine what type of treatment modality is appropriate for the client when teletherapy or "distance counseling" is being provided. The teletherapy policy is as follows.

> Guidelines include the generally accepted principle that treatment occurs where the client is located. A therapist-client relationship needs to be established through electronic communication. An appropriate mental health evaluation and review of history needs to be conducted to establish diagnoses and underlying conditions. The Mandatory Disclosure Statement must be signed by the client, as required by Colorado law, no later than the second session. Continuity of care needs to be provided to the client. Emergency planning needs to occur, including a plan for referral of a client to an Emergency Department for evaluation and treatment, if necessary. Mental health records must be maintained, as required by Licensing Board Rule 16. Privacy and security of records should comply with HIPAA Standards. Disclosures to the client should comply with "state and federal law."
>
> Once a mental health professional chooses to provide psychotherapy via electronic means, the mental health professional is expected to carefully identify and address issues that involve:
>
> 1) The agreed upon therapeutic means of communication between the client and the mental health professional (i.e. when will face-to-face contact be appropriate, what method(s) of electronic communication will be utilized, what is the structure of the contractual relationship);

2) Implementing written consent form(s) and proper disclosure(s) including, but not limited to the client's knowledge regarding security issues, confidentiality, structure, etc.;
3) Ensuring that the therapeutic means of communication includes confidentiality and computer/cyber security;
4) Determining the basis and ability for the mental health professional to support the rationale for the decision to choose a particular therapeutic method;
5) Ensuring that the mental health professional is practicing within his/her scope of practice;
6) Ensuring that the therapeutic means of communication that is chosen does not cause any potential harm to the client.

The mental health professional may encounter specific challenges while providing psychotherapy through electronic means. The mental health professional must realize that these challenges may include, but are not limited to:

1) Verifying the identity of the client and determining the client's age;
2) Providing the client with procedures for alternative modes of communication when there is possible technology failure;
3) Assessing how to cope with potential misunderstandings when the visual cues that would normally occur during face-to-face visits do not exist;
4) Assessing how to address crisis intervention when necessary;
5) Ensuring that clients are knowledgeable with regard to encryption methods, firewall, and backup systems to help secure communication and educate clients on the risk of unsecured communications;
6) Establishing a means to retain and preserve data;
7) Upon request, have the ability to capture and provide client treatment notes, summaries or other information that is received via the electronic technology;
8) Disclosing that health insurance coverage may not exist for psychotherapy service that is provided through technological means.

Although this Policy does not mandate that a Consent Form for Teletherapy be signed by the client that discusses the process of teletherapy and the emergency plan that should be made in the event that a client has a mental health crisis while receiving this treatment, it has become a generally accepted practice for therapists nationwide to obtain informed consent for teletherapy through the use of such a form. You will find a Consent Form for Teletherapy in Appendix A, the Forms Section of this book, Form 11.

DORA's teletherapy policy, Policy 30-1, is similar to the provisions contained in the AMHCA Code of Ethics (2010). The AMHCA provision regarding technology-assisted counseling requires that therapists "ensure that clients are intellectually, emotionally, and physically capable of using technology-assisted counseling services, and of understanding the potential risks and/or limitations of such services." It also requires that therapists confirm that "technology-assisted counseling services are not prohibited by or otherwise violate any applicable state or local statutes, rules, regulations, or ordinances."

FAQs on Teletherapy

1. Do I need a Consent Form for clients who are doing teletherapy?

   Answer: Yes, you should use a Consent Form that obtains informed consent for teletherapy and describes the treatment process. Be sure to review Board Policy 30-1 regarding teletherapy and comply with it. The Consent Form, Form 11 in Appendix A, tracks DORA's Policy 30-1 and is an excellent informed consent form.

2. What disclosures should be made in providing informed consent to clients receiving teletherapy?

   Answer: The Consent Form for Teletherapy must be used in addition to your Client Disclosure Statement, which is also an informed consent form. See Form 2 in Appendix A. If a client has already been in treatment with you before beginning teletherapy, have the client sign the Consent Form for Teletherapy in addition to your standard Client Disclosure Statement.

   The elements of informed consent for distance counseling should include: the benefits and risks of teletherapy; the confidentiality rules that apply, including a disclaimer that no guarantee can be made that electronic communication will not be compromised; the fact that written notes of treatment will be kept, just as if you were doing in-person therapy; and the fees that will be charged. Although most health insurers have been covering teletherapy during the COVID-19 crisis, you should disclose that health insurance may not cover this treatment. Informed consent needs to include an emergency plan in the event of a client crisis. The client should be encouraged to disclose any thought of self-harm and any history of suicide attempts or of hospital treatment for suicidal thoughts. In case of any emergency, the client should sign a release authorizing an emergency contact to be involved with you; and a referral for hospital evaluation and treatment should be prepared and included in the Form.

3. How should I get clients or client representatives to sign my Consent Form for Teletherapy?

   Answer: You can have clients sign the Form, scan it and email it to you, if they have the proficiency to do so. They can type their name on the Form as an e-signature, and send you a copy. Or if you are using video conferencing, a client can sign the form in front of the camera, so that you can take a screen shot of it, and then document in your Note for the session that the client signed the Form.

4. Can I practice teletherapy across state lines in a jurisdiction where I am not licensed?

   Answer: It is not advisable to practice therapy in a jurisdiction where you are not licensed. Treatment is considered to occur where the client is located. In some states it is a crime to practice as a health care provider or therapist if you are not licensed or approved to provide treatment in that state. Insurance coverage may not apply to claims involving a criminal act or to treatment provided in a state where you are not licensed. You may be able to contact the other state to seek approval to provide teletherapy across state lines. Document any such approval carefully.

5. What are good resources for learning the legal and ethical standards for teletherapy?

   Answer: In order to comply with standards for teletherapy, consult Colorado laws and DORA's Licensing Board Rules and Policies. In addition, consult the Codes of Ethics for professional associations such as the American Mental Health Counselors Association (AMHCA), the American Association for Marriage and Family Therapy (AAMFT), the American Psychological Association (APA), the American Counseling

Association (ACA), and the National Association of Social Workers (NASW). The U.S. Department of Health and Human Services (HHS.org) has adopted policies during the COVID-19 crisis to make telehealth in general an easier process, one in which HHS states that it will not strictly enforce HIPAA Regulations regarding the platform used for telehealth and teletherapy. The HHS website includes FAQs for dealing with COVID-19 in businesses that are very practical and provide the guidance that the Centers for Disease Control (CDC) has issued for the safety of the public. Of course, workshops and seminars on teletherapy are offered by professional associations at national, state, and local levels, online.

6. Do therapists have a role in "contact tracing"? Are we required to report to the Colorado Department of Health (CDPHE) if a client has been diagnosed with COVID-19 or has tested positive for the virus?

   Answer: Not at this time. Colorado does not currently have a Statute requiring health care providers to make such reports Such a law could be passed during this pandemic. The purpose of enacting such a requirement would be to allow the Health Department to conduct contact tracing, by asking an infected person who they have had contact with, and then to test those individuals for the coronavirus.

7. I am a grief counselor and too many of my elderly clients had spouses who died from COVID-19. One of my clients is planning to do counseling with me, using her cellphone. She does not have a computer. She says that she mailed all of the consent forms for treatment to the agency a week ago, but staff informs me that only a signed Client Disclosure Statement was received, not the Consent Form for Teletherapy. What should I do? This grieving woman needs help.

   Answer: Make sure that your client read the Consent Form, understands its disclosures, and agrees with it. You can proceed with teletherapy when your client informs you on the phone that she consents to counseling over the telephone. Document the client's record with the fact that you discussed the teletherapy process with her; that she understood the disclosures, and wants to proceed with telephone counseling.

LPC Board Policy 30-3, Electronic Supervision

The mental health licensing boards have been adopting policies regarding electronic supervision, similar to Board of Licenses Professional Counselors Policy 30-3, which states:

> Supervision by electronic means includes only methods such as Skype or similar means that provide for uninterrupted, secure, means to communicate utilizing voice and video simultaneously over the internet (communication solely by telephone is not sufficient).
>
> Supervision by electronic means is acceptable if:
>
> (1) the system utilized is an interactive, real-time, system that provides for visual and audio interaction between the licensee and the supervisor;
>
> (2) the first two meetings are face-to-face and in-person;
>
> (a) the initial meeting with any supervisor shall be a minimum of two (2) hours;
>
> (b) all subsequent meetings shall be sufficient length as determined by the supervisor and in accordance with generally accepted standards of practice for supervision;
>
> (c) additional face-to-face meetings should occur not less than every six (6) months in conjunction with the regularly scheduled electronic meetings.
>
> (d) cases are reviewed in the same manner as when meeting in person.
>
> This policy in no manner relieves a mental health professional from adhering to all statutory, rule, policy or disciplinary requirements, including but not limited to adhering to generally accepted standards of practice for supervision, ensuring confidentiality, adequate record-keeping as well as recording only with permission of both parties.

Use of Social Media in Marketing

Social media has proven to be an effective method for therapists to use in marketing their practices. Therapists who have created their own websites to promote themselves and their practice can link their website to professional pages on Facebook, LinkedIn, and other social media. On these professional pages, therapists can post articles of general interest to prospective clients and a list of frequently asked questions and answers concerning counseling and its benefits. Therapists can also include blogs on their professional pages containing information of interest to prospective clients. By linking all of these sites together and keeping their websites and professional pages current with monthly updates, therapists can elevate their profile on Google to a great extent.

Online Counseling

AAMFT has adopted Ethical Principle 6.1, Technology Assisted Services, which applies to online counseling. Principle 6.1 provides:

> Prior to commencing therapy or supervision services through electronic means (including but not limited to phone and Internet), marriage and family therapists ensure that they are compliant with all relevant laws for the delivery of such services. Additionally, marriage and family therapists must: (a) determine that technologically-assisted services or supervision are appropriate for clients or supervisees, considering professional, intellectual, emotional, and physical needs; (b) inform clients or supervisees of the potential risks and benefits associated with technologically-assisted services; (c) ensure the security of their communication medium; and (d) only commence electronic therapy or supervision after appropriate education, training, or supervised experience using the relevant technology.

Clients who will receive counseling over the internet need to receive a disclosure in writing that the confidentiality of information in online counseling cannot be guaranteed. Online counseling is not considered appropriate, in general, for a client who has severe, chronic mental health problems or who may be suicidal.

Websites: Practical Tips

1. Make certain that all marketing information on a website regarding your specialty areas, educational background, and experience is accurate. Codes of ethics and Colorado statutes prohibit the use of advertising that is inaccurate, misleading, or false.
2. Do not use clients' photographs on your website. This could lead to claims that confidentiality was breached, or that clients were exploited in the promotion of your business.
3. Do not use testimonials from clients. This could be seen as an ethical violation in which clients were exploited for your financial gain.

4. If your website has a "contact us" feature that allows prospective clients to make contact to inquire about services or to schedule an appointment, include a disclaimer on the website that contacting your office through your website does not establish a professional relationship.

Top Tips for Use of Social Media and Technology

No matter how often we discuss the use of social media and technology, reminders are helpful regarding legal and ethical standards. Stay up to date with board rules, policies, and ethical code rules regarding the use of social media and technology in consulting practice. Here are the top tips:

1. Review Board Policy 30-1 concerning teletherapy on the DORA website for your regulatory board.
2. Maintain a policy limiting the use of e-mails or text messages to logistics and the scheduling of client sessions.
3. Inform clients that you are *not* available 24/7 to triage client crises, and that in the event of a crisis, clients are to call 911 or go to the local hospital emergency room.
4. On your website, do *not* have a chat room. This may imply that you are available to triage crises, if communicated by a member of the public in a chat room.
5. Be extremely careful using Skype, Facetime, or other media to conduct counseling sessions with clients in other states, which may prohibit therapists from outside the state from providing services to residents within the state. Short-term psychotherapy, for 30 days or less, to keep a client stable when a client has moved or relocated is permissible in order to maintain continuity of care until a client can obtain a new therapist.
6. Obtain an e-mail encryption system in the event that, on occasion, treatment information is transmitted electronically by e-mail.
7. Do not friend clients on Facebook.
8. Do not post client pictures on your website or on business social media sites, because this may be considered "exploitation" of the clients.
9. Inform clients that the use of technology for counseling, including telephone, Internet, Skype, etc., may not be a confidential process.
10. If treatment information or client records are maintained in the cloud and the process requires the use of two separate servers, the use of the cloud may constitute a HIPAA violation.

11. Teletherapy in any form, including Skype or Facetime, cannot be used to assess a client in crisis.

6.16 AAMFT Telehealth Standards

The AAMFT Code of Ethics (Effective January 1, 2015) contains a new section regarding Standards for Technology-Assisted Professional Services.

- Standard 6.1 provides that MFTs must ensure that they are compliant with all relevant laws for the delivery of services through electronic means, including telehealth services provided by phone, the internet, and video conferencing. Specifically, Standard 6.1 requires that MFTs must: (a) determine that technologically-assisted services or supervision are appropriate for clients or supervisees, considering professional, intellectual, emotional, and physical needs; (b) inform clients or supervisees of the potential risks and benefits associated with technologically- assisted services; (c) ensure the security of their communication medium; and (d) only commence electronic therapy or supervision after appropriate education, training, or supervised experience using the relevant technology.
- Standard 6.2 requires informed consent in writing that advises clients and supervisees of the risks associated with technology-assisted services, and that advises clients and supervisees of the responsibility for minimizing such risks on the part of the therapist, the client, and the supervisee.
- Standard 6.3 provides that it is the responsibility of the therapist or supervisor "to choose technological platforms that adhere to standards of best practices related to confidentiality and quality of services."
- Standard 6.5 requires that MFTs "follow all applicable laws regarding location of practice and services," and do not use technologically-assisted means for practicing outside of their allowed jurisdictions.
- A number of states including New York, New Jersey, California, North Carolina, Ohio, and Idaho have all adopted state statutes that prevent healthcare providers who are not licensed by these states from providing treatment to their state residents.
- Standard 6.6 provides that MFTs ensure that they are "well trained and competent in the use of all chosen technology-assisted professional services."

Confidentiality of Telehealth Services

- When a computer is used for videoconferencing or other forms of internet counseling, the computer must be protected by security software in an effort to protect client confidentiality. Although it is impossible to prevent the hacking of a computer, at a minimum computers must be password protected and protected by security software in order to safeguard treatment information.
- When MFTs and clients use the telephone for a counseling session or consultation, only a landline provides for confidential communication, because a cell phone call is a form of radio communication that can be intercepted.
- If e-mail communication is used for online counseling or consultation, the e-mails must be encrypted for the communication to be secure. Regular e-mails are not confidential.

Videoconferencing

- Videoconferencing has become a popular medium for the delivery of telehealth services, in appropriate cases, and a HIPAA-compliant platform for providing therapy for videoconferencing with a client can be found at Vsee.com.
- Telehealth is not considered an appropriate way to evaluate an individual who is in crisis; and a face-to-face crisis evaluation must be conducted for individuals who may be dangerous to self or others.

6.17 Colorado Law Prohibiting Conversion Therapy for Minors

In 2019 the Colorado General Assembly passed HB 19-1129, which prohibits either medical doctors or psychotherapists from providing conversion therapy to minors. C.R.S. § 12-43-201(1.5), which will be codified as 12-245-202(1.5), effective October 1, 2019, defines conversion therapy as "any practice or treatment . . . that attempts or purports to change an individual's sexual orientation or gender identity, including efforts to change behaviors or gender expressions or to eliminate or reduce sexual or romantic attraction or feelings towards individuals of the same sex."

Conversion therapy does not, by definition, include practices or treatments that provide: "Acceptance, support and understanding for the facilitation of an individual's coping, social support, and identity exploration and development, including sexual orientation-neutral interventions to prevent or address unlawful conduct or unsafe sexual practices, as long as the counseling does not seek to change sexual orientation or gender identity," or assistance to a person undergoing gender transition.

The General Assembly also enacted C.R.S. § 12-245-224(1)(t), which prohibits any psychotherapist from providing "conversion therapy with a client who is under eighteen years of age."

If therapists have questions about the propriety of providing conversion therapy to adults, they should consult the Code of Ethics, Position Statement, or Policy of the national professional association to which they belong. The APA, AAMFT, AMHCA, AAMFT, and NASW have cautioned their members not to utilize conversion therapy with clients because they have stated that no scientific basis exists to demonstrate that people can change their sexual orientation or gender identity through this treatment modality, and clients can be harmed by being subjected to this approach.

6.18 Board Certified Behavior Analysts

In May 2019, DORA announced its policy that Board Certified Behavior Analysts (BCBAs) who perform Applied Behavior Analysis (ABA) are not required to register with the mental health database as registered psychotherapists, so long as their practice is confined to ABA and no psychotherapy is conducted as that term is defined in C.R.S. § 12-245-201(14). This DORA policy states: "The practice of applied behavior analysis (ABA) differs from the practice of psychotherapy. The Association of Professional Behavior Analysts defines ABA as 'the design, implementation, and evaluation of instructional and environmental modifications to produce socially significant improvements in human behavior. The practice of ABA includes the empirical identification of functional relations between behavior and environmental factors, known as functional assessment and analysis. ABA interventions are based on scientific research and direct and indirect observation and measurement of behavior and environment. They utilize contextual factors, motivating operations, antecedent stimuli, positive reinforcement and other procedures to help individuals develop new behaviors, increase or decrease existing behaviors, and emit behaviors under specific environmental conditions.'" This policy further states that ABA practitioners (*e.g.*, those certified by the Behavior Analyst Certification Board) are not required to register as a psychotherapist pursuant to C.R.S. § 12-245-703, unless they engage in psychotherapy, as defined in § 12-245-202(14), in addition to their ABA work.

Caveat. BCBAs who are not licensed, certified, or registered as psychotherapists in Colorado need to be careful not to bill clients or their insurance plans for psychotherapy using CPT Codes for therapy, such as 90801, 90802, 90837, etc., as this could cause problems for the individual who risks being accused of the unauthorized practice of psychotherapy or of billing fraud.

6.19 Licensed Professional Counselor Compact

In 2022, the Colorado General Assembly enacted the Interstate Licensed Professional Counselor Compact, which is designed to enable LPCs to practice in other states that have adopted the compact in order to make professional counseling practice more portable. The compact takes effect when at least 10 states have adopted it. As of May 2022, Colorado is the third state to adopt the compact, along with Maryland and Georgia. A Counseling Compact Commission has been created to regulate and administer the process of applications by LPCs and to coordinate the exchange of information between State Boards of professional counseling and the Commission.

This statute provides that the practice of professional counseling occurs in the state where the client is located at the time of the counseling services. Among the objectives that the compact is designed to achieve is to increase public access to the services of LPCs by providing for the mutual recognition of member state licenses. The Compact is also intended to support spouses of relocating active duty military personnel. In addition the compact allows for the use of telehealth technology to facilitate increased access to the services of LPCs by granting them a "privilege to practice telehealth."

6.20 The Behavioral Health Administration

In 2022, the Colorado General Assembly created the Behavioral Health Administration (BHA) in the Department of Human Services to establish a coordinated, cohesive, and effective behavioral health system in Colorado. The BHA will handle most of the behavioral health programs that were previously handled by the Office of Behavioral Health (OBH) in the department.

By 2024, the bill, HB 22-1278, requires the BHA to be the licensing authority for all behavioral health entities; to establish a behavioral health performance monitoring system; and to create a comprehensive behavioral health safety net system.

Chapter 7:
Business Aspects

Psychotherapists are employed by a variety of employers. These employers include governmental bodies, corporations, nonprofit corporations, professional corporations, partnerships, and sole proprietors. The legal aspects and status of these entities are outlined in this chapter.

7.01 Government Employment

There are numerous government agencies that employ psychotherapists. These bodies include federal and state agencies, county and city governments, and school districts. A psychotherapist employed by the government is required to follow numerous policies and procedures, which are detailed and comprehensive and which encompass service requirements, documentation, and reporting. Additionally, these agencies have established certain civil service procedures and employee rights that are not generally available to non-governmental psychotherapists. Other than these requirements, there are no other unique legal or business issues associated with government employment.

Occasionally, a governmental agency will order an employee to disregard a Colorado law or rule and regulation pertaining to psychotherapy. If this occurs, a psychotherapist should immediately consult a private attorney, since the jurisdictional issues are complex.

7.02 Nonprofit Corporations

Nonprofit corporations employ a number of psychotherapists as caseworkers, counselors, therapists, or direct care staff. These organizations are generally organized solely and exclusively for charitable, educational, or eleemosynary purposes. In order to be a nonprofit corporation, no part of the corporation's income or profit may be distributed to its members, directors, or officers.

The major advantage of a nonprofit corporation is its ability to seek tax-exempt status. If such status is granted, the nonprofit corporation pays no tax on its income or profit. Additionally, charitable contributions made to such nonprofit corporations are tax deductible by the donor.

A common misperception about nonprofit corporations is that these entities may not legally make a profit. Although in reality many such organizations suffer this financial consequence, there is no such requirement. Nonprofit corporations are managed by a board of directors, whose members serve without compensation. These directors are responsible for the overall guidance, direction, control, and management of the nonprofit corporation's affairs. Typically, the directors are community volunteers chosen to serve because of some special interest in the organization's mission or because of some skill or expertise they bring to the board.

The nonprofit corporation's directors elect a president or board chair, who is responsible for presiding over the board meetings. Other officers may be elected to fulfill other board responsibilities, such as treasurer, vice president, or secretary. All of these officers serve without compensation.

The actual day-to-day affairs of the nonprofit corporation are managed by an executive director or chief executive officer, selected by the board of directors. This executive officer is a salaried employee of the nonprofit corporation who hires, fires, and supervises the nonprofit corporation's other employees.

Because of the charitable nature of the nonprofit corporation's work, psychotherapists who work for such agencies are typically dedicated, competent professionals who have chosen to forego the potentially huge financial rewards that are available to those psychotherapists who have chosen to practice their profession in the for-profit world.

7.03 Business Entities

A psychotherapist who wants to establish a private practice that is not associated with a government or nonprofit agency may establish that practice as a sole proprietorship, partnership, limited liability company, or corporation. These forms of doing business are compared and contrasted in sections 7.04, 7.05, and 7.06 of this book.

7.04 Sole Proprietorship

A sole proprietorship is a business having a single owner who has chosen not to do business in the corporate form (*i.e.*, as a corporation).

Other than procuring any licenses that may be required to engage in the particular business, there are no other legal requirements that must be met in order to establish a sole proprietorship. For example, there is no legal requirement that a separate business checking account be established. However, good accounting practice would dictate such. Hence, a person desiring to do business under this form simply commences the business without having to undertake any legal formalities.

Likewise, in order to cease doing business as a sole proprietor, one need only stop the business activity with the intent to terminate the business. A sole proprietorship, unlike a corporation, ceases to exist upon the death of the proprietor. As such, there is no continuity of the business after death.

Because of the singularity of ownership, control of the sole proprietorship remains undiluted in the hands of the owner. Because there is only one owner, the potential for capital is limited to the financial resources of the sole owner and his or her ability to borrow funds.

In the event the proprietor desires to sell or transfer the business to a third party, such transaction can occur without undue delay.

A sole proprietor may employ others to work as independent contractors or employees. A discussion of the differences between independent contractors and employees can be found in section 7.07 of this book. The reader should carefully review section 7.07, since there are important tax and liability consequences that result from each type of employment.

From a tort liability standpoint, a sole proprietor is personally liable for his or her own negligent and intentional actions, as well as the negligent actions of his or her employees when they occur within the scope of the employment relationship. Hence, not only are the business assets of the sole proprietor at risk, but the sole proprietor's personal assets (*e.g.*, house, car, boat, bank accounts, etc.) are also available to satisfy a judgment resulting from a lawsuit filed by an injured third party.

This rule imposing personal liability upon the sole proprietor for the negligent actions of his or her employees may be avoided by choosing the corporate form of doing business. Under the corporate form of business, the corporation is the employer and is liable for its employees' actions. This protects the shareholder-owner, who enjoys limited liability in this instance. Unfortunately, the corporate shield of limited liability does nothing for the owner's own negligent or intentional actions, since a person is always personally liable for such actions. As a practical matter, if a psychotherapist who employs others in his or her practice elects to do business as a sole proprietor, adequate insurance should be carried to protect any personal wealth that would be at risk.

A sole proprietor's income is taxed at his or her ordinary tax rate. Hence, only one federal tax return is filed for an individual doing business as a sole proprietor. This is less cumbersome and complicated than the tax requirements for a partnership or corporation.

In summary, a sole proprietorship is ideal for an individual without employees. Its simplicity and lack of legal formalities and requirements make it an attractive option. However, personal liability for the actions of employees and a limited ability to raise capital make it less desirable for the proprietor who seeks the greater financial returns that are possible through the efforts of employees.

7.05 Partnerships

A partnership is defined as two or more persons who agree to carry on a business for profit with joint rights of management and control.

This is a business entity that is used frequently by professionals such as physicians, lawyers, accountants, and others who possess specialized skills and knowledge. It is also a popular entity in real estate. It is not used as much by psychotherapists, although a basic understanding of its essential features is necessary in order to select the appropriate business entity for a psychotherapist.

A partnership requires greater effort to form than a sole proprietorship. In comparison to forming a corporation, however, it requires slightly less effort. The essential requirement in formation is that two or more persons must agree to do business as a partnership. Although there is no requirement that this agreement be in writing, the better practice is to reduce the agreement to a writing that is signed by all partners.

The agreement should, at a minimum, address the following issues:

1. What will be the name of the partnership?
2. Where will the principal office be located?
3. How much will each partner contribute as an initial capital contribution?
4. What will be each partner's obligation to make future capital contributions?
5. What happens if a partner is unable to provide future capital as needed?
6. How will partnership decisions be made?
7. What will be the authority of each partner to enter into contracts for and on behalf of the partnership?
8. What happens in the event of a partner's death or disability?
9. What happens in the event a partner wants to sell his or her partnership interest or withdraw, resign, or retire?
10. How will profits and losses be distributed or handled?
11. What happens upon termination of the partnership?

These issues should be discussed and legal advice obtained prior to signing any partnership agreement. In the absence of an agreement with respect to such issues, the Colorado Uniform Partnership Law (C.R.S. §§ 7-60-101, *et seq.*) will control and provide the law that will be followed to resolve any disagreement between the parties.

Once an agreement is reached to do business as a partnership, no other formalities are required other than obtaining the appropriate business or professional licenses.

A partnership may exist for any specifically defined period of time chosen by the partners (*e.g.*, five years). However, upon the death of a partner, the partnership ceases to exist and, in the absence of an agreement to the contrary, the surviving partners are required to terminate all partnership business, sell assets, pay creditors, return to each partner his or her initial capital contributions, and distribute the profits. In most cases the surviving partners do not want to cease doing business and dismantle the partnership in this fashion. Hence, most partnership agreements will contain some provision for the surviving partners to have an option to purchase the deceased partner's interest in the partnership so that the dissolution procedure need not disrupt the partnership business. If the surviving partners elect to continue the partnership business and buy the deceased partner's interest, a new partnership consisting of the surviving partners is created and the prior partnership ceases to exist.

A partner's interest in a partnership cannot be sold or transferred to a third party without the unanimous consent of the other partners. This consequence results from the legal requirement that all partners must agree to be partners; therefore, one partner cannot simply sell his or her partnership interest to a third party if one of the other partners objects to the third party. Consequently, a partner who wants to withdraw from the partnership will trigger a process by which the partnership business is terminated and dissolved in the same manner as that which occurs when a partner dies. Here again, a provision in the partnership agreement that allows the other partners to purchase the interest of the partner desiring to leave can eliminate the disruption that is inevitable in the absence of such a clause.

Unlike a sole proprietorship, partnership decision-making is much more complicated. The Colorado Partnership Law provides that each partner has joint rights to management and control. C.R.S. § 7-60-109. This means that each partner is vested with the authority to make partnership decisions. In practice, most partnership agreements provide that a partner will not exercise such right without the consent of a majority of the other partners. Consequently, decision-making in a partnership can be a time-consuming and laborious democratic process.

One of the advantages of a partnership is that a partnership's ability to generate capital for operations is not limited to a single partner, as is the case in a sole proprietorship. Each partner brings his or her own wealth to the partnership, and therefore the potential to raise capital is greater than that of a sole proprietor.

The greatest disadvantage of a partnership is that each partner is jointly and severally liable for the acts of the partnership's employees and the actions of each of the other partners, even though he or she may not have participated in the wrongful action. In other words, a psychotherapist who is a partner in a partnership is liable for the negligence or malpractice of the other partners regardless of his or her level of involvement with the particular client-victim. This means that any judgment obtained against the partner committing the negligence can be satisfied or paid out of the personal wealth of the other partners.

This aspect of joint and several liability is a dangerous element of partnership law and should be carefully considered before jumping into a partnership. Although this danger can be minimized by the use of malpractice insurance, such insurance will not provide coverage for a partner who binds the partnership to purchases, contracts, or other debts. Although the innocent partner may sue the guilty partner and attempt to recover the loss, such lawsuits are successful only to the extent that the guilty partner has financial resources and is able to pay the judgment.

A partnership's income and losses are passed through to the partners in accordance with their respective agreement. This means that each partner's share of the profits and losses are reported as ordinary income on each partner's individual tax return. Consequently, a partnership itself pays no income tax on its earnings since these are passed along to the partners.

There are advantages to doing business as a partnership. The combination of resources, skills, and talents enables individuals who otherwise could not compete in the business world to do so. However, these advantages must be balanced against the management control and liability issues that are inherently present in a partnership.

7.06 Corporations for Profit

The Traditional Corporate Entity

A corporation is an artificial, fictitious person that exists by operation of law. As a legal entity, it is recognized to have certain rights, privileges, and obligations. A corporation may own and dispose of property. It may employ others and engage in business. It has certain constitutional rights such as the right to be free from unreasonable searches and seizures, although it has no right to vote, as do natural persons. It has the obligation to pay taxes and obey the law. In most respects, then, it can legally do what any natural person could do.

A corporation may be thought of as consisting of people and property.

The shareholders contribute capital or money to the corporation so that it can engage in its business. Because of these contributions, the shareholders are the owners of the corporation. Their ownership is evidenced by a stock certificate indicating how many shares are owned. Shareholders have certain rights, which exist by virtue of ownership. The most important right of shareholders is the right to elect the board of directors. Additionally, the shareholders have the right to receive dividends and to inspect the corporate books and records.

The board of directors is elected annually by the shareholders and meets periodically to review corporate activities. The board of directors also appoints the corporate officers, who are responsible for the actual day-to-day affairs of the corporation.

There are several corporate officers. The president is the presiding officer of the corporation and is in charge of all day-to-day affairs. The president may be assisted by one or more vice presidents. The secretary is responsible for the corporate books and records, as well as the corporate minutes. There may be a Treasurer who is responsible for the management of the corporation's financial activities.

The officers are assisted by employees, whom they hire and fire. The employees are considered to be agents of the corporation.

In a small, closely held corporation such as might be contemplated for a psychotherapist, the shareholders also serve as the directors, officers, and employees.

In Colorado and in most states, a corporation's legal existence commences when the Secretary of State reviews and approves a document known as Articles of Incorporation. If these articles are in proper form and contain the required information, the Secretary of State will issue a Certificate of Incorporation, which is evidence of the corporation's legal existence. In many respects, it is similar to a birth certificate, which is nothing more than evidence of the existence of a natural person.

The Articles of Incorporation are generally drafted by an attorney who acts as the incorporator. These articles must contain the following information in order to be approved by the Secretary of State:

1. The name of the corporation;
2. The period of existence;

3. The name and address of the corporation's registered agent and the corporation's principal place of business;
4. The amount of stock the corporation wants to have available for issuance;
5. The names and addresses of the initial board of directors; and
6. The name and address of the incorporator.

Unlike sole proprietorships and partnerships, whose legal existence ceases upon death or transfer of ownership, a corporation's legal existence is not affected by the death of a shareholder or by his or her sale or transfer of stock. Hence, the corporation may be thought of as having perpetual existence if such is desired by the incorporator.

A corporation may issue as much stock as it desires. Thus, its ability to raise capital is potentially unlimited. There is no requirement that the shareholders consent to any new stockholders. This is one of the key advantages of the corporate form of business.

Another advantage is that the shareholders are generally not liable for the actions and conduct of the other owners, directors, officers, and employees. This legal principle is known as the shield of limited corporate liability. Under this doctrine, a shareholder's personal wealth, such as a house, boat, or car, is not subject to any judgment that might be obtained against the corporation or any other person associated with the corporation. However, a shareholder is liable for his or her own negligence or malpractice when it is committed as an employee or director.

The law requires that certain legal formalities be followed in order to maintain the corporate existence. For example, regular meetings of the shareholders and directors must be held and minutes recorded of the decisions of each. Corporate funds must not be commingled with the personal funds of the shareholders. Corporate documents must be signed by persons who have received authority to do so, and the signature must identify the fact that the person is signing as an agent for the corporation. If such formalities are not followed, the corporate shield will be disregarded and the shareholders will be found to be personally liable for the corporation's debts.

A corporation must file a corporate tax return and pay taxes on its earnings. If there are sufficient after-tax earnings, the board of directors may declare dividends for the shareholders. These dividends are taxable to the shareholders as ordinary income. This second tax on dividends is considered by many individuals to be a double taxation of corporate income. Consequently, dividends are often disfavored and ways are sought to avoid this double taxation. Accountants are best equipped to advise a psychotherapist on the best way to avoid dividends with respect to that worker's particular corporation.

The U.S. Tax Code permits certain corporations to elect to have their profits and losses passed through the corporation without taxation, provided all shareholders report their respective shares of such on their individual tax returns. Corporations that make this election are known Subchapter "S" corporations. Those that choose the normal form of taxation are known as "C" corporations. An accountant should be consulted with respect to whether a "S" or "C" election is appropriate.

Corporations are also permitted to establish a variety of pension and/or profit sharing plans, which provide for the legitimate tax sheltering of income if it is for retirement purposes. Again, an accountant should be retained to determine the appropriateness of such plans.

Other Corporate-Like Entities

Colorado has enacted legislation (C.R.S. §§ 7-80-101, *et seq.*) that allows for the establishment of a type of corporation known as a Limited Liability Company (LLC). This type of corporation was created in order to allow for a greater number of companies to take advantage of "S" corporation tax treatment. A Limited Liability Company is taxed much like an "S" corporation. Many of the eligibility requirements for "S" treatment, however, have been relaxed for Limited Liability Companies. The advantage of operating as an LLC is that the owners, who are referred to as "members," are not personally liable for the alleged improper actions of the LLC or its employees.

Of more recent creation than the LLC is the Limited Liability Partnership (LLP), which provides the same advantage of limited liability that an LLC possesses. Limited liability is achieved through compliance with state laws that require both an LLC and an LLP to maintain required amounts of liability insurance. You should consult with an attorney who specializes in business transactions if you need to set up either type of limited liability business organization.

Special Requirements

A psychotherapist seeking to use the corporate form of business must comply with the particular licensing requirements for his or her particular profession. For example, psychologists, social workers, professional counselors, and marriage and family therapists must comply with the provisions of C.R.S. § 12-245-213, while psychiatrists must comply with the provisions of C.R.S. § 12-240-138. Such corporations are known as "Professional Service Corporations." The specific requirements are outlined in section 6.09 of this book for licensed psychologists, licensed clinical social workers, licensed marriage and family therapists, and licensed professional counselors, and in section 6.10 of this book for psychiatrists. A corporation or professional service corporation offers many advantages for a psychotherapist, particularly if the psychotherapist wants to be affiliated with other psychotherapists but wants to avoid the joint and several liability associated with partnerships. There are trade-offs for this protection, namely, the added costs associated with forming and maintaining the corporate existence and the procedural formalities that must continually be followed.

Professional Liability Insurance for a Corporation

Any corporation under which you practice as an employee must be covered by professional liability insurance. Make certain that your professional liability insurance policy provides coverage for you individually and also for your corporation under which you practice as an employee.

7.07 Employees or Independent Contractors

A psychotherapist doing business as a sole proprietor, partnership, or corporation and employing others in the practice has a financial responsibility under the Colorado Employment Security Act, the Colorado Workers' Compensation Act, the United States Code, and the Colorado Tax Code to make monthly payments to fund unemployment and workers' compensation, as well as other federal and state assistance programs. Although these payments are mandatory for employers whose work is performed by employees, businesses that contract their work to independent contractors generally are not required to make such contributions. Consequently, many businesses attempt to characterize their employees as independent contractors. Unfortunately, this is easier said than done.

In a Colorado Court of Appeals case, *Dana's Housekeeping v. Butterfield*, 807 P.2d 1218 (Colo. App. 1990), an employer attempted to avoid liability under the Colorado Workers' Compensation Act by seeking independent contractor status for its employees. The employer, Dana's Housekeeping, argued that it was a referral service for domestic housekeepers that did not have or exercise control over Butterfield's work. Thus, Dana's Housekeeping contended that Butterfield was an independent contractor. When Butterfield was injured, she sought workers' compensation on the basis that she was an employee. The court held that Butterfield was an employee of Dana's Housekeeping rather than an independent contractor.

In determining that Butterfield was an employee, the court applied a "right to control" test, which provides that a person shall be considered an employee if the employer has retained the right to control the manner, method, or means of the employee's duties. Although Dana's Housekeeping signed a contract with Butterfield that characterized their relationship as being that of an independent contractor, the court ruled that the way in which parties may refer to themselves does not determine whether a person is an independent contractor or an employee. In deciding this case, the court considered the following factors as to whether a person is an employee or independent contractor:

1. Whether the employee gives all or any part of his or her time to the work;
2. Whether the worker or the employer controls the detail;
3. Whether the employee furnishes his or her own necessary tools and equipment;
4. Whether either may terminate employment without liability to the other; and
5. Whether compensation is measured by time, piece, or lump sum for the entire task.

In 1989, the Colorado Court of Appeals considered the case of *Locke v. Longacre*, 772 P.2d 685 (Colo. App. 1989). In this case, the court considered whether a person was an independent contractor or an employee under the Colorado Employment Security Act.

The defendant, Longacre, was a licensed practical nurse who had entered into an agreement with Locke to provide substantial home care and nursing services for Locke's mother. The parties had signed an agreement purporting to create an independent contract relationship between themselves. During a three-year period, Longacre provided constant care for Locke's mother. On one occasion, she provided similar services for a neighbor for approximately one week. When Longacre sought unemployment benefits, Locke argued that Longacre was an independent contractor providing professional nursing services with the potential to provide services for other individuals, but that she chose not to do so for personal reasons. In rejecting Locke's arguments, the court noted that in order to obtain independent contractor status, the claimant must be engaged in a business venture at the same time the claimant is providing services for the employer. Thus, if a person is providing services to a *sole* employer, even if the employer does not retain the right to control the manner, method, or means of the other party, an employer-employee relationship may exist.

There is much uncertainty in the law as to whether a psychotherapist who employs other therapists can achieve independent contractor status for them and avoid the financial obligations associated with employee status. Certainly, if the psychotherapist-employer retains the right to control the manner, method, or means of the therapy, an employee relationship would exist and there would be liability for the unemployment, workers' compensation, and FICA contributions. This would be particularly true if the professional rendering the services was not working for any other psychotherapist.

In order to substantiate to the Colorado Division of Employment that the individual is free from direction and control, the business should have given a written document to the independent contractor, preferably prepared by legal counsel, and signed by both parties. The document and actual practice should demonstrate that the business does *not*:

1. Require the individual to work exclusively for that business;
2. Establish a quality standard, except to the extent of plans and specifications (*i.e.*, work cannot be overseen by the person for whom the services are performed);
3. Establish a salary or hourly rate but rather pays a fixed or contract amount;
4. Terminate the work during the contract period, unless the individual fails to produce a result that meets the specifications of the contract;
5. Provide any training for the individual;
6. Provide small tools or benefits, except that materials and equipment may be supplied;
7. Dictate the time of performance (a completion schedule may be established);
8. Pay the individual personally, but rather makes checks payable to the trade or business name of the individual; and
9. Combine business operations in any way with the individual's business, but instead maintains separate and distinct operations.

The IRS has developed a 20-factor test used to characterize workers. The American Institute of Certified Public Accounts, Tax Division, has developed a guide, based on the IRS criteria, to help in determining work status. A majority of the following questions should be answered "yes" in order to indicate potential independent contractor status:

1. Have the parties signed an independent contractor agreement?

2. Does the contract state that the company has no right to control the work performed?
3. Does the contract state that the independent contractor cannot be fired as long as he or she meets contractual obligations?
4. Does the contract state that the independent contractor has a right to hire and fire assistants?
5. Does the contract provide that the independent contractor is solely responsible for providing the labor to achieve the intended result?
6. Is the independent contractor paid by the job rather than by the hour?
7. Is the company ensuring that the company provides no type of training for inexperienced workers?
8. Is the independent contractor hired for a specified time period?
9. Is the independent contractor free to work for any number of persons or firms simultaneously?
10. Does the independent contractor advertise and project himself or herself to the public as an independent contractor in business for himself or herself?
11. Does the independent contractor perform his or her job off the company premises?
12. Does the contract provide that the customer will pay the independent contractor directly rather than pay the company, which then pays the contractor?
13. Does the company refrain from sending supervisors or inspectors to the field on a regular basis to check on the work progress?
14. Does the company refrain from requesting that the independent contractor do the same type of work as its regular employees?
15. Is there evidence that the company's competitors are treating similar workers as independent contractors?

Because the delinquent taxes and penalties can be significant for non-compliance with any of the foregoing government programs, a psychotherapist is cautioned to consult an accountant prior to attempting to characterize any worker as an independent contractor.

For further information regarding employee versus independent contractor status, and contract provisions in employment and independent contractor agreements, see Kimberlie Ryan, *Employment Law Guidebook: For Colorado Business Owners and Human Resource Professionals* (Bradford Publishing Co. 2006).

7.08 Employment Law

Prior to the evolution of modern-day service and technology-based economies, the employment relationship reflected the dominance of the employer that existed in the agricultural and industrial economies. In both of these economic states of development, the employee had no ability to influence the nature of the employment relationship. The landowner and the industrialist, by virtue of their economic power, were able to dictate working conditions, wages, and hours. The workers in such economies had no economic or political power and therefore became subservient to the landowners and capitalists. From this historical perspective, it is not surprising that the law originally characterized the employment relationship as being one of "Master-Servant."

One of the earliest laws to emerge from the Master-Servant characterization of the employment relationship was the doctrine of "employment-at-will." Under this legal doctrine, employees served at the will of the employer, who possessed the unfettered and absolute right to terminate the employee with or without cause. Hence, an employee had no recourse for the employer's decision to terminate the employment relationship, even if done in bad faith.

Modern judicial interpretations of the employment-at-will doctrine have imposed certain limitations upon the doctrine and have affirmed the right of employees to seek recourse against employers who fail to follow their own policies and procedures regarding discipline and termination. Additionally, the courts have declared that employers who terminate employees for reasons that are found to be against public policy may not invoke the employment-at-will doctrine as justification for such terminations. Hence, in many states, an employee cannot be discharged for refusing to commit an unlawful act, for reporting criminal activities, or for disclosing illegal, unethical, or unsafe business practices.

The erosion of the Master-Servant relationship and the employment-at-will doctrine may also be traced to the creation of employee rights through federal and state legislation. The following represent some of the more significant federal laws that have changed the employment relationship and eroded the employment-at-will doctrine.

The Davis-Bacon Act. Signed in 1931, this act requires the payment of "prevailing wages" to employees of contractors or subcontractors working on government construction projects. In 1936, the Walsh-Healey Act extended the Davis-Bacon Act and required a minimum wage, as well as overtime pay of time and a half, to employees of manufacturers or suppliers entering into contracts with agencies of the federal government.

The Norris-LaGuardia Act. The Norris-LaGuardia Act was passed in 1932 and removed the power of federal courts to enjoin union activity, unless such activity involved fraud or violence.

The National Labor Relations Act. In 1935, Congress enacted the National Labor Relations Act, which established the right of employees to form, join, or assist labor organizations; to bargain collectively with their employers; and to engage in concerted activity for the purpose of collective bargaining or mutual aid and protection. The Act also required employers to bargain and deal in good faith with unions and created the National Labor Relations Board to oversee union elections and prevent employers from engaging in unfair and illegal union-labor activities and unfair labor practices.

Fair Labor Standards Act (1938). This Act prohibits oppressive child labor and provides that a minimum hourly wage rate be paid to covered employees and requires individuals working over 40 hours per week to be paid overtime wages of no less than one and a half times the regular pay for hours worked beyond 40 hours a week (with some exceptions).

Equal Pay Act of 1963. In 1963, Congress enacted the Equal Pay Act as an amendment to the Fair Labor Standards Act to eliminate discrimination between employees on the basis of sex (*i.e.*, by paying wages at a rate less than the rate at which an employer pays wages to employees of the opposite sex for equal work on jobs, the performance of which requires equal skill, effort, and responsibility and which are performed under similar working conditions).

Title VII of the Civil Rights Act of 1964. This Act prohibits discrimination by most employers on the basis of race, color, national origin, religion, or sex.

Age Discrimination in Employment Act. In 1967, the Age Discrimination in Employment Act was enacted, which prohibits discrimination against job applicants or employees falling within the 40-70 age category by those employers whose business affects interstate commerce and who employ 20 or more employees.

Rehabilitation Act of 1973. This Act prohibits discrimination in employment against handicapped persons by those who receive federal contracts or assistance. The Act requires a covered person to hire a handicapped person who can, after reasonable accommodation, perform a job at the minimum level of productivity expected of a normal person performing the job. Further, contractors with federal contracts in excess of $2,500 are required to take "affirmative action" to hire handicapped persons.

Americans with Disabilities Act. This Act provides that effective July 26, 1992 (for employers with at least 25 employees), and July 26, 1994 (for employers with at least 15 employees), employers may not discriminate on the basis of disability and must make reasonable accommodations similar to those required by the Rehabilitation Act of 1973.

Employee Polygraph Protection Act. This Act, which was passed in 1988, prohibits employers from requiring, suggesting, or causing employees or prospective employees to take lie detector tests. It also forbids discharging, disciplining, discriminating against, refusing to promote or hire, or threatening to take any action against any employee or applicant because he or she refuses to take a lie detector test. The Act contains exceptions for security employees, government employers, and FBI contractors, as well as employees with access to controlled substances and investigation of a specific employer's economic loss if the employee had access to the property and the employer has a reasonable suspicion of the employee's involvement.

Pregnancy Discrimination Act of 1978. This Act amended Title VII of the Civil Rights Act of 1964 to prohibit discrimination on the basis of pregnancy.

Worker Adjustment and Retraining Act. This Act requires that employers with 100 or more employees give each employee at least 60 days' notice of a plant closing or mass layoff.

Other Laws. A variety of other federal laws impinge upon the employment relationship. These laws include the Social Security Act, Employee Retirement Income Security Act, and the Occupational Health and Safety Act. Additionally, each state has passed laws covering workers' compensation and unemployment.

Other Resources. For further information about federal and state laws affecting employers, including discrimination laws, see Kimberlie Ryan, *Employment Law Guidebook: For Colorado Business Owners and Human Resource Professionals* (Bradford Publishing Co. 2006).

7.09 Workers' Compensation

The Colorado Workers' Compensation Act is designed to provide a remedy for job-related injuries without regard to fault. Under the Act, an employer is granted immunity from common-law negligence with respect to employees, provided the employer assumes the burden of compensating workers for all job-related injuries through private insurance. In essence, an injured employee may not sue the employer for negligence, but receives a fixed compensation for any injury that is work-related.

Compensation for injured workers is funded by premiums paid by the employer to a private insurance carrier. A psychotherapist should consult a competent insurance broker to determine the most economical means of fulfilling this obligation.

7.10 Employer Payroll Taxes

Employers are required to pay FICA taxes for each employee. The rates change with some regularity. A psychotherapist should consult an accountant to determine the prevailing rates, and to plan appropriately for fulfilling these obligations.

State Unemployment

The Colorado Employment Security Act sets forth a comprehensive legislative scheme for providing unemployment benefits for qualified individuals who become unemployed. The funding for this program comes from insurance taxes levied against employers. An employer's tax is based upon the employer's total payroll and unemployment history. An accountant should be consulted for planning purposes with respect to such taxes.

7.11 Employee Withholdings

Employers are currently required to withhold from each employee's wages and deposit through a bank depository the following:

1. FICA employee taxes; and
2. Federal and state income taxes, depending on the declaration of the employee on his or her W-4 form.

Employers are required to obtain from each employee a W-4 form and an I-9 immigration form. Failure to comply with these requirements can result in civil penalties and fines.

For further information regarding employee withholdings, see Kimberlie Ryan, *Employment Law Guidebook: For Colorado Business Owners and Human Resource Professionals*, Ch. 4 (Bradford Publishing Co. 2006).

7.12 Insurance

A psychotherapist who is in private practice should seriously consider the need for the following types of insurance:

1. Professional liability insurance;
2. Health insurance for himself or herself and all employees;
3. Property casualty insurance to insure against loss and theft of property;

4. Overhead expense insurance, which will provide a source of funds to meet ongoing business expenses in the event the psychotherapist is disabled and unable to generate fees for a period of time;
5. Personal disability insurance, which will provide a stream of income for the psychotherapist in the event he or she is disabled and unable to generate fees;
6. Life insurance, particularly if the psychotherapist provides the income to pay the bills for his or her family and currently lacks personal wealth to support such family in the event of his or her death; and
7. Comprehensive general liability coverage, which insures against losses due to ordinary negligence, and covers claims for a slip and fall at the therapist's office, for automobile accidents that result from business travel, etc.

7.13 Use of Professionals

Throughout this book, references have been made to the need to obtain advice from attorneys, certified public accountants, insurance brokers, and other business advisors. These professionals generally work at an hourly rate and are compensated for time actually devoted to rendering advice. The psychotherapist is urged to seek out and retain such professionals, since their advice can result in substantial savings.

In retaining a professional, the following facts should be considered:

1. The professional's expertise in a particular area;
2. The compatibility of the professional's personality with that of the psychotherapist;
3. The professional's reputation for timeliness and accuracy; and
4. The professional's hourly rate.

The psychotherapist should not hesitate to request a written fee engagement letter that outlines the scope of the services to be rendered and the basis for calculating the fees and terms of payment.

Attorneys frequently ask for a "retainer." This term means different things to different attorneys. For example, it may mean the client pays a non-refundable amount for that attorney's availability for legal services. For others, it may mean an advance deposit against which hourly charges are billed. Most legal work for psychotherapists will be billed at hourly rates ranging from $150 to $250 per hour, depending upon the attorney's experience. Some attorneys will charge a flat fee for certain types of work, such as incorporating a business or drafting a will.

Psychotherapists should not hesitate to inquire about these matters before engaging or retaining an attorney or any other professional.

7.14 Billing Standards and Billing Practices

Because of the complexity of HIPAA standards and managed health care billing practices, therapists nationwide have had many questions regarding billing standards and billing practices. In addition, frequent questions have arisen concerning the Current Procedural Terminology (CPT) Codes that should be used by therapists in billing for different types of treatment. The information that follows concerning the use of CPT Codes is not meant to be a substitute for purchase of the manual, *Current Procedural Terminology,* published by the American Medical Association (2017 Edition). The following questions are frequently posed by psychologists, licensed clinical social workers, MFTs, and professional counselors.

Q. Can a clinical supervisor, who is a licensed mental health professional and who is on insurance panels, bill for treatment or professional services provided by a supervisee or contract employee who is not on the insurance panel?

A. No, only the individual who actually provides treatment can bill for those services. It is generally considered fraud if a person other than the treatment provider bills for those services.

Q. As a licensed psychologist, I am a panel provider on most insurance panels. I am required by the contracts with insurance panels to be available in emergencies for my clients. When I provide counseling over the telephone to clients in emergencies, can I bill for this service using the 90832 CPT Code for brief psychotherapy (30 minutes) or the 90834 CPT Code for a 50-minute session with a client?

A. These CPT Codes all require "face-to-face" contact with the client. In addition, the HCFA billing form used for insurance billing requires you to indicate the place of service (POS). It is essential that bills for services be accurate in every respect. When you are billing for a telephone session with a client that is not conducted "face-to-face," check with the insurance company representative to see if you are allowed to use one of these CPT Codes, or if another Code can be used for telephone sessions. Confirm in writing any directions that you are given in this regard. Also check with the insurance representative to see if the place of service should be listed as your office, or if you should reference the telephone as the place of service. Insurers generally have agreed to pay for teletherapy sessions conducted on video conferencing platforms, as well as phone sessions and online counseling.

Q. None of the insurance panels with which I contract will pay for missed appointments. My written policies, which every client receives, state that the client is responsible for payment for any missed appointments. However, the insurance panel contracts also prohibit me from billing their insureds directly or collecting fees from them, except for deductibles or co-pays. Under these circumstances, can I charge clients for missed appointments?

A. Any contractual provisions should be negotiable between the contracting parties. When you receive a contract from an insurance panel, you must read it thoroughly to make certain that you can agree with all of its provisions and to ensure that you have no questions concerning the agreement. Therefore, if a contract presents this dilemma, stating that you cannot collect fees directly from an insured and that you cannot bill for missed appointments, you should insert in the contract that you will collect fees for missed appointments from the insured-client.

Under no circumstances can you bill for a missed appointment as if psychotherapy occurred when it did not: this would constitute fraud.

Q. I am a marriage and family therapist who specializes in couples counseling, marital therapy, and family counseling. Can I bill insurance panels for marriage counseling? What procedural code would I use? I know that 90847 is the CPT Code for family therapy (conjoint). Can this also be used for marriage counseling?

A. First of all, not many insurance panels will pay for marriage counseling, although some do. Marriage and family therapists who bill for couples counseling do use 90847, since this Code for family therapy comes the closest to this specific type of treatment. Other MFTs bill using the more generic 90832 or 90834, depending on the length of the session. A difficulty that may arise is how to fill in the block on the HCFA bill where an ICD diagnostic code must be inserted. If the treatment is for marital problems, and not for depression, anxiety, or an adjustment disorder, can one of these three diagnoses be inserted? If the goal of treatment is not to resolve symptoms of depression, anxiety, or an adjustment disorder, can a bill be submitted that implies that a client is receiving treatment for such problems? These are difficulties inherent in insurance billing. The best practice in such a situation is to have clients pay for marital counseling the old-fashioned way: out of their own pocket. An alternative approach would be to inform an insurance company representative directly, with client consent, of the services being provided, and ask what CPT Code or Diagnostic Code should be used. If you are informed that the health insurance policy does not cover marriage counseling, abide by that decision, and do not attempt to construct a creative but fraudulent way to bill the insurance carrier.

Q. When a client cannot pay their co-pay, am I required to turn the client away, and not let them attend a treatment session? I know that I cannot waive a co-pay or a deductible, but what do I do if a client does not have the funds to pay it?

A. You should not turn the client away from an individual or group therapy session because the client lacks funds to pay a required co-pay. When clients need treatment, they need to receive treatment. Although you cannot waive a co-pay, you can carry it on your books as a balance due from the client, when he or she has the funds to pay it.

Q. Are sliding-scale fee policies required? I know that I cannot bill an insurance company more than I bill my individual clients. But I am not certain if it is ethical for me to bill some clients less than I bill others.

A. That is an excellent question. In Colorado, sliding-scale fee policies are a generally accepted practice. In fact, the Domestic Violence Offender Management Board Standards require DVOMB-approved therapists to have a sliding scale for clients, based on income. Yes, this is an ethical practice, and sliding-scale fee policies are used by therapists nationwide.

Q. I know that I cannot bill an insurance company a rate higher than that which I bill to self-pay clients. Is there anything wrong with me charging everyone the same rate: $100 per hour? If an insurance company will not pay that rate, then I am required to accept whatever the contract with insurance panels will pay. Is there anything wrong with this practice?

A. No, this is acceptable. But you may want to make an exception for any indigent clients or low-income individuals, who may need a sliding-scale fee.

Q. When clients do not pay their bills, can I turn them over to a collection agency? Can I sue them in small claims court?

A. No you cannot sue them, for two reasons. First, there is no way that you can sue without breaching confidentiality. Secondly, if you sue a client in small claims court, it is likely that the client would file a counterclaim against you for malpractice, claiming that the treatment did not provide any benefit to the client. Even if such a counterclaim could easily be defended and dismissed, you would still be required to report it to your professional liability insurance company, and to answer in the affirmative when filling out applications in the future when you are asked, "Have you ever been sued for malpractice?" Therefore, you never want to sue a client.

The use of collection agencies is a common practice for medical doctors and hospitals. Ethical Codes for mental health professionals allow psychologists and other therapists to use collection agencies, so long as informed consent is given to the client, informing that this practice will be used. Sometimes, a client's failure to pay bills becomes a clinical issue: Why isn't the client paying, when the client has a clear ability to do so? The best practice is not to allow clients to get behind by more than three sessions. It certainly is ethical for you to treat the problem as a clinical issue, find out why the client has not paid, and encourage the client to either pay any balance immediately or to institute a payment plan.

Q. Recently, I received a letter from Medicaid, requiring me to provide a copy of all client records for the last calendar year as part of an audit. I do not know if this was a quality assurance review or if some other issue was being investigated. When I called the representative from whom I received the letter, she would not inform me what the purpose is for the audit. Client records, of course, have very personal and private information. Do I need to turn over all of the client records that have been requested?

A. This is certainly a problem with our managed healthcare system, and has been for many years. You will often find that contracts for panel providers, including not only private health insurance but also government health insurance programs, contain provisions requiring panel providers to turn over copies of client records when requested. HIPAA disclosure statements generally state that such audits constitute exceptions to the confidentiality of private healthcare information (PHI).

Can you trust the government or the government contractor that administers federally funded health insurance programs? The generally accepted standard of practice is to trust that any records provided during the audit will be kept confidential. In fact, federal law generally requires that the confidentiality of such records be protected. HIPAA standards were enacted by Congress in order to protect the confidentiality of all PHI.

The difficulty that arises if you refuse to provide the client's records in response to this request is that Medicaid will demand back from you all the payments that you received for treatment of any client(s) involved. If you refuse to pay, your name will be placed on a "hold up list" and payments from other clients' treatment will be retained by Medicaid until all funds demanded have been paid.

Private health insurers should not be engaging in such a practice, however. HIPAA standards should prevent such practices. In compliance with HIPAA, whenever a request is made for treatment information, therapists are to respond by providing the least amount of information sufficient to satisfy the request. That is an excellent standard, and should be remembered by mental health professionals whenever they are responding to requests for treatment information.

Chapter 8: Standards for Domestic Evaluations and for Domestic Violence Treatment Providers

Psychotherapists are increasingly being employed by the courts to assist judges with evaluation of issues relating to parental responsibilities, parenting time, and domestic violence. The legal standards and best practices for child and family investigators, parenting coordinators, and approved domestic violence treatment providers are outlined in this chapter.

8.01 Allocation of Parental Responsibilities

In the late 1990s, the Colorado General Assembly made sweeping changes to the statutes regarding custody actions and custody evaluations, and changed the term "custody" to "parental responsibilities." The entire statute that provided for "joint custody" was repealed. In its place, C.R.S. § 14-10-124 provides that courts shall "determine the allocation of parental responsibilities, including parenting time and decision-making responsibilities, in accordance with the best interests of the child giving paramount consideration to the child's safety and the physical, mental, and emotional conditions and needs of the child."

With regard to parenting time, C.R.S. § 14-10-124 requires that courts "make provisions for parenting time that the court finds are in the child's best interests unless the court finds, after a hearing, that parenting time by the party would endanger the child's physical health or significantly impair the child's emotional development," based upon various factors set forth in the statute. This statute also provides, "In order to implement an order allocating parental responsibilities, both parties may submit a parenting plan or plans for the court's approval that shall address both parenting time and the allocation of decision-making responsibilities." In addition, the court may order mediation in order "to assist the parties in formulating or modifying a parenting plan or in implementing a parenting plan."

The statute that previously provided for custody evaluations (C.R.S. § 14-10-127) now provides for evaluations and reports concerning the allocation of parental responsibilities. Such an evaluation may be conducted pursuant to a court order by "any county or district social services department or a licensed mental health professional" who is qualified. C.R.S. § 14-10-127 further provides, "When a mental health professional performs the evaluation, the court shall appoint or approve the selection of the mental health professional."

In preparing a report concerning the allocation of parental responsibilities, the evaluator may "consult with and obtain information from medical, mental health, educational, or other expert persons who have served the child in the past *without obtaining the consent of the parent . . . ; but the child's consent must be obtained if the child has reached the age of fifteen years unless the court finds that the child lacks mental capacity to consent."* [Emphasis added.] This means, for example, that a mental health professional conducting such an evaluation need not obtain the parent's consent before speaking with another mental health professional, but he or she must obtain the child's consent if the child has reached the age of 15 years. The mental health professional consulted by the evaluator must, of course, obtain consent from his or her client before providing to the evaluator any information that was gained during the course of a professional relationship involving the child.

In order to be qualified to testify regarding an evaluation of parental responsibilities or parenting time, the court must find that the evaluator is an expert, by training and experience, in the following areas: the effects of divorce and remarriage on children, adults, and families; appropriate parenting techniques; child development, including cognitive, personality, emotional, and psychological developments; child and adult psychopathology; applicable clinical assessment techniques; and applicable legal and ethical requirements of parental responsibilities evaluation.

C.R.S. § 14-10-127 requires that the written report of the evaluator be mailed to the court, to counsel, and to any party not represented by counsel at least 21 days prior to the hearing. The evaluator must make available to counsel and to any party not represented by counsel the file of underlying data and reports, complete texts of diagnostic reports, and the names and addresses of all persons consulted for the evaluation. The written report must include, but need not be limited to, the following information:

1. A description of the procedures employed during the evaluation;
2. A report of the data collected;
3. A conclusion that explains how the resulting recommendations were reached from the data collected, with specific reference to criteria listed in the statute and their relationship to the results of the evaluation;
4. Recommendations concerning custody, parenting time, and other considerations; and

5. An explanation of any limitations in the evaluations or any reservations regarding the resulting recommendations.

The standard to be followed by courts in allocating the decision-making responsibilities between the parties is "the best interests of the child," based upon specific factors enumerated in C.R.S. § 14-10-124. In making such a determination, "the court shall not presume that any person is better able to serve the best interests of the child because of that person's sex."

In the past, mental health professionals who performed custody evaluations have at times become embroiled in misunderstandings regarding their role, after interviewing parents and family members. Family members have filed complaints in the past to the grievance board, alleging that they believed information provided to the evaluator would be confidential. Such evaluations are not confidential, since information will be shared with the court, with attorneys for the parties involved, and with guardians *ad litem*. In order to avoid these unfortunate misunderstandings, an evaluator should provide any person who is interviewed for purposes of such an evaluation with a statement disclosing the fact that information provided in such an interview is not confidential, and will be shared with the court and other appropriate professionals.

It should go without saying that a therapist who has previously provided treatment to any family members involved in a dispute regarding parenting time or allocation of parental responsibility should not accept an appointment as an evaluator, since such would constitute a dual relationship.

Decision-Making Authority

When a potential client brings his or her children to see an MFT and provides information that he or she and the children's other parent have recently divorced, careful efforts must be made to ensure that the parent has decision-making authority. Pursuant to C.R.S. § 14-10-124, courts are empowered to allocate parental responsibilities when a divorce is awarded. Parental responsibilities include the residential care of children and the authority to make decisions concerning the children's treatment providers, schools, or church.

When this statute was enacted and went into effect in 1999, its purpose was to avoid conflicts and court hearings involving disputes between the parents over therapists, schools, and church attendance. In the vast majority of cases, judges do not necessarily allocate decision-making authority to one parent or the other, choosing instead to award "joint decision-making authority."

The best practice in determining whether a parent has decision-making authority is to require the parent to provide the divorce decree or an order entered by the court. If one parent has been given exclusive decision-making authority, that is the only parent who can select a treatment provider and sign a therapist's Disclosure Statement. Where joint decision-making authority has been granted to both parents, both parents must consent to treatment by signing a therapist's Disclosure Statement. By securing the permission of both parents for treatment, both will be entitled to receive treatment information and will be involved in the treatment process, which is generally in the best interests of the children involved.

Pursuant to C.R.S. § 14-10-124(6), either parent may consent to treatment of a child in an emergency. This affords treatment providers the opportunity to evaluate a child and determine what treatment is needed on an emergent basis. When a therapist determines that mental health services are needed on an emergent basis, the therapist should document the facts and circumstances that justify the need for treatment, and also document the harm that would result if services are not provided.

When parents have been awarded joint decision-making authority and one of the parents refuses to consent to mental health treatment, an interesting ethical issue is posed: Is the parent who is refusing to consent to treatment committing medical neglect? Should that parent be reported to DHS for neglecting his or her child?

The public policy in the State of Colorado, established by the child abuse reporting statute contained in the Children's Code, C.R.S. § 19-3-304, requires that the basic needs of children be met by their parents. Any parent who fails to provide for a child's medical or mental health needs is potentially engaging in neglect. When domestic situations become adversarial and conflictual, children can be harmed by a parent's refusal to consent to the provision of mental health services needed by a child.

8.02 Parenting Time

The courts are frequently asked to resolve disputes concerning parenting time. This normally arises when one parent is not complying with the visitation schedule. When presented with such a motion, the court will resolve the motion based on what is in the best interests of the child.

C.R.S. § 14-10-129(1) provides that the court must not restrict a parent's visitation rights (parenting time) unless it finds that the parenting time would endanger the child's physical health or significantly impair the child's emotional development. For example, if a non-custodial parent has been convicted of the crimes listed below or any crime in which the underlying factual basis has been found by the court on the record to include an act of domestic violence, it constitutes a potential threat or endangerment to the child.

The crimes allowing the court to restrict parenting time include the following: murder in the first degree; murder in the second degree; enticement of a child; sexual assault in the first, second, or third degree; sexual assault on a child; incest; aggravated incest; child abuse; trafficking in children; sexual exploitation of children; procurement of a child for sexual exploitation; soliciting for child prostitution; pandering of a child; procurement of a child; keeping a place of child prostitution; pimping of a child; inducement of child prostitution; and patronizing a prostituted child.

8.03 Standard of Care for Testifying in Domestic Cases

Section 8.01 discusses the factors to be considered by a parental responsibilities/parenting time evaluator. It also discusses the procedures to be followed in conducting an evaluation, the factors to be considered in making recommendations to the court, and the basic qualifications that an evaluator must possess. Although the law regarding domestic evaluations changed in 1999, the practices of many attorneys who handle domestic cases have not changed. They still subpoena therapists to court, expecting them to give opinions regarding who would be the better parent. In many cases, this creates a problem for the therapist involved when the therapist has not conducted a thorough parental responsibility/parenting time evaluation and thus does not have the appropriate basis for providing recommendations to the court concerning the issues that should be addressed. If you are called to court by an attorney in a domestic case and you are asked who would be the better parent or caregiver, do not express an opinion. You may simply answer, "I have not conducted the evaluation necessary to address these issues, and therefore do not have an opinion to give you."

You must not accept a court appointment or a request by counsel to conduct an evaluation concerning allocation of parental responsibilities if you have provided treatment to the parties or the children involved in the litigation, because this would constitute a dual relationship. In addition, your professional judgment in conducting the evaluation might be impaired by your loyalty to a former client. Remember that any time you are asked to testify in court concerning your assessment of a client or your opinions concerning a client, you are entitled to an expert fee. Arrangements for payment of your fee by the attorney who requests your testimony should be made before you go to court, and you should demand payment in advance.

8.04 Standards for Child and Family Investigators

In November 2011, Colorado Supreme Court Chief Justice Bender amended Chief Justice Directive 04-08. In his Introduction to the revised standards, Chief Justice Bender identified the purpose of CFI investigations, in contrast to parental responsibility evaluations: "The purpose of a CFI investigation is to provide a brief assessment that is non-intrusive, efficient, and cost effective." CJD 04-08 (last revised 11/21) contains procedures for complaints against CFIs, which are to be reported to the Colorado Supreme Court Administrative Office (SCAO) and to the District Court that appointed the CFI. The SCAO will determine if a complaint is founded or not. The Introduction to these revised standards states: "Violation of a standard should not in and of itself give rise to a cause of action nor should it create any presumption that the CFI breached a legal duty or committed a professional ethical violation."

Revised CJD 04-08 Standards

1. **Maximum Fee for Privately Paid CFIs.** The standards provide, "[T]he presumptive maximum fee for the investigative and reporting work of privately paid CFIs is $2,750 per appointment. The fee shall not exceed this presumptive $2,750 cap without prior court approval in the form of a written order with specific findings concerning the extraordinary circumstances justifying the excess fees." When the testimony of a privately paid CFI is sought by a party or deemed necessary by the court, a presumptive maximum fee of $500 per appointment applies. The standards state that the total fees for a CFI's testimony and preparation time "shall not exceed this presumptive $500 cap without prior court approval in the form of a written order with specific findings concerning the extraordinary circumstances justifying the excess fees."
2. **Placement on Eligibility Roster.** To be eligible for appointment, all CFIs must be listed on a state eligibility roster, which is maintained by the SCAO, based upon the application and background check that will be conducted by the Supreme Court. To be eligible for appointment, all CFIs must be listed on both the statewide Eligibility Roster and also the Eligibility Roster of one or more judicial districts. The eligibility list for judicial districts is maintained by each judicial district.
3. **Complaints.** Any complaint regarding the performance of a CFI must be submitted electronically to the judicial district and to the SCAO, using the "Child and Family Investigator Complaint Form" located on the SCAO website. A paper copy of the complaint form may be submitted to the

judicial district's District Administrator. The judicial district's District Administrator "shall forward the complaint to the judge presiding over the matter in which the CFI was appointed so that the judge may determine whether to take any immediate preventative or corrective action." The judicial district shall then conduct an investigation "to determine whether the complaint is founded, and what action, if any, to take in resolving the concerns raised by a founded complaint." If the judicial district determines that the complaint against an attorney CFI is founded, "the District Administrator shall inform the Colorado Supreme Court Office of Attorney Regulation Counsel," and notify the complainant of the action taken.

If the complaint involves a mental health professional licensed by the Department of Regulatory Agencies, and if it is determined that the complaint concerning the CFI was founded, "the District Administrator shall inform DORA and shall notify the complainant." In addition, the District Administrator shall request that DORA inform the judicial district and the SCAO of the final outcome of any investigation.

If a judicial district fails to conduct an investigation pursuant to the procedures established by CJD 04-08, then the SCAO may conduct its own investigation. Sanctions that may be imposed in the complaint process include removal of the CFI from the Statewide Eligibility Roster, from one or more of the judicial eligibility rosters, or from the OCR District List.

4. **Malpractice Insurance.** The revised CJD 04-08 requires that all attorney and non-attorney CFIs with professional liability insurance "must provide written notice to the SCAO within five days if such insurance coverage terminates and must not accept CFI appointments until reinstatement of coverage." In addition, all CFIs "shall notify the SCAO in writing within five days of his or her notification of any malpractice suit or criminal charge brought or filed against him or her or notification of any grievance, formal complaint or disciplinary action that is under investigation."
5. **No Psychological Testing or Referrals by the CFI.** It is clear from the revised standards that CFI investigations are to be non-intrusive. Accordingly, Standard 13 provides:

The CFI shall not conduct psychological testing. The CFI shall not perform or require drug, alcohol, polygraph or other testing, inspection or evaluation unless specifically ordered by the court.

> If the CFI believes testing, inspection, or evaluation would benefit the parties or child/ren and would assist the court,

> the CFI shall notify the court and parties as soon as possible and shall include this information in the CFI report. This prohibition does not prevent the CFI from conducting domestic violence screening the CFI is competent to perform.

> The Comment to Standard 4 provides that the CFI is the "investigative arm of the court," and that it is therefore inappropriate for CFIs to "make referrals or recommendations to the parties or to the court for specific professionals, unless the party makes a written request for referral or recommendation or unless the court requests a referral or recommendation."

The remaining standards for the conduct of CFI investigations have not changed. However, Chief Justice Directive 04-08 does require the parties and counsel be informed of the CFI's policies and procedures, which include a disclosure of the new complaint process, the cap on fees, and the other revised standards discussed in this section.

CJD 04-08 Standards for CFI investigations

These Standards apply to the work of both attorneys and mental health professionals who assist judges in domestic relations cases by conducting investigations and advise the court concerning the best interests of children involved in family law matters. CFIs, appointed by the court, make recommendations regarding the allocation of parental responsibilities and parenting time. Two questions that these Standards resolve concern whether it is appropriate for CFIs to have *ex parte* contact with the judge and whether CFIs must turn over a copy of their file to the parties involved. The Standards prohibit *ex parte* contact with the judge; that is, personal communication with the judge without involving the attorneys and any *pro se* party (unrepresented by counsel) in the case. Any communication by a CFI with a judge in writing is appropriate, so long as all attorneys and any *pro se* party are copied with the written communication. Similarly, CFIs are allowed to address concerns to the court at scheduled hearings in the case.

The Standards clarify what materials from the investigator's file must be disclosed, upon request, to attorneys and *pro se* parties. They require that a copy of all data and reports upon which an investigator has relied in formulating opinions and recommendations be turned over. "Data" would undoubtedly include the contemporaneous notes made by the investigator when interviewing parents, children, etc., but would not include notes made while drafting a report.

In regard to raw data from psychological testing, the standards provide that the release of raw data from any psychological testing should be done in compliance with the requirements of the relevant ethical standards for the professional.

The Standards require that an investigator, in assisting the court, shall:

- Collect data and conduct an investigation to allow the investigator to provide competent opinions to the court;
- Have age-appropriate communication with the children involved;
- Report child abuse to the proper agency and the court;
- Prepare a clear and timely report;
- Provide copies of his or her files upon request;
- Request termination of the appointment when permanent or post-decree orders are entered;
- Maintain competence through training; and
- Acknowledge when an issue is beyond his or her competence.

Do child and family investigators need to worry about being sued by parents who are dissatisfied with the investigation or who seek damages in a lawsuit because they are unhappy with either the process or the court's ruling? Under existing case law, a professional appointed by the court is considered to be an agent of the court who is entitled to the same judicial immunity that the judge is entitled to receive, since the professional's function is to assist the court in the judicial process.

The Standards also answer another question, previously unresolved, concerning whether an investigator could subsequently serve in a role as a parenting coordinator. As drafted, the Standards state that this is permissible; however, before an investigator can move to the role of parenting coordinator, the appointment of the child and family investigator must be terminated by the court and both parties must consent.

The Colorado Supreme Court Standards currently provide that an investigator "shall develop written policies for the parties" and for counsel. Anyone serving as a child and family investigator needs to have a contract that explains the parties' financial obligations, deadlines for payment of fees and costs, and appropriate disclosures concerning the investigator's role, as well as the process involved. Such a contract should also disclose that a therapist is not conducting therapy, nor establishing a professional relationship with any of the parties, when serving as an investigator.

The Colorado Supreme Court's Standards specifically provide that an investigator "shall not serve dual roles" and, therefore, shall not serve as a formal mediator in the case, provide psychotherapy to any of the parties or children in the case, nor accept an appointment from the court if he or she has had a prior personal relationship or a prior professional role with the family.

Communication with the Court and Counsel

According to Colorado Supreme Court Standard 19, "The CFI shall have no private or *ex parte* communications with the court." A child and family investigator may need to communicate with the court concerning various issues, which include the receipt of information from the court concerning the order appointing the professional; submitting information to the court concerning a party's refusal to pay or to cooperate in the investigative process; or reporting to the court concerns relating to the potential for harm to children. The Colorado Supreme Court's Standards require that an investigator communicate with the court in a process that includes the attorneys involved in the case and any *pro se* party. Suggested methods of communication include "a short written report with copies to the parties and counsel"; attendance at a status conference or hearing in court, where issues can be raised; or arranging a conference call with the court and all counsel or *pro se* parties.

Communication with counsel for the parties is meant to facilitate the investigative process, not complicate it. The drafter of the Standards, however, states in the Comment to Standard 17: "A CFI may not engage in non-disclosed communications with one party or one party's counsel." This means that any matter discussed with one attorney must be disclosed to all other counsel or *pro se* parties through a written communication that confirms and discloses any subject matter discussed. In this way, an investigator is careful to avoid any bias or the appearance of bias in the eyes of parties engaged in a high-conflict domestic relations case.

Records to be Disclosed by Child and Family Investigators Upon Request

Colorado Supreme Court Standard 12 mandates: "Upon written request of the parties or their counsel, the CFI shall make the CFI file available after filing the CFI report and prior to the hearing in the case. The CFI file shall include CFI notes, data, witness statements, completed questionnaires, and any information underlying the CFI's report." As stated above, the release of raw data from any psychological testing should be done in compliance with the requirements of the relevant professional ethical standards.

Disclosure of Potential Bias

Pursuant to C.R.S. § 14-10-116.5, within seven days after being appointed by the court, a CFI must disclose to each party, attorneys of record, and the court any familial, financial, or social relationship that the CFI has or has had with the child, either party, the attorneys of record, or the judicial officer and if a relationship exists, the nature of the relationship.

8.05 Access to Treatment Information

C.R.S. § 14-10-123.8 contains provisions that you need to know if you provide therapy to families and children. This statute provides:

> Access to information pertaining to a minor child, including but not limited to medical, dental, and school records, shall not be denied to any party allocated parental responsibilities, unless otherwise ordered by the court for good cause shown.

Applying this statute, if you are providing treatment to the children of a mother to whom the court granted the authority to select treatment providers, and you receive a request for records from the children's father who has been allocated the responsibility to pay child support, you should obtain the mother's consent to provide treatment information, or a summary of it, to the father. How can you do this? One way is to provide your client with a Disclosure Statement that contains the following provision: "When parents are divorced, Colorado law allows any parent who has been assigned parental responsibilities access to medical records. Therefore, in compliance with C.R.S. § 14-10-123.8, you authorize me to provide access to treatment information to such an individual by authorizing me to provide services to a child in your custody." Of course, if it is your policy to have both parents provide you with informed consent for treatment of their children, then you can have both parents sign an authorization for release of information, allowing the other parent to have access to treatment information.

8.06 Parenting Coordinators

C.R.S. § 14-10-128.1 provides that the court may appoint a parenting coordinator to assist in the resolution of disputes between the parties concerning parental responsibilities or implementation of the court-ordered parenting plan. The duties of the parenting coordinator are listed as follows:

(a) Assisting the parties in creating an agreed-upon, structured guideline for implementation of the parenting plan;

(b) Developing guidelines for communication between the parties and suggesting appropriate resources to assist the parties in learning appropriate communication skills;

(c) Informing the parties about appropriate resources to assist them in developing improved parenting skills;

(d) Assisting the parties in realistically identifying the sources and causes of conflict between them . . . ; and

(e) Assisting the parties in developing parenting strategies to minimize conflict.

The court must appoint the parenting coordinator for a specific period of time, not to exceed two years. C.R.S. § 14-10-128.1 mandates that the court order appointing a parenting coordinator "shall include apportionment of the responsibility for payment of all of the parenting coordinator's fees between the parties."

The parenting coordinator *cannot* be compelled to testify in the domestic proceeding. In this regard, C.R.S. § 14-10-128.1(7)(c)(I) states, "[A] parenting coordinator shall not be competent to testify and may not be required to produce records as to any statement, conduct, or decision that occurred during the parenting coordinator's appointment to the same extent as a judge of a court of this state acting in a judicial capacity." Thus, a parenting coordinator cannot be cross-examined by either of the parties concerning recommendations made to the parties or concerning the nature of the conflicts and problems that the parenting coordinator has been attempting to resolve with the parties. There are three exceptions to this rule. The parenting coordinator can be compelled to testify when: (1) the testimony or production of records by the parenting coordinator is necessary to determine a claim of the parenting coordinator against a party; (2) the testimony or production of records by the parenting coordinator is necessary to determine a claim of a party against a parenting coordinator; or (3) both parties have agreed in writing authorizing the parenting coordinator to testify. C.R.S. § 14-10-128.1(7)(c)(II).

The procedures for communication with the court (including the prohibition on *ex parte* communication), which are discussed in section 8.04, also apply to parenting coordinators.

The Standards issued by the Colorado Supreme Court for child and family investigators specifically state: "These CFI standards do not apply to service as a [parenting coordinator] or [decision-maker]." However, the court's Standards state that an investigator may agree to serve in the "role of parenting coordinator . . . or decision-maker . . . or arbitrator after completing all CFI duties and after termination of the CFI appointment," with the parties' consent. In a Comment to the Standards, the drafters discussed the pros and cons involved in this changing of roles. A therapist who had served as an investigator would be immediately familiar with the family dynamics, which would facilitate service in the role of parenting coordinator. On the other hand, if an issue arose in the future requiring further exploration by an investigator, then the previous investigator, with a wealth of knowledge about the family, would be unavailable because, as the drafter's Comment notes, the new parenting coordinator would then be in a "prior professional role" that would prevent him or her from accepting an appointment as the investigator once again.

Because of the important work performed by a parenting coordinator, resolving disputes between parents relating to the specifics and the logistics of parenting issues and making recommendations to the court concerning permanent orders, a parenting coordinator should have the same credentials as a child and family investigator and, in the opinion of this author, should adhere to the same legal and ethical standards that have been adopted for court-appointed professionals.

New Standards for Parenting Coordinators

The Colorado Supreme Court has issued Draft Guidelines for Parenting Coordinators. Parenting coordinators are appointed by the court in divorce and family court cases pursuant to C.R.S. § 14-10-128.1. Therapists who accept appointments as parenting coordinators should adopt these Guidelines as the standards to be followed pending issuance of a Chief Justice Directive from the Colorado Supreme Court.

According to the Draft Guidelines, the objective of parenting coordination is "to assist high conflict parents in implementing court orders concerning allocation of parental responsibilities in a timely manner." The appointment of a parenting coordinator (PC) is reserved for "high-conflict parents who have demonstrated difficulty in making parenting decisions together, who are unable to comply with court-ordered parenting plans, who cannot or will not reduce their child-related conflicts, and those who are unable to protect their children from the impact of that conflict."

The role of the PC is to assist the parties in implementing the terms of a parenting plan. Pursuant to the Guidelines under consideration, the court will apportion the PC's fees between the parties, and the court will enforce its order requiring payment of the PC's fees. General principles and duties established by the Guidelines are as follows:

1. To observe all applicable statutory duties and act professionally;

2. To maintain neutrality;
3. To maintain competence through appropriate training;
4. To have no private or *ex parte* communication with the court;
5. To review court orders;
6. To maintain confidentiality;
7. To report child abuse to proper agencies;
8. To not serve dual roles; and
9. To develop written policies for the parties.

To be qualified to serve as a court-appointed PC, a therapist may not have served previously in the role of parental responsibility evaluator or as a therapist for any of the parties or children involved in a case. It is recognized that the work of a parenting coordinator does not constitute the practice of psychotherapy. Under traditional principles of immunity for judges and court-appointed professionals, a PC should be entitled to immunity from suit for serving in this role.

8.07 Decision-Makers

C.R.S. § 14-10-128.3 provides for the appointment of a "qualified domestic relations decision-maker." A professional serving in this role has the authority, on behalf of the court, "to resolve disputes between the parties as to implementation or clarification of existing orders concerning the parties' minor or dependent children, including but not limited to disputes concerning parenting time, specific disputed parental decisions, and child support." The statute provides, "The decision-maker appointed pursuant to the provisions of this section may be the same person as the parenting coordinator appointed pursuant to section 14-10-128.1." The court appoints the decision-maker for a specific period of time, not to exceed two years, and may apportion "the responsibility for payment of all of the decision-maker's fees between the parties."

This statute requires the decision-maker's procedures for making determinations to be "in writing and [to] be approved by the parties prior to the time the decision-maker begins to resolve a dispute of the parties." All decisions made by the decision-maker must be in writing, dated, and signed by the decision-maker, and must be filed with the court and mailed to the parties or their counsel. The statute also provides, "All decisions shall be effective immediately upon issuance and shall continue in effect until vacated, corrected, or modified by the decision-maker or until an order is entered by a court pursuant to a de novo hearing."

Under C.R.S. § 14-10-128.3, a decision-maker is barred from testifying in the domestic proceeding, to the same extent that a judge acting in a judicial capacity is not competent to testify. In addition, a decision-maker "may not be required to produce records as to any statement, conduct, or decision, that occurred during the decision-maker's appointment."

Immunity

The Colorado General Assembly has conferred statutory immunity upon decision-makers. C.R.S. § 14-10-128.3(7) states:

> A decision-maker shall be immune from liability in any claim for injury that arises out of an act or omission of the decision-maker occurring during the performance of his or her duties or during the performance of an act that the decision-maker reasonably believed was within the scope of his or her duties unless the act or omission causing such injury was willful and wanton.

The legislature created provisions for a sanction to be imposed in the event that a litigant files suit against a decision-maker. Section 14-10-128.3 provides, "If a person commences a civil action against a decision-maker arising from the services of the decision-maker, or if a person seeks to compel a decision-maker to testify or produce records . . . the court shall award to the decision-maker reasonable attorney fees and reasonable expenses of litigation."

8.08 Caselaw Concerning Domestic Evaluations

In *Ryder v. Mitchell*, 54 P.3d 885 (Colo. 2002), the Colorado Supreme Court upheld the dismissal of a lawsuit against a therapist, which the court determined to be frivolous. This is a case where a mother (Mitchell) took her children to a therapist (Ryder) and informed Ryder that she was convinced the children were being abused by their father. Mitchell asked that Ryder evaluate the children to determine the harm done to them by their father and prepare a treatment plan to remedy the effects of the abuse.

After Ryder evaluated the children and commenced treatment, she prepared a report in which she expressed her opinion that the children's father had not been abusing them, as well as her opinion that Mitchell was engaging in parental alienation. At the time, these parents were involved in a high-conflict battle over their children.

When Mitchell sued Ryder for negligence and breach of a fiduciary duty, the trial court dismissed the claims. The dismissal was upheld by the Colorado Supreme Court, which awarded Ryder attorney fees for her defense of a lawsuit that the trial court had termed "a disturbing example of truly vexatious litigation clearly warranting the imposition of fees against both Mitchell and her counsel." *Mitchell v. Ryder*, 104 P.3d 316, 321 (Colo. App. 2004).

8.09 Limitations on Testimony by Mental Health Clinicians in Domestic Actions: Practical and Ethical Considerations for Attorneys

Attorneys who practice in the domestic relations courts need to understand the limitations imposed by the Standards for Child and Family Investigators (CFIs) on mental health professionals who have provided counseling or treatment to family members involved in a divorce or parental responsibilities action. These Standards were adopted in Chief Justice Directive (CJD) 04-08, issued by the Chief Justice of the Colorado Supreme Court in 2004. Attorneys for family court litigants also need to know the ethical limitations imposed on therapists by their professional codes of ethics, which restrict a clinician's ability to express opinions concerning the allocation of parental responsibilities or parenting time. This section discusses the application of both the CFI Standards and ethical codes for therapists, and the appropriate role for therapists subpoenaed to testify in family court cases.

The Application of CFI Standards and Ethical Codes for Therapists

Attorneys understand the bounds of legal ethics in the representation of clients, and we adhere to basic ethical principles instinctively. Mental health professionals do the same in providing treatment to clients. Attorneys are aware of the boundaries created by a professional relationship and avoid the most basic taboo—a conflict of interest. For a therapist in a professional relationship with a client, basic ethical principles prohibit a "dual relationship" or a "boundary violation." A prohibited dual relationship for a therapist, for example, would occur if a clinician were to provide counseling to a close friend, colleague, or relative. Such relationships might impair the therapist's professional judgment in providing treatment to a client or in adhering to legal duties, such as the reporting of suspected child abuse and neglect. A boundary violation would occur if a therapist were to engage in an intimate relationship with a client, or to exercise "undue influence on the client, including the promotion of the sale of services, goods, property, or drugs in such a manner as to exploit the client. . . ." C.R.S. § 12-245-224(1)(j). These ethical principles for therapists, therefore, prohibit a clinician who has provided counseling to a family, to a couple, to individuals, or to children from conducting an evaluation and making recommendations to a court concerning the allocation of parental responsibilities and parenting time.

CJD 04-08, Standard 4 also prohibits a mental health professional who has "had a prior professional role with the family" (other than as a CFI) from serving in the role of CFI.

Too often, parents involved in domestic litigation engage in "therapist shopping." They will take their children to a therapist, establish trust and rapport with the professional, and try to appear as the model parent. Then they will make critical comments about their estranged spouse, emphasizing how uncaring or abusive that individual is. Finally, they make a plea to the therapist for assistance in court: "Will you testify for me at the final orders hearing? I need you to make a recommendation to the judge that I should have sole custody of my children." Or the parent may request that the therapist make a recommendation that the other parent should only have supervised parenting time. This plea is accompanied by a request from that parent's attorney for a letter to the court by the therapist, making favorable recommendations on behalf of the client.

Such pleas by parents and requests by counsel put clinicians in an untenable position. No matter how great the therapist's desire to be supportive, a therapist cannot go to court and assume the role of a CFI or other court-appointed evaluator. To do so would violate the therapist's ethical principles and the CFI Standards, referred to above. For a clinician providing therapy to make ultimate recommendations on issues relating to parental responsibilities would also violate the legal principles embodied in C.R.S. § 14-10-127(6). This statute provides for the appointment by the court in domestic cases of licensed mental health professionals who meet the qualifications specified in this statute to conduct an evaluation of issues concerning the allocation of parental responsibilities. C.R.S. § 14-10-127(6)(a) authorizes a court-appointed mental health professional to make specific recommendations to the court "when the mental health professional has interviewed and assessed all parties to the dispute, assessed the quality of the relationship, or the potential for establishing a quality relationship, between the child and each of the parties, and had access to pertinent information from outside sources." Since a clinician who has provided services to a family member is prohibited from conducting an evaluation of these issues, any recommendations by the therapist would violate the clear intent and provisions of C.R.S. § 14-10-127.

The role of a therapist, who is compelled by subpoena to appear in court for a hearing on parenting issues, is therefore limited. The American Association for Marriage and Family Therapy (AAMFT) Code of Ethics, Principle 7.7, provides:

> Marriage and family therapists avoid conflicts of interest in treating minors or adults involved in custody or visitation actions by not performing evaluations for custody, residence, or visitation of the

> minor. Marriage and family therapists who treat minors may provide the court or mental health professional performing the evaluation with information about the minor from the marriage and family therapist's perspective.

While it is appropriate, then, for CFIs or other court-appointed professionals to conduct evaluations of parenting issues and to make recommendations to the court regarding them, that is their role, and not the role of a clinician who has provided treatment to a family member.

What information or input is appropriate for therapists to provide the court from their clinical perspective? The Colorado Children's Code, which mandates the reporting of suspected child abuse and neglect by all licensed and unlicensed therapists, contains statutes designed to protect children. Various provisions of the Colorado Children's Code encourage therapists to provide information to social services or law enforcement officials to promote the purposes intended by these statutes: to keep children safe from harm. Consistent with these statutory provisions, therefore, clinicians may provide input to the court or to court-appointed professionals in domestic cases that will help the court in implementing parenting plans designed to keep children safe. While it is the role of a CFI, GAL, or Child Representative to make recommendations to the court in the best interests of children, it would be appropriate for a therapist to express concerns for a child's safety from a clinical perspective by suggesting to the court that a CFI may need to be appointed to investigate problems arising from a family's history of violence, abuse, drug use, or the like, when no one has yet been appointed in one of these roles. Since therapists reporting suspected child abuse are encouraged to provide input to child protection professionals concerning safety plans to prevent the risk of harm to children, then it is reasonable for clinicians to provide the same input to the court. This has long been a "generally accepted" practice among mental health professionals. Certainly, judges and magistrates welcome such information in order to keep children safe.

What factual information or opinions might therapists provide to the court from their clinical perspective in a domestic case? To the extent that it may be admissible, and assuming that the therapist-client privilege has been waived, therapists may express opinions concerning their assessment of clients, their treatment plan, and clients' progress in treatment. For all the reasons discussed above, therapists may not express opinions or recommendations on ultimate issues regarding parental responsibilities. Such testimony would not only exceed the clinician's role, but would also lack the necessary foundation: a thorough investigation and evaluation conducted by a competent court-appointed professional in compliance with the Standards set forth in CJD 04-08 or by an evaluator appointed pursuant to C.R.S. § 14-10-127.

Practical and Ethical Considerations for Attorneys

As stated above, sometimes domestic attorneys ask therapists for letters expressing recommendations on parenting issues, in the expectation that the therapists will advocate the client's position regarding these matters. Such requests, as well as the client's pleas for support in court, place therapists in conflict, torn between their loyalty to the client and their ethical duty. Harm to the therapeutic relationship inevitably results when therapists explain that they cannot go to court as an "advocate" for the client.

Domestic relations practitioners need to respect therapists' boundaries and comply with the Standards established by CJD 04-08 by ensuring that they not make requests of therapists that create ethical conflicts for them and undermine their clinical relationships. Since legal ethics require that our conduct as attorneys must "conform to the requirements of the law," domestic practitioners would be well advised to comply with the spirit and intent of CJD 04-08 Standard 4 and of C.R.S. § 14-10-127 by acknowledging that clinicians cannot express opinions or recommendations regarding custodial arrangements in violation of these legal provisions.

Is it practical to subpoena therapists to testify in family court matters in view of these legal and ethical limitations? Keeping in mind that a clinician who is called to provide testimony concerning treatment issues is an expert witness who must be compensated as such, attorneys may question the cost-effectiveness of such evidence. Too often, therapists subpoenaed to testify in domestic matters complain that the attorney who issued the subpoena informed them, when advised of the clinician's fee schedule for court appearances, "Oh, you're not an expert. You're just going to be called to testify concerning your treatment." It is true that on occasion a healthcare professional may be a fact witness, called to court to provide testimony concerning a statement made by a party or regarding an eyewitness account of an incident. However, mental health professionals who testify in court regarding clinical matters that require their education, training, and expertise are expert witnesses who, like attorneys, are entitled to be paid their hourly rates for the task at hand.

Conclusion

The Standards established by CJD 04-08, the Colorado statutes, and ethical principles for therapists prohibit clinicians who have treated family members from making recommendations to the court regarding parenting issues. It is the role of

CFIs and other court-appointed professionals, who have conducted an appropriate investigation and evaluation, to make recommendations to the court regarding the allocation of parental responsibilities and parenting time.

Domestic relations attorneys, understanding therapists' limitations, should respect clinicians' ethical boundaries and avoid undermining their therapeutic relationships with parents, children, or families involved in domestic cases.

8.10 Approved Domestic Violence Treatment Providers

Domestic violence treatment providers are approved and regulated by the Colorado Domestic Violence Offender Management Board (DVOMB), created in July 2000 pursuant to C.R.S. § 16-11.8-103. This statute states that the consistent and comprehensive evaluation, treatment, and continued monitoring of domestic violence offenders at each stage of the criminal justice system is necessary in order to lessen the likelihood of re-offense, enhance the protection of potential victims, and work toward the elimination of repeat offenses. The DVOMB has the authority to formulate standards for the evaluation, treatment, and monitoring of convicted domestic violence offenders, and the Board has published Standards for Treatment with Court-Ordered Domestic Violence Offenders.

The DVOMB has issued standards that specify the qualifications for treatment providers, the specific education and training required for approval by the Board, and requirements for experience and supervision that must be met when an application is filed with the DVOMB for approval as a domestic violence treatment provider. In addition, the Board Standards require all approved treatment providers to complete 32 hours of CEUs every two years in topic areas relevant to treatment with court-ordered domestic violence offenders.

"Domestic violence" is defined by C.R.S. § 18-6-800.3 as "an act or threatened act of violence upon a person with whom the actor is or has been involved in an intimate relationship." It also includes any other crime against a person or property, including an animal, when the act is "used as a method of coercion, control, punishment, intimidation, or revenge directed against a person with whom the actor is or has been involved in an intimate relationship." The DVOMB has issued standards for the evaluation of a domestic violence offender who has pled guilty or been convicted of a domestic violence offense, where the offender has been ordered to undergo evaluation prior to sentencing in order to assist the court in determining an appropriate sentence. In addition, the DVOMB has set forth separate standards for an intake evaluation to assess appropriateness for treatment, treatment amenability, and the best intervention strategy. Numerous factors are considered in this assessment, including alcohol and drug abuse history, financial stability, employment stability, history of all violent behavior, previous counseling, a mental health inventory, conflicts in relationships, assessment for risk of re-offense, and an interview with the victim.

The DVOMB Standards establish treatment goals for domestic violence offenders, which include educating offenders about domestic violence and its dynamics; self-management techniques to avoid abusive behaviors; education to increase the offender's skills and problem-solving and conflict resolution; cognitive-behavioral skills to improve communication and to promote healthy relationships; and education of the offender concerning the potential for reoffending. The treatment standards require offenders to be placed in gender-specific groups generally and in a group specifically designed to address issues regarding sexual orientation. The DVOMB Standards may be found at https://dcj.colorado.gov/dcj-offices/domestic-violence-and-sex-offender-management/dvomb-standards-approved-revisions.

8.11 Record-Keeping Practices for DVOMB Approved Treatment Providers

In compliance with mental health board rules and ethical standards for therapists, Approved Treatment Providers must keep individual notes for each group session, as well as a group session note. In each individual client's chart, mandated entries include a note concerning each disclosure of information made, to whom information was provided, and the nature of the information disclosed. In compliance with DVOMB Standards, every contact with a victim must be summarized in a chart entry, and every attempt to contact a victim must be charted. Retain all records, including intake forms, treatment contracts, evaluations, reports to probation and the court, authorization forms for releases of information, group notes, individual notes, etc., for a minimum of seven years or any longer period of time mandated by a licensing board rule. Remember that any report mandated by law must be charted thoroughly, as discussed in section 4.16.

8.12 DVOMB Standards for Couples Counseling

For years the Domestic Violence Offender Management Board (DVOMB) has had a standard that prohibits couples counseling for a DV offender who is involved in DV offender counseling. The basic rationale expressed by the DVOMB in the past for this prohibition was the fact that a victim of domestic violence did not have the ability to engage in couples counseling freely and voluntarily, due to the fact that the victim would presumably be under the control of the offender.

Revisions were made to the DVOMB *Standards and Guidelines for Domestic Violence Offenders*, but this prohibition of couples counseling is still a requirement in the Offender Contract, in which the DV offender must agree not to engage in couples counseling during the court-ordered offender treatment.

During presentations at mental health board meetings by DVOMB officials, board members are told that the prohibition of couples counseling during offender treatment applies to all mental health professionals in Colorado, including therapists who are not engaged in DV offender treatment. So, if couples counseling is requested by members of a couple in which one of the individuals is involved in DV offender treatment, the best course is to wait until that treatment program is completed before assessing whether couples counseling is appropriate or not.

8.13 Potential Parental Alienation and the Best Interests of Children

I have been consulted by counselors from across the country on an issue that seems to be arising in high-conflict domestic situations. It concerns the report of a child, communicated to the child's therapist, that the child hates one of the parents and does not want to see that parent. The context for these reports inevitably is high-conflict divorce or custody litigation. These are not situations in which the parent whom the child does not want to see has been physically abusive, or a perpetrator of sexual abuse or domestic violence. The child's therapist then communicates this information to courts or family court-appointed evaluators.

Where are these reports coming from? Are they the product of parental alienation? How should a child's therapist deal with these situations and these reports?

These are truly clinical issues for clinicians to consult upon, discuss, and address. When a child provides a therapist with a list of all the reasons that the child hates the parent and does not want to see the parent, prepared in advance of a treatment session, how should a therapist respond? Should the response include the affirmation: "I am sure that your dad/mom loves you very much, and wants to see you?" or "Can you now make up a list for me of all the reasons why you love your dad/mom?" In addition to assessing whether the child in question, who has reported animosity towards a parent, demonstrates symptoms of anxiety, stress, or fear, should the therapist ask the non-offending parent what prompted the child to write out the list? Should the therapist also inquire how the parent responded to the situation, when presented with the list? Would it be proper for the therapist in this situation to suggest to this parent: "Did you reassure your child that s/he is loved by the other parent, and that it is important that they have a relationship?"

Under Colorado law, one of the most important factors that a court considers in determining custodial arrangements is which parent will foster a relationship between the children and the other parent. Parental alienation is the antithesis of this. Regardless of whether "parental alienation" is a syndrome, judges and court-appointed professionals who evaluate custodial issues are deeply concerned when they hear of parental behaviors that may harm children or a child's relationship with the other parent. Whose role is it to evaluate whether parental alienation has occurred? The judge in any domestic litigation and court-appointed professionals.

What is the role of the child's therapist in this situation where a child has expressed animosity towards a parent? To remain clinically objective and impartial, providing appropriate treatment and any referrals needed. It is not the role of the therapist to make recommendations to the court concerning the allocation of parental responsibilities, concerning who should have custody, or concerning parenting time. And, of course, a therapist must report any child abuse or neglect that a therapist suspects has occurred or is occurring.

Chapter 9: Frequently Asked Questions and Answers on Ethics

This chapter discusses basic ethical standards for mental health professionals in Colorado.

9.01 ABCs of Ethics for Mental Health Counselors in Colorado

The ethical principles discussed in this section are based upon Colorado Statutes, Colorado licensing board rules, HIPAA Standards, and the Code of Ethics for the American Mental Health Counselors Association (AMHCA), revised in 2015.

A. **Abuse Reporting** – All therapists in Colorado are Mandated Reporters of Suspected Child Abuse and Neglect, in compliance with C.R.S. § 19-3-304. Such reports must be made to Child Protective Services (CPS) or to law enforcement immediately, when a therapist suspects that child abuse or neglect has occurred. Document the information reported.

B. **Bartering** is defined in AMHCA Code of Ethics Section I.E.2 as "accepting goods or services from clients in return for counseling services." The Code cautions that "such arrangements may create the potential for conflicts, exploitation, and distortion of the professional relationship." The Code further states that "[b]artering may occur if a client requests it, there is no exploitation, and the cultural implications and other concerns regarding the practice are discussed with the client and agreed upon in writing."

C. **Confidentiality** is essential in a professional relationship, in compliance with C.R.S. § 12-245-220. Basic exceptions to confidentiality include the reporting of suspected child abuse and neglect, compliance with the Tarasoff duty, initiating a 72-hour hold for a client, reporting of elder abuse for seniors 70 years of age or older to law enforcement, and disclosing information to third parties with client consent in writing.

D. **Dual Relationships** are to be avoided, because they may exploit clients financially, create conflicts between a therapist and client, or take advantage of a client's trust. Examples of dual relationships include: providing treatment to family members, friends, close colleagues, or business associates, or having multiple relationships with a counseling client, in violation of DORA's Policy 30-2.

E. **Ethical Codes** contain the generally accepted standards of practice for mental health professionals. The American Association for Marriage and Family Therapy (AAMFT) Code of Ethics (2015) provides excellent guidance for therapists in their counseling practice. The 2015 revisions to the Code of Ethics provide guidance regarding the use of technology, social media, and standards for clinical supervision. When an ethical conflict arises with another professional, the Code of Ethics requires that you confer with that professional in an effort to resolve the conflict, if possible.

F. **Fees** for treatment services must be fair and reasonable, and can only be billed by the therapist who actually provided services to the client. Informed consent for treatment should provide information to clients regarding the fees to be charged. Counselors should not hire a bill collector or take action to collect fees without first informing the client that such action may be taken, and providing the client with an opportunity to settle the debt or agree to a payment plan.

G. **Goals of Treatment** need to be formulated, based upon the counselor's assessment of the client's presenting problems. This will inform the treatment plan prepared by the counselor in order to accomplish the treatment goals (objectives).

H. **HIPAA Privacy Rule** provides that clients are not entitled to access their "psychotherapy notes," which are defined in 45 C.F.R. § 164.524, the same as session notes. This Privacy Rule provides that clients may receive a Progress Report, which basically contains a summary of treatment information and the client's progress and treatment. This Rule also provides that "psychotherapy notes" be kept in the client's chart separate from the rest of the treatment records.

I. **Informed Consent** is required for treatment in Colorado, except in emergencies, in compliance with C.R.S. § 12-245-216, which requires that a client or client representative sign a disclosure statement no later than the second treatment session. The disclosures to clients in a disclosure statement must set forth the limits of confidentiality. When obtaining informed consent for children whose parents are divorced, counselors need to obtain a copy of the court order that provides for "decision-making authority" to select children's treatment providers. If parents have joint decision-making authority, they both need to consent to treatment. If one parent is granted sole decision-making authority, then that parent is the person who must provide informed consent for treatment.

J. **Join** your Professional Association, and participate in its activities. This will enhance your knowledge of ethical standards, and will afford you the opportunity to obtain training, seminars, or workshops concerning practice issues, changes in Colorado law, and trends in the profession. Participation in a

Professional Association is an excellent way for counselors to contribute to the profession.

K. Kickbacks may not be received or given by counselors in exchange for referrals. Such conduct is unethical, and constitutes a prohibited activity, in violation of C.R.S. §§ 12-245-224(1)(o) & (q).

L. Liability Insurance protects counselors by providing insurance coverage for malpractice claims and for payment of attorney fees in responding to licensing board complaints. Such insurance is needed to protect the personal assets of counselors. When a professional is practicing as an employee of a corporation, the corporation, too, must have professional liability insurance coverage.

M. Mental Health Commitments – All counselors have a duty to initiate a 72-hour hold evaluation of a client in compliance with C.R.S. § 27-65-105 when the client is dangerous to self or others due to a mental disorder. Licensed counselors, medical doctors, and police officers have the authority to sign an M-1 form, authorizing an individual to be taken into custody and transported to a hospital ER or crisis unit for evaluation and treatment. Document carefully all evaluations of the client's suicidal ideation, suicide threats, history of hospital treatment, suicide attempts, episodes of violence, and the action taken by the counselor to initiate a 72-hour hold.

N. Neglect is defined as the failure of a parent or caretaker to provide appropriate housing, food, clothing, medical care, and supervision for a child. Suspected neglect must be reported to Child Protective Services or to law enforcement. Improper supervision includes leaving children home alone when they lack the maturity and the responsibility to care for themselves.

O. Objectivity must be maintained by counselors in their relationships with clients, especially when clinical services are provided to children whose parents are separated or divorced. Both parents may be assured that the counselor will be objective while providing treatment to a child, and will be striving to achieve the child's best interests. When conducting assessments or writing reports regarding treatment and when testifying in court, counselors must remain objective, and not let any personal feelings or bias influence their professional opinions.

P. Patient's Rights – The AMHCA Code of Ethics provides in Section I.B that "clients have the right to be treated with dignity, consideration and respect at all times." Clients have the right to refuse treatment; the right to provide informed consent for treatment; and, when hospitalized, the right to receive treatment in the "least restrictive environment."

Q. Questions regarding ethical issues may be discussed in consultation with clinical supervisors, administrative supervisors, professional colleagues, or attorneys. Some professional liability insurance programs, including CPH (www.CPHIns.com), may be able to arrange a legal consultation with an attorney to discuss legal and ethical issues, in order to avoid potential liability.

R. **Referrals** must be provided to clients whenever clients need services that a counselor is not qualified to provide or whenever treatment is terminated due to a conflict, in compliance with C.R.S. § 12-245-224(1)(l). Provide the referral to the client in writing, with contact information for healthcare providers, and document in the chart the need for the referral, the fact that the referral was given to the client, and other information that is pertinent.

S. **Supervision** provides excellent training for supervisees in clinical settings, as counselors gain experience and learn to comply with the clinical, legal, and ethical standards applicable. Obtaining supervision or a consultation is essential when difficult clinical, ethical, or legal issues arise. Excellent standards for clinical supervision have been adopted by AMHCA in its Code of Ethics (2020).

T. **Termination** of treatment is mandated in compliance with C.R.S. § 12-245-224(1)(k) when it is reasonably "clear that the client was not benefiting from the relationship and is not likely to gain such benefit in the future."

U. **Unauthorized Practice** – According to the provisions of C.R.S. § 12-245-228, it is a criminal offense for any person to practice as a mental health professional in Colorado "without an active license, registration, or certification" issued by DORA.

V. **Values** – All counselors are trained that it is unethical for them to impose their values on a client, whether the therapist's values arise from religious beliefs, cultural traditions, or other factors. Counselors must use their own values in making a determination concerning whether suspected child abuse has occurred, recognizing that a professional's values inform the individual's professional judgment. Such value judgments are based upon our shared values, based upon laws and ethical standards.

W. **Waiver** of a right by a client occurs, for example, when the individual authorizes the release of confidential information and consents to its disclosure, in writing. Confidential treatment information is protected by the therapist-client privilege, which can only be waived by the client, and not by the counselor.

X. **Expert Witnesses** are entitled to be paid for their time, when required to testify in court. Who is an expert? A counselor, subpoenaed to testify in court concerning the assessment of a client, the client's presenting problems, the treatment goals, and the treatment plan, is an expert witness, based on the individual's education, training, and experience. The fact that a counselor qualifies as an expert witness does not mean that the professional is conducting a forensic evaluation, it simply means that the person's credentials and knowledge qualify that individual as an expert.

Y. Your best defense in the event of a complaint to a licensing board may be provided by treatment notes and records. Keeping good treatment records enables a professional to explain any decision that has been made and to justify the treatment provided, whether it is your assessment of the client's problems, or your treatment plan. S.O.A.P. Notes are an excellent way of capturing a client's presentation during a treatment session, and recording your observations, assessment, and plan for treating a client. When insurance companies conduct utilization reviews or audits of treatment providers, they may demand that you provide treatment records in order to justify that the treatment that you provided was "reasonable and necessary." Maintaining good notes and records, which reflect the treatment process accurately, should enable you to successfully complete an insurance audit.

Z. Zero Tolerance for Threats of Violence – When a client makes a threat of violence by expressing, "I am going to kill myself" or by saying, "I am going to kill my children and myself," those statements demonstrate that an imminent danger to self or to others exists. Such statements indicate the clear intention of the client to either commit suicide or harm others. When confronted with such situations, conduct a thorough evaluation of the danger that exists and the risk posed by the client, so that appropriate action may be taken. Keep in mind that when clients make threats of violence in airports, in schools, in the home, or in the workplace, zero tolerance exists for such threats. When threats of violence are communicated, we must err on the side of protecting people – both clients and the public.

9.02 FAQs on Ethics for Marriage & Family Therapists

The ethical principles discussed in this section will be based upon Colorado Statutes, the Colorado MFT Board Rules, HIPAA Standards, and the Code of Ethics for the American Association for Marriage & Family Therapy (AAMFT), revised in 2015.

Informed Consent

Q. Do *both* parents need to sign a disclosure statement, providing consent to treat a child?

A. AAMFT ethical standards do not require both parents to authorize treatment for their children. Either biological parent can provide informed consent for treatment of their children, unless a court has intervened and ruled otherwise. When parents are divorcing, the court will generally assign parental responsibilities to the parents, including "decision-making authority." If joint decision-making authority is granted to both parents, then both parents need to sign a disclosure statement consenting to treatment. If sole decision-making authority is granted to one parent or the other, then that individual is the only individual who can consent to treatment. If parents have joint decision-making authority, then they jointly hold the privilege for their children, and, in such a case, both parents need to sign release of information forms, consenting to disclosure of confidential treatment information.

Q. I am teaching a parenting class, and members of the class want to see me for treatment. Can I provide counseling to my students?

A. No. AAMFT Ethical Standard 4.2 provides, "Marriage and family therapists do not provide therapy to current students or supervisees." After the class has concluded, however, former students may seek treatment from you, if they so desire.

Q. At what age is a client legally competent to consent to treatment and to sign a disclosure statement?

A. An adolescent, 15 years of age or older, is authorized by law, C.R.S. § 27-65-103, to consent for treatment provided by a licensed mental health professional, for treatment in a hospital, and for treatment at a community mental health center. The 15-year-old adolescent then would hold the privilege, and would have the authority to authorize the release of treatment information by providing consent in writing on a release of information form. In addition, Colorado law authorizes a licensed Marriage and Family Therapist to provide outpatient treatment to a 12-year-old without parental consent when the MFT determines: (1) the minor is knowingly and voluntarily seeking mental health services; and (2) the provision of psychotherapy services is clinically indicated and necessary for the minor's well-being. C.R.S. § 12-245-203.5. See Section 4.14 for more details regarding disclosures to parents and documentation required.

As discussed in Section 4.14, a 12-year-old may consent to outpatient therapy provided by a licensed mental health professional when the therapist determines that that treatment is needed and that the 12-year-old client is voluntarily consenting to the services.

Q. When I am providing treatment to a minor, and a parent asks for information concerning my client's problems or requests treatment records, what information – and how much information – should I disclose?

A. When a parent has authorized treatment for his or her child, the parent is entitled to information concerning the services given or needed. In particular, a parent needs to be informed concerning any referrals for other services needed by the child.

Best Practice: When you first see a minor who has been brought in by a parent for counseling, let both of them know that you will need some degree of confidentiality with the adolescent, so that you can discuss basic issues and problems such as use of drugs or alcohol, sexual experience, or parent-child issues in confidence with the minor. At the same time, let both the adolescent and the parent know that you will, in the exercise of your professional judgment, advise the parent of any "services given or needed." You may state this policy in writing in your disclosure statement, and have both the parent and minor sign it.

Q. If a client refuses to sign my disclosure statement, can I then provide services to that individual?

A. One of the most basic patient's rights is the right to refuse treatment. When a client refuses to sign your disclosure statement, which is your "consent to treat form," the client is not providing you with any consent for treatment and is thereby refusing treatment.

Mandatory Reporting

Q. When am I required to make a report concerning child abuse or neglect?

A. In compliance with the Colorado Children's Code, § 19-3-304, an MFT is required to report *suspected* child abuse or neglect *immediately*, within 24 hours of forming the suspicion that abuse or neglect has occurred. The report must be made to county DHS, Child Protective Services; to local law enforcement; or to the state reporting hotline that has been set up. Make sure that you document all information regarding the report, including the name of the CPS caseworker or the law enforcement officer to whom the report is made.

Q. What constitutes "child abuse" or "neglect"?

A. "Child abuse" means an act or omission that threatens the health or welfare of a child, including injury to a child evidenced by skin bruising, bleeding, malnutrition, failure to thrive, burns, etc. Child abuse also includes subjecting a child to sexual assault or molestation, sexual exploitation, or prostitution.

"Neglect" occurs when a child's parent or custodian fails to provide adequate food, clothing, shelter, medical care, or supervision that a parent should provide.

Q. When do I have the duty to warn of a threat by my client or a duty to protect against violence that may be committed by a client?

A. In compliance with the Tarasoff duty to warn and protect, established by Colorado law, C.R.S. § 13-21-117, an MFT has a duty to warn and protect when a client makes a serious threat of imminent physical violence against a specific person or location. When this occurs, an MFT has a duty to initiate a 72-hour hold of the client; to report the threat to law enforcement; and, if possible, to warn the person threatened or to warn the person in charge of premises that have been threatened of the risk that exists. When an MFT has complied with this duty, the professional is entitled to immunity from suit or from a licensing board complaint.

Q. Do I have a duty to report another therapist if I know of ethical misconduct on his or her part?

A. It depends. If the information is known first hand by an MFT, who has observed unethical conduct, or who has been told of unethical conduct by another therapist, then a duty exists to make a report in compliance with licensing board rules. If the information regarding unethical violation by a therapist comes from a counseling client, that client must consent to waive confidentiality, thereby allowing a complaint to be made to the appropriate licensing board. If the client prefers, the client can initiate a complaint against a former therapist.

Q. In conducting family counseling, the children tell me that their parents have a Meth lab in the home. The children tell me that they have had breathing problems because of their exposure to chemicals in the house. Am I required to report this information to law enforcement? Is this a situation that constitutes child abuse or neglect?

A. Yes, because of the health problems that result from Meth labs, and the risk that the house could explode or catch fire, Colorado law now requires that mandated reporters make reports regarding Meth labs in homes where children live. Such a report should be made to law enforcement.

Record-Keeping Requirements

Q. What specific records must I keep?

A. AAMFT Code of Ethics Principle 3.6 requires MFTs to maintain "accurate and adequate clinical and financial records." In order to comply with the MFT Board's record-keeping rules, therapists should keep the following records:

1. Assessment data.
2. Client disclosure statements.
3. Treatment plans.
4. Signed authorizations for release of treatment information.
5. Notes concerning any disclosure of information, including the date, the person to whom information was disclosed, and the specific records or information disseminated.
6. Billing and payment information.
7. Information concerning referrals made to other professionals for services.
8. Session notes concerning each treatment session.
9. Information concerning consults with other professionals on a client's case.
10. When the client has been discharged, the MFT needs to keep a "closing statement," stating either that the treatment services have all been paid in full, or identifying any balance due for services that have been provided.
11. Additional information that MFTs must maintain includes: identifying data, to include the therapist's name and the client's name, address, and age; reason(s) for the marriage and family therapy-psychotherapy services; the date of each contact with primary client(s), to include the date on which marriage and family therapy-psychotherapy services began and the date of last contact with client; adequate and reasonable case management records; and the name of any test administered, each date on which the test was administered, and the name(s) of the person(s) administering the test.

Q. When a client demands a copy of my file, must I copy it for him or her?

A. Neither AAMFT ethical standards, federal law, nor HIPAA regulations require that you provide a client with your records concerning treatment. You are entitled to use your judgment in responding to a request for records by deciding whether to provide a copy of records or to provide a treatment summary. Colorado law, C.R.S. § 25-1-802, provides that when a client or client representative requests treatment records that involve mental health problems, a therapist may comply with the request by providing a treatment summary, instead of the actual notes and records.

Domestic Relations Evaluations

Q. I have been subpoenaed to testify in a domestic relations case involving former clients whom I saw for couples counseling. The subpoena also requires that a copy of my records concerning the couples counseling be brought to court. The wife has consented to my testimony and to the release of records to her attorney, but the husband has refused to consent to my disclosing any information concerning the couples counseling. What should I do?

A. The AAMFT Code of Ethics Standard 2.3 prohibits the disclosure of information received from clients during couples counseling unless consent is obtained from both individuals in the client group. This ethical Standard provides, "When providing couple, family, or group treatment, the therapist does not provide access to records without a written authorization from each individual competent to execute a waiver." Thus, without both the wife's and the husband's consent, you cannot testify or release any records.

Q. I provided family counseling to a family that is now going through a divorce. An MFT has been appointed by the court to conduct a custody evaluation. The evaluator has asked me for a copy of my records concerning this family; the wife consents and has signed an authorization for the release of treatment records, but the husband has refused for me to provide any information. The children are all under the age of 10, so they are too young to consent. What should I do?

A. In compliance with AAMFT Code of Ethics Standard 2.3, which provides that an MFT "not disclose information outside the treatment context without a written authorization from each individual competent to execute a waiver," you should protect the confidentiality of treatment information and refuse the request for disclosure of treatment information, on grounds that you lack client consent.

Q. I have been seeing Mom and her children in counseling to deal with issues concerning parent-adolescent problems and divorce issues. Mom and Dad are separated. Mom's attorney wants me to testify in court that Mom should have all parenting rights and responsibilities. I have never met the husband, and know little about him, except for information provided by

Mom concerning his drug problems and his acts of domestic violence. Can I testify as an expert witness for Mom in the divorce case?

A. No, you cannot. AAMFT Code of Ethics Standard 7.7 states, "MFTs avoid conflicts of interest in treating minors or adults involved in custody or visitation actions by not performing evaluations for custody, residence, or visitation of the minor. MFTs who treat minors may provide the court or mental health professional performing the evaluation with information about the minor from the MFT's perspective as a treating marriage and family therapist, so long as the MFT obtained appropriate consents to release information."

If your client's attorney does call you as a witness at the divorce hearing and insists on asking you questions that you do not feel adequately prepared to answer under the circumstances, you may simply respond, "I do not have an opinion on that subject." Or you could simply state, "I do not have the information necessary to make a recommendation to the court on that."

Q. Mom has brought in her children so that I can make a recommendation to the court. She has full custody of her children and is opposing Dad's motion to modify parenting time for more time with his children. I have met with the children, and they do not want to spend more time with Dad. Mom's attorney has asked me to prepare a letter to the judge, summarizing the children's opposition to their father's motion and his request for additional parenting time. Can I prepare such a report?

A. No, you may not. AAMFT Code of Ethics Standard 7.7, which is quoted above, prohibits an MFT who is providing clinical services from making recommendations to the court regarding custody or parenting time ("visitation"), so you may not make any such recommendations.

Supervision

Q. I am an AAMFT-approved supervisor. What should I do to protect myself from liability, in case I am sued for the actions of a supervisee? For example, how could I defend myself if a therapist that I was supervising was having an intimate relationship with a client – without my knowledge?

A. You need to have a supervision contract in writing, which explains the supervisor-supervisee relationship and specifies the terms of your agreement. You can protect yourself, first and foremost, by making certain that you have professional liability insurance that covers you; and you want to ensure that your supervisee also maintains professional liability insurance. The form Clinical Supervision Contract at Form 7 in Appendix A is an excellent contract and is designed to protect clinical supervisors from potential liability. Note that in the contract, the supervisee promises to comply with the AAMFT Ethical Code, with the Colorado Statutes contained in the Mental Health Act, and with the MFT Board's Rules.

Q. What should my supervisee's disclosure statement disclose in regard to clinical supervision and my role as supervisor?

A. The disclosure statement should state that treatment information will be shared with you, in order to assure that all legal and ethical standards for therapy are being met. The disclosure statement must identify you, in order to ensure that no conflictual dual relationship exists between you and the client who is receiving services, and should also disclose the basic information concerning your qualifications and experience as an MFT. That helps to establish the client's confidence in you and your ability to direct the treatment.

Q. Am I required to sign the supervisee's treatment notes during clinical supervision?

A. No, this is not required, unless a counseling agency, treatment facility, hospital, or community health center has a policy requiring supervisors to sign a supervisee's notes.

Q. I am an MFT who receives weekly clinical supervision from a licensed mental health professional as part of my job. In discussing a confidentiality question with my supervisor, he told me that I had breached confidentiality, and that he had a duty to file a grievance against me. The complaint that he filed was dismissed, but I am still upset, because I thought that a supervisor-supervisee relationship was confidential. Am I right or wrong in that belief?

A. You are correct; the entire supervisor-supervisee-client relationship is confidential. The AAMFT Code of Ethics is clear in this regard. Standard 4.7 states, "Marriage and family therapists do not disclose supervisee confidences except by written authorization or waiver, or when mandated or permitted by law." The training that occurs in clinical supervision is extremely valuable. Supervisees need to know, of course, that they can raise questions to their supervisor about legal and ethical issues without having a grievance filed against them.

Q. I have had several clinical and administrative supervisors during my years in practice. Each has had different methods, styles, and procedures. Is there a basic protocol for supervision? What are the essential duties of a clinical supervisor?

A. The standards for clinical supervision published by the Colorado State Board of Marriage and Family Therapist Examiners and the AAMFT Code of Ethics constitute the protocol. The basic duties of a clinical supervisor are to:

1. Monitor the supervisee's clinical activities to ensure therapy provided meets basic standards.
2. Direct the services provided by the supervisee, based upon appropriate clinical, legal, and ethical standards.
3. Assure that the supervisee provides the disclosure statement at the initial client contact, and that the disclosure statement is signed by the client no later than the second visit.
4. Assure that clients are informed concerning any changes in the supervisory relationship, and that the process of termination of supervision is undertaken with both the supervisee and the clients.
5. Assure that records documenting supervision are kept that meet generally accepted standards.
6. Assure that a supervision contract is prepared, which establishes the supervisor-supervisee relationship and specifies rules, procedures, and financial agreements.
7. Assist the supervisee in becoming aware of and adhering to all legal, ethical, and professional responsibilities.
8. Assure that all bills or insurance forms are filled out accurately, and correctly state who provided the therapy and who provided the supervision.
9. Have adequate knowledge of legal, ethical, and professional standards relating to the clients being served.
10. Ensure that no conflictual dual relationship exists between the client and therapist, supervisor and supervisee, and supervisor and client.

Q. I will need to be tape-recording and videotaping treatment sessions for purposes of supervision. I am concerned that tape-recording sessions may affect the dynamics of interactions, and may affect clients' willingness to disclose information. Do I need to let clients know that they are being tape-recorded, or can I record sessions surreptitiously?

A. AAMFT Code of Ethics Standard 1.12 requires that therapists "obtain written informed consent from clients before videotaping, audio recording, or permitting third-party observation." Therefore, you must obtain informed consent from your client in writing before you may record a treatment session. If a client refuses to allow you to record treatment sessions, then you may not do so.

Best Practice: As soon as the videotape or tape-recording has been used for supervision, tape over it or erase the recording.

Ethical Standards for Business Practices

Q. Am I allowed to trade services with a client or engage in bartering?

A. AAMFT Code of Ethics Standard 8.5 states, "Marriage and family therapists ordinarily refrain from accepting goods and services from clients in return for services rendered. Bartering for professional services may be conducted only if (a) the supervisee or client requests it; (b) the relationship is not exploitative; (c) the professional relationship is not distorted; and (d) a clear written contract is established." If a client of yours were ever to claim that you took advantage of him or her in a bartering situation, it would obviously be a problem.

Q. If a client fails to pay for professional services, can I turn the account over to a collection agency or sue in order to collect the debt?

A. AAMFT Code of Ethics Standard 8.3 requires that you disclose to a client "the use of a collection agency or legal measures for nonpayment" prior to entering into a professional relationship with a client or supervisee. In addition, Standard 8.3 requires that AAMFT members "give reasonable notice to clients with unpaid balances of their intent to seek collection by agency or legal recourse." Two obvious problems are created if you sue a client: (1) Standard 8.3 provides that if collection action is taken, "therapists will not disclose clinical information"; and (2) a lawsuit may invite a counterclaim for malpractice, which you would then be required to report to your malpractice insurer.

Q. A former client has requested that I send records to her new therapist. This client still has a balance owed for treatment services. Can I demand that the balance be paid before I comply with my client's request for treatment information?

A. No. The AAMFT Code of Ethics Standard 8.6 is clear that you may not withhold records because payment has not been received for past services.

Q. I have completed a graduate program in marriage and family therapy and an internship in a clinic. How do I know what problems I am competent to treat, since I have limited experience?

A. The AAMFT Code of Ethics Standard 3.10 states that therapists may not "diagnose, treat or advise on problems outside the recognized boundaries of their competence." So long as you have a clinical supervisor, who is an MFT and who is competent to handle your clients' presenting problems and to direct you in the therapy being provided, you can treat the clients involved and obtain experience in the process. This ethical standard is consistent with C.R.S. § 12-245-224(1)(h), which states that it is unethical if a therapist "performed services outside of such person's area of training, experience, or competence." In such a situation, the MFT needs to refer a potential client to others who would be competent to provide the services needed.

Q. I have a client who is being seen in couples counseling. His unwillingness to make a serious attempt to cooperate with counseling has been an obstacle to the process of therapy. His flirtatious remarks to me make me very uncomfortable. I feel that I should refer this couple to another therapist, but I do not want to be seen as abandoning these clients. Can I terminate my services and refer the couple out?

A. AAMFT Code of Ethics Standard 1.11 states, "Marriage and family therapists do not abandon or neglect clients in treatment without making reasonable arrangements for the continuation of treatment." Standard 1.9 prohibits continuing a professional relationship with clients when it is reasonably clear that the clients are no longer benefitting from the relationship. When clients are no longer benefitting from your services or other reasons exist for referring clients to another professional, you can terminate your relationship with the clients and refer them to other appropriate professionals. When you have terminated your relationship appropriately, and have referred your clients to other therapists who can provide services that are needed, you are not abandoning your clients. Whenever you make a referral, do it in writing, so that it is properly documented.

Q. What can I do to protect myself from being sued or grieved?

A. There are many things that you can do:

- Keep good records, using S.O.A.P. notes or their equivalent;
- Consult whenever ethical issues arise;

- Refer clients to appropriate professionals when you do not have the experience or competence necessary to help them;
- Never sue a client;
- Maintain active membership in professional associations;
- Maintain professional liability insurance with a minimum of $1,000,000 coverage;
- If you are in private practice, set up an LLC or professional corporation to protect your personal assets; and
- Practice with informed consent, explaining to your client any presenting problems, the goals of treatment, the methods of treatment used to achieve treatment goals, and your treatment plan. Maintain good professional liability insurance. The AAMFT Group Policy is issued through CPH & Associates. Information concerning this policy can be obtained online at www.cphins.com.

9.03 FAQs on Ethics for Mental Health Counselors

Q. If a client refuses to sign my treatment contract, can I then provide services to that individual?

A. In general, no. Counselors must respect client rights, and as stated in the AMHCA Code of Ethics (Code), Principle I.B.7.i, a basic right of clients is "to refuse any recommended services, techniques or approaches and to be advised of the consequences of this action." Clients may, of course, give informed consent to treatment if they choose to do so. Code section I.B.2 provides excellent guidance regarding the informed consent process, and the disclosures that should be made to clients.

In Colorado, C.R.S. § 12-245-216 requires a disclosure to clients that they may terminate treatment or seek a second opinion at any time, which guarantees this basic right to refuse treatment. If treatment of the client is court ordered, there may, of course, be consequences if the client refuses treatment in violation of a court order.

Q. When do I have the duty to warn of a threat by my client or a duty to protect against violence that may be committed by a client?

A. The Tarasoff duty to warn and protect against serious threats of imminent violence by a client has been adopted in various forms in state laws and licensing board Rules. Counselors need to comply with their state law or licensing board Rules regarding the duty to hospitalize a client who is dangerous to others, in order to prevent threatened violence and to protect the potential victim. By doing this, you comply with Code Principle I.A.2.c, which contains an exception to confidentiality "for the protection of life," and provides: "mental health counselors are required to comply with state . . . statutes regarding mandated reporting." Colorado law does impose on counselors a "duty to warn and protect," according to C.R.S. § 13-21-117, when a client makes a serious threat of imminent physical violence against a specific person or location. The counselor then has a duty to initiate a hospital hold on the client, or cause one to be made; to warn the potential victim, or the manager of a location that was threatened; and to notify law enforcement.

Q. I have been seeing a Mom and her children in counseling to deal with issues concerning parent-adolescent problems and divorce issues. Mom and Dad are separated. Mom's attorney wants me to testify in court that Mom should have custody of her children. I have never met the husband, and know little about him, except for information provided by Mom concerning his drug problems and his acts of domestic violence. Can I testify as an expert witness for Mom in the divorce case?

A. No, a counselor who is serving in a clinical role, providing treatment to a Mom and her children in family counseling, cannot also take on the role of forensic expert. To do so would violate Code principle I.D.4.g, which prohibits counselors from evaluating, for "forensic purposes, individuals whom they are currently counseling or have counseled in the past." To express an opinion on custody, which Mom's attorney has requested, would also result in a violation of Code section I.A.3, which prohibits counselors from having dual relationships in serving clients. A dual relationship would result if a counselor served the same client in both a clinical and forensic role.

Mom's attorney should ask the court to appoint an unbiased, objective, forensic evaluator; or the attorney can retain a forensic expert to evaluate custody issues and make recommendations to the court in the best interests of the parties' children.

Q. Part of my practice as a counselor involves providing clinical supervision to people who are seeking licensure. What should I do to protect myself from liability, in case I am sued for the actions of a supervisee? For example, how could I defend myself if a therapist that I was supervising was having a personal relationship with a client – without my knowledge?

A. The best defense against any potential risk in a situation such as this is for the clinical supervisor to have a thorough Clinical Supervision Contract with the supervisee in compliance with Code section III.B.2. The contract needs to have a requirement that the supervisee will comply with the AMHCA Code of Ethics; and the supervisor should provide the supervisee with a copy of the Code as stated in Principle III.B.2.b. Exploitative relationships, such as an intimate relationship between the supervisee and client, are "strictly prohibited" according to Code section I.A.4. Thus, the AMHCA Code of Ethics is an excellent learning device in the clinical supervision process, and the supervisee's commitment to comply with the Code assures that the clinical supervisor in not responsible if the supervisee crosses boundaries with the client without the supervisor's knowledge, after the supervisee has promised to comply with the Code of Ethics. An excellent clinical supervision contract is contained in Appendix A: the Forms section of this book.

Q. I have a client who is being seen in couples counseling. His unwillingness to make a serious attempt to cooperate with counseling has been an obstacle to the process of therapy. His flirtatious remarks to me make me very uncomfortable. I feel that I should refer this couple to another therapist, but I do not want to be seen as abandoning these clients. Can I terminate my services and refer the couple out?

A. Trust your judgment and refer the client couple to another counselor. By doing this, you are not abandoning the couple, you are complying with Code section I.A.3.a, which requires that "mental health counselors make every effort to avoid dual/multiple relationships with clients." Flirtatious clients can create any number of problems, even when the counselor is not crossing boundaries. By terminating treatment and referring the couple to another counselor, no abandonment occurs. The best practice in terminating a clinical relationship and providing referrals to a client is to do it in writing.

Q. In disclosing my fee to clients, am I required to inform them concerning my sliding scale or may I withhold that information until a client asks for it?

A. Informed consent is intended to be a transparent process in which information about treatment is disclosed to clients. Accordingly, counselors should disclose billing practices, including a sliding scale fee in compliance with I.B.2.a of the Code, which requires disclosure of information to clients including "counselor credentials, issues of confidentiality, the use of tests and inventories, diagnosis, reports, billing, and the therapeutic process." Similarly, counselors need to comply with section I.E.2, which provides that counselors "clearly explain to clients, early in the counseling relationship, all financial arrangements related to counseling."

Q. I am a devoutly religious person, and I do not believe in divorce. When working with couples who have marital problems, I make every effort to preserve the marriage, and counsel my clients not to seek a divorce because of the guilt and emotional problems that this will cause the couple and their children. Is this permissible?

A. Counselors cannot impose their values on others. The Code, section I.A.4.d, cautions counselors to be "aware of their own values, attitudes, beliefs, and behaviors, as well as how these apply in a society with clients from diverse ethnic, social, cultural, religious and economic backgrounds." Then, of course, you must respect the client and be mindful that you are not imposing your attitudes, beliefs, or values on them.

Q. How do I handle confidentiality in conducting group therapy, and what do I tell group members will be the consequences if confidentiality is breached?

A. The Code provides that "in working with . . . groups, the right to confidentiality of each member should be safeguarded" according to section I.A.2.l. Inform each group member in the treatment contract or disclosure statement that group counseling is confidential, disclose the exceptions that apply, and also disclose that what is said in group stays in group, because the information is personal, private, and confidential. Then, at the beginning of each group session, remind the members again that all information shared in sessions is confidential, and stays in group. If a member talks outside of group about what someone else had said in a session, then often the consequences are left up to the group to decide what should be done. However, the counselor should reserve the right to determine if group counseling should be terminated for the member who violated another's confidentiality, in order to prevent a repetition of the breach of confidentiality.

Q. When I engage in couples counseling, can I share information with the husband that is confided to me by the wife in order to facilitate communication between them?

A. The Code provides in section I.A.2.l: "In working with families . . . , the right to confidentiality of each member should be safeguarded." When you meet with a member of a couple individually to obtain information for purposes of couples counseling, get an agreement immediately at the end of the session regarding what information can be shared to the other member of the couple, and what information may not be shared. Document this agreement in the session note for that meeting. This best practice is recommended, even if a client has signed a "No Secrets Policy."

Q. I am counseling a man who is experiencing marital problems. His wife is having an affair, and he is devastated. He wants to preserve his marriage, but his wife is not willing to seek counseling. He wants for me to meet with her, and she has agreed to do so. Will she be my client, too?

A. No, the wife is unwilling to take part in counseling, so she would be a "collateral," not a client, in the husband's individual counseling process. The Code states in section I.B.3.b: "Collateral consent informs family members or others . . . of the parameters and limitations of confidentiality." The client husband needs to sign a Release (ROI) authorizing his wife to attend a session and to receive treatment information. Any collateral in a situation such as this should receive a Collateral Disclosure informing that the collateral is not a client and will not be receiving treatment; and that any treatment information shared with her will be part of the client husband's confidential treatment record, and is not confidential information belonging to her. This clarifies the roles of the two spouses in the treatment process. So, any notes or records regarding the wife/collateral's involvement in the husband's individual counseling are part of the husband's treatment record, and he can use the information or authorize its release since it is his confidential treatment information. A Collateral Disclosure Form is found in Appendix A: the Forms section of this book.

Q. I am providing services online through email with clients. Is this practice ethical? Are there any special disclosures that I need to give these clients?

A. At a minimum, two disclosures are needed regarding the security of email communication. First, in compliance with Code principle I.A.2.o, disclose that only encrypted email is secure in communicating online and conducting treatment sessions; and that unencrypted email is not secure because it can be hacked more easily. Section I.A.2.o states: "Mental health counselors take necessary precautions to ensure client confidentiality of information transmitted electronically through the use of a computer, e-mail, fax, telephone, voicemail, answering machines," or other media such as video conferencing platforms. The second disclosure that should be made pursuant to I.B.6.c concerns "the benefits and risks of entering into distance counseling" including "e-mail contact with a client." The risk that a breach of confidentiality may occur if unencrypted email is used is well known to most email users, but should still be discussed in making this disclosure. Counselors in Colorado need to review and comply with the guidance provided in LPC Board Policy 30-1, the Board's Teletherapy Policy.

Q. For years, I have been asking whether I am required to report a client who is HIV-positive and who is having unprotected sex with his partner. Recently this issue arose, and my client refused to allow me to disclose to his partner that he is HIV-positive. We have treated this as a clinical issue. Do I have a duty to report this situation, or am I required to maintain my client's privacy and the confidentiality of this information?

A. Comply with state law in determining whether you are required to report information regarding a client in treatment who has been tested and found to be HIV-positive, or whether, on the other hand, state law requires that such information be kept confidential. The Code addresses this issue in section I.A.2.n which provides: "Mental health counselors may justify disclosing information to identifiable third parties if clients disclose that they have a communicable life-threatening illness. However, prior to disclosing such information, mental health counselors must confirm the diagnosis with a medical provider. The intent of clients to inform a third party about their illness and to engage in possible behaviors that could be harmful to an identifiable third party must be assessed as part of the process of determining whether a disclosure should be made to identifiable third parties." In view of the legal risks of informing the client's partner that he is HIV-positive without his written consent, a counselor would be well advised to seek legal counsel before taking any such action. Other issues regarding HIV/AIDS reporting under Colorado law is found in § 2.09 of this book.

Q. How should I disclose to clients the limitations on confidentiality, such as the mandatory reporting of suspected child abuse or neglect, and other exceptions to confidentiality?

A. The Code requires in section I.B.2 that counselors obtain informed consent for treatment by providing disclosures to clients, which include "issues of confidentiality." These disclosures may be made in the "counselor's professional disclosure statement," which should list the basic exceptions to confidentiality and any special exceptions that may apply in a particular client's situation. Appendix A contains a Form Disclosure Statement for clients that includes a thorough discussion of the exceptions to confidentiality under Colorado law.

Q. Am I required to report another counselor if I know that the counselor cannot practice competently or if I know of an ethical violation that a professional has committed?

A. The Code addresses this problem in II.A.7, which provides: "When mental health counselors have knowledge of the impairment, incompetence, or unethical conduct of a mental health professional, they are obliged to attempt to rectify the situation. Failing an informal solution, mental health counselors should bring such unethical activities to the attention of the appropriate state licensure board and/or the ethics committee of the professional association." If the information about the unethical conduct of another professional comes from a client and constitutes confidential treatment information, obtain consent in writing in a release by the client before disclosing it.

In compliance with Colorado law, C.R.S. § 12-245-227 and LPC Board Rule 1.6, which is discussed in § 6.05 of this book, a counselor has a duty to report another therapist if the individual commits a violation of the Prohibited Activities listed in C.R.S. § 12-245-224, so long as the information that forms the basis of the report is not confidential treatment information. If the information is confidential, then client consent is needed.

Q. What am I required to do when I receive a subpoena for my records?

A. The Code provides excellent guidance in this situation in section I.A.2.d, which states: "Mental health counselors are advised to seek legal advice upon receiving a subpoena in order to respond appropriately." A counselor should check with their professional liability insurer to determine if their insurance policy contains coverage for the counselor to retain an attorney to handle the subpoena, and provides that the insurer will pay the attorney fees involved. An attorney may need to file a motion to quash if the subpoena was not properly served, or to file a motion for protective order if the subpoena seeks confidential treatment information or records, and the client does not consent to these disclosures. A subpoena does not compel the production of counseling records and does not compel testimony by a counselor: client consent is needed, in writing, in order to disclose confidential treatment information. A subpoena, properly served, does compel a counselor to appear at the time and place indicated in it.

Legal advice can assist a counselor to determine if the subpoena was properly served, and should assure that the counselor's response to the subpoena is proper, in order to avoid a breach of confidentiality through the disclosure of confidential information without client consent.

In Colorado, a subpoena must be served personally to a counselor for service to be valid, unless the counselor has authorized a third party, such as an office manager, to accept service of subpoenas.

Q. My client has sent me a letter containing a written request for a copy of her treatment records. This client's diagnosis is paranoid schizophrenia. I am afraid that she will feel stigmatized by this label, and that she will be confused not only by the diagnosis in her file, but also by the test data contained in it. Am I required to give this client a copy of her chart?

A. Code section I.A.2.b apples in this instance. It states: "The information in client records belongs to the client and shall not be shared without permission granted through a formal release of information. In the event that a client requests that information in his or her record be shared, mental health counselors educate clients to the implications of sharing the materials." Some state laws require that health care providers and counselors give a copy of their treatment records to clients, upon request; however, many state laws agree with HIPAA standards, which provide that the counselor's "psychotherapy notes" need not be shared with clients, who are entitled to a progress report, which is a treatment summary. Disclosure to this client of her treatment notes and records could be harmful to her, due to the client's inability to process diagnoses, labels, or discussions of her history. Thus, if state law allows a counselor to provide the client with a treatment summary in this instance, it would undoubtedly be an appropriate judgment on the part of the counselor to do that.

Under C.R.S. § 25-1-802, a counselor may comply with a client's request for treatment records by providing a treatment summary, which is similar to the "progress report" authorized by HIPAA standards.

Q. I have several clients in my drug and alcohol treatment agency who are indigent and cannot afford to pay me. Can I put them to work for me in my agency, and trade services with them?

A. No, this would not be advisable, due to the dual relationship that would result in violation of principle I.A.3.a, which prohibits multiple relationships arising out of "familial, social, financial, business, or close personal relationships with the clients." Putting these clients to work in the agency would create dual relationships between the counselor-client and employer-employee. Supervising the client in the workplace would lead to foreseeable problems. Code provision I.E.2.b states that "counselors usually refrain from accepting goods or services from clients in return for counseling services, because such arrangements may create the potential for conflicts, exploitation and distortion of the professional relationship." Bartering is problematic because it can only occur "if there is no exploitation," and whenever a client complains to a licensing board that they were exploited in such a situation, the client will be believed, and the counselor may be punished for engaging in a dual relationship. In Colorado, bartering is never recommended, because of the Licensing Boards' history of imposing discipline on therapists who have engaged in bartering.

Q. I have a client who continues to schedule appointments with me every week, even though I have suggested that she does not need counseling any longer. She says that it makes her feel better and that she enjoys our interaction. What should I do?

A. Code section I.B.5.b applies in this analysis: "Mental health counselors terminate a counseling relationship when it is reasonably clear that the client is no longer benefiting," or "when services are no longer required." Clients can become dependent on counselors and counseling, which is not healthy as it does not promote client autonomy. Schedule a termination session with this client, thank the client for her excellent work that resulted in treatment goals being reached, discuss her progress in treatment, and suggest that she can return if she should need additional services.

It is a violation of the Prohibited Activities Statute under Colorado law, C.R.S. § 12-245-224 to continue with treatment when a client no longer needs services.

Q. I have a client who has not been paying for his sessions. I know that he can afford to pay, because he has a good job, drives an expensive car, and is always well-dressed. What can I do?

A. The AMHCA Code provides that "counselors may terminate a counseling relationship when clients do not pay fees charged," according to section I.B.5.c. "In such cases referrals are offered to the clients" in order to prevent abandonment of the client. If the counselor intends to use a collection agency to obtain payment of treatment invoices, the counselor must first disclose the intention to use a collection agency, and try to work out a payment plan, an approach that can be used prior to terminating the professional relationship with the client. This approach is acceptable in

Colorado, but it is never advisable to sue a client for various reasons, including breach of confidentiality, and also the prospect that a client might file a counterclaim for malpractice, claiming that the client did not pay for the treatment because it was no good.

Q. I know that doctors carry pagers, and that they have other physicians to take calls for them after hours when the doctor is not available. Are counselors required to do the same? Many of my colleagues have messages on their answering machines that direct callers to go to the nearest hospital emergency room or call 911 if they are in crisis. Do counselors have to be available to their clients 24/7?

A. The Code does provide that assistance be "given in making appropriate arrangements for the continuation of treatment, when necessary, during interruptions such as vacations and following treatment," according to section I.B.5.a. Regarding after hours calls or texts from clients, be aware that some managed health care companies enter into fee for service contracts with counselors that require them to be available to respond to calls from the insured/client after hours in case of a crisis or emergency. Check any provider contract carefully to see if it has such a requirement, and comply with the contract if it does.

It is a generally accepted practice, however, in the absence of such a contract, for counselors to inform clients to call 911 or to go the nearest hospital emergency room for treatment in the event of a crisis. In general, that is the safest approach, since counselors are not available on a 24/7 basis to triage client's problems and emergencies after hours, and clients need to know what to expect in these situations.

Q. Is the possession or use of child pornography reportable?

A. Yes, the possession or use of child pornography is illegal; it is a crime, pursuant to C.R.S. § 18-6-403, which prohibits sexual exploitation of a child. This statute states in part: "The mere possession or control of any sexually exploitative material results in continuing victimization of our children by the fact that such material is a permanent record of an act or acts of sexual abuse of a child; that each time such material is shown or viewed, the child is harmed; that such material is used to break down the will and resistance of other children to encourage them to participate in similar acts of sexual abuse; . . . it is necessary for the state to ban the possession of any sexually exploitative materials. . . ."

Therefore, whenever a therapist knows or suspects that a person is viewing or using child pornography, it must be reported to law enforcement.

Q. Is sexting reportable, that is, emailing or texting photos or video of a person's genital area or the intimate parts of the body to another?

A. It depends on the situation, according to Colorado law: Sometimes it may be; sometimes it is not, depending on the age of the individuals and the provisions of C.R.S. § 18-7-109, which prohibits the offense of posting a private image by a juvenile. This statute provides in part:

> (1) A juvenile commits the offense of posting a private image by a juvenile, if he or she, through digital or electronic means:
>
> (a) Knowingly distributes, displays or publishes to the view of another person a sexually explicit image of a person other than himself or herself who is at least 14 years of age or is less than 4 years younger than the juvenile:
>
> (I) Without the depicted person's permission; or
>
> (II) When the juvenile knew or should have known that the depicted person had a reasonable expectation that the image would remain private; or
>
> (b) Knowingly distributes, displays or publishes to the view of another person who is at least 14 years of age or is less than 4 years younger than the juvenile, a sexually explicit image of himself or herself, when the recipient did not solicit or request to be supplied with the image and suffered emotional distress.
>
> (2) A juvenile commits the offense of possessing a private image by a juvenile if he or she, through digital or electronic means, knowingly possesses a sexually explicit image of another person who is at least 14 years of age or is less than 4 years younger than the juvenile without the depicted person's permission, except that it is not a violation of this subsection (2) if the juvenile:
>
> (a) Took reasonable steps to either destroy or delete the image within 72 hours after initially viewing the image.
>
> (3) A juvenile commits the civil infraction of exchange of a private image by a juvenile if he or she, through digital or electronic means:
>
> (a) Knowingly sends a sexually explicit image or images of himself or herself to another person who is at least 14 years

of age or is less than 4 years younger than the juvenile and the image or images depict only the sender and no other person, and the sender reasonably believed that the recipient had solicited or otherwise agreed to the transmittal of the image or images; or

(b) Knowingly possesses a sexually explicit image or images of another person who is at least 14 years of age or is less than 4 years younger than the juvenile, and the image or images depict only the sender and no other person and the juvenile reasonably believed that the depicted person had transmitted the image or images or otherwise agreed to the transmittal of the image or images.

In adopting § 18-7-109, the Colorado General Assembly amended the statute that prohibits sexual exploitation of a child, C.R.S. § 18-6-403, stating: "A juvenile's conduct that is limited to the elements of the petty offense of possession of a private image by a juvenile, as described in section 18-7-109(2), or limited to the elements of the civil infraction of exchange of a private image by a juvenile, as described in section 18-7-109(3), is not subject to prosecution pursuant to [C.R.S. § 18-6-403(3)(b) or (3)(b.5)."

A therapist who has questions about whether or not to report a suspected violation of these laws can contact law enforcement or CPS and present the factual scenario without disclosing the identities of the individuals involved, and ask if the situation is reportable Then, if directed to provide the names of the individuals involved, the therapist should do so.

Q. Can I be held liable if a client or other person sues me and claims that they contracted COVID-19 by coming to my office after I reopen it?

A. A claim that a person contracted COVID-19 at a specific location due to the negligence of a business owner would be extremely difficult to prove. "Negligence" is defined as a failure to maintain the care that a reasonable person would provide under the circumstances; and it includes the failure to protect against a foreseeable risk of harm. Practical solutions to avoid liability for this type of claim are contained in the answer to the next question regarding the steps to take in reopening your office after conducting teletherapy exclusively for the sake of safety. You would be well advised to obtain premises liability insurance coverage for your office, which might afford greater coverage for a claim of this type. If you are sued, do not make any statement to anyone regarding the case to anyone except to your insurance company representative, or to an attorney hired or appointed to represent you and to defend the claim. In particular, do not make any apology or admission to the claimant. Inform your insurance company immediately if you are sued, and provide a copy of the summons and complaint to the insurer or to your insurance agency. If you are sued by a current client, the conflict created requires that you terminate services appropriately and refer the client to another therapist.

Q. What steps should I take to reopen my office after conducting teletherapy exclusively during the COVID-19 crisis?

A. The Centers for Disease Control (CDC) has issued specific guidelines for reopening a business. Before you reopen your office, follow those guidelines as well as state and local orders and laws for maintaining safety in public spaces. In addition, take care to follow the national, state, and local guidelines for safety issued by CDC, HHS, and local governments, which include instructions for cleaning office space; for protective equipment to be worn; and for screening clients to promote safety. Both the CDC and HHS websites have FAQs and practical information to assist you in making this decision and in staying safe after you have reopened. You would be well advised to purchase premises liability insurance coverage, if you do not have it.

Q. As a therapist with many years of experience, I have had many situations where former clients and others harassed me, sending me offensive text messages, emails, and voicemails, sometimes dozens of them. They threaten to "take my license," or file a complaint if I refuse their demands, and even threaten my safety. Do I have any rights as a therapist?

A. Yes, you have rights: the right to protect yourself from harassment. Harassment is a crime in Colorado, defined as the making of offensive statements to another, with the intent to harass or annoy them; and includes both stalking and threats of harm. The protocol that law enforcement often requires is that you notify, in writing, the person who is harassing you that their contacts or the content of their communications is offensive; that you want them to stop contacting you; and that harassment is a crime in Colorado. In that communication, you can also inform the individual, if you choose to do so, that if they do not stop contacting you, you will notify the police and ask that they file charges for harassment. Depending on the severity of any threats, you may be able to apply for a civil protection order in the local county court. If criminal charges are filed against the offender, an automatic restraining order is entered, requiring that the offender not have any contact with you, and that they stay away from you, your residence, and your office. Law enforcement officials consider that stalking is a serious offense. Online stalking is serious, as well. In the event that you need to call the police, do not inform them that the offender is a former counseling client; you can simply state that you had a business relationship with the person, and that your business relationship with them has ended. That way no one can accuse you of a HIPAA violation or of a breach of ethics.

Appendix A: Forms

In this appendix, you will find the following forms:

Form 1. **Motion for Protective Order:** This motion discusses doctrines of confidentiality, the therapist-client privilege, and judicial decisions from both the U.S. Supreme Court and the Colorado appellate courts. The purpose of this motion is to protect against unauthorized disclosure of treatment information, where a client has not consented to any courtroom testimony regarding treatment issues or to any release of information.

Form 2. **Client Disclosure Statement:** This disclosure statement complies with the requirements of C.R.S. § 12-245-216 and provides information to the client concerning the basic exceptions to confidentiality that may apply. Keep in mind that your disclosure statement is an informed consent form. When your client or your client's representative signs it, consent is thereby given for treatment. You may, therefore, include any additional disclosures in this form that are appropriate.

Form 2a. **Surprise Billing Disclosure Form:** This form became a mandated disclosure for Mental Health Professionals and other providers in 2020. You can incorporate this form in your Client Disclosure Statement (Form 2), or have clients sign it at the same time they sign the Client Disclosure Statement.

HIPAA forms. These forms include:

Form 3-1. **HIPAA Privacy Statement**: This is to be given to clients at the inception of treatment in order to explain the limitations on confidentiality and the potential uses of treatment information.

Form 3-2. **HIPAA Business Associate Contract:** This is to be signed by independent contractors who provide services to mental health professionals and who may come into the possession of confidential information relating to clients' identities, their diagnoses, or other privileged information. This form may be used by billing clerks, maintenance contractors, or contract therapists working in an agency to give assurances that they will protect confidential, privileged information, and that they will not make any unauthorized disclosure of confidential information.

Form 3-3. **Accounting of Disclosures:** This form can be used by HIPAA-compliant therapists when clients exercise their right to request an accounting of any disclosures of confidential information. A form is also provided to use in responding to the client's request for an accounting. (See section 2.25 for more information concerning the use of this form.)

Form 3-4. **Request for Confidential Treatment Information:** This form is provided for use by clients in requesting access to their treatment records.

Form 3-5. **Authorization to Disclose Protected Mental Health Information:** This form may be used by clients to authorize the release of records to treating professionals or attorneys and to authorize mental health professionals to disclose confidential information to third parties or to testify in court.

Form 4. **Form M-1:** This form is essentially a symptom checklist and report used to document a person's mental health history and information relating to either an imminent threat of physical violence made by a client; or a client's homicidal or suicidal ideation, which makes a person imminently dangerous to self or others.

Form 5. **Disclosures for Forensic Evaluation:** This form is designed for forensic evaluations where the person being evaluated is *not* a patient and no professional relationship is being established.

Form 6. **Professional Will:** This form is designed to be used by a therapist in conjunction with the therapist's own personal will, to give directions to the professional executor of the therapist for closing down the therapist's practice in the event of death; or to enable a mental health professional, acting as a business associate, to transact business and handle client matters in the event of a therapist's disability.

Form 7. **Contract for Clinical Supervision.**

Form 8. **Collateral Disclosure Form:** This form contains information for collaterals, when the client has signed a release authorizing the therapist to share confidential treatment information with a collateral, or when the client has signed a release that authorizes a collateral to attend a treatment session. The form discloses to the collateral that the individual is not a counseling client, and that the therapist will not be assessing or treating that person's needs. *See* sections 1.09 and 2.02.

Form 9. **Fee Policy:** This form is for use when therapists agree to testify in court concerning their opinions as to treatment information, whether they agree to testify or receive a subpoena to testify. The therapist needs to fill in the blanks on the form regarding the hourly rate that the therapist charges when asked to prepare a report, or when required to testify either in court or at a deposition.

Form 10. **Policies for CFIs re Communication with Counsel:** In compliance with CJD 04-08, Standard 17, a CFI must send to counsel or pro se parties a statement about how communications with counsel or pro se parties will be arranged and how sensitive information will be handled.

Form 11. **Teletherapy Consent Form:** This explains the teletherapy process and contains information regarding teletherapy. Use of a consent form is recommended by Mental Health Board Policy 30-1. Clients need to sign this Consent Form when they will be receiving teletherapy. Refer to § 6.15 in the book.

Form 1. Motion for Protective Order

<table>
<tr><td>District Court, __________ County, Colorado
Court Address:

Petitioner:

v.
Respondent/Co-Petitioner:</td><td>

▲COURT USE ONLY▲</td></tr>
<tr><td>Attorney or Party Without Attorney

Phone Number: E-mail:
FAX Number: Att. Reg.#:</td><td>Case Number:

Div: Ctr:</td></tr>
<tr><td colspan="2">MOTION FOR PROTECTIVE ORDER</td></tr>
</table>

Pursuant to C.R.S. § 13-90-107(1)(g), ______ moves this Court for a Protective Order, protecting against disclosure of confidential information sought by the Board. This Motion seeks protection against disclosure of any documents sought by the Board, on grounds that any such information of the type requested in the subpoena is personal, private, privileged, and confidential pursuant to the provisions of C.R.S. § 12-245-220 and C.R.S. § 13-90-107. The grounds for issuance of a Protective Order are as follows:

1. All records in the possession of Movant, ________________, are confidential pursuant to the provisions of C.R.S. § 12-245-220, which provides in relevant part:

    12-245-220. Disclosure of confidential communications. (1) A licensee, registrant, or certificate holder shall not disclose, without the consent of the client, any confidential communications made by the client, or advice given to the client, in the course of professional employment. A licensee's, registrant's, or certificate holder's employee or associate, whether clerical or professional, shall not disclose any knowledge of said communications acquired in such capacity. Any person who has participated in any therapy conducted under the supervision of a licensee, registrant, or certificate

> holder, including group therapy sessions, shall not disclose any knowledge gained during the course of such therapy without the consent of the person to whom the knowledge relates.

The legislative intent and public policy supporting confidentiality of mental health records is based upon the premise that participants in such therapy need reassurance that they can disclose information concerning emotional issues and psychological problems within the professional relationship to a psychotherapist, who will not disclose the confidential information shared by the client. *See Jaffee v. Redmond,* 518 U.S. 1, 116 S. Ct. 1923 (1996). In *Jaffee,* the U.S. Supreme Court held that a psychotherapist-client privilege exists, which shall be recognized as an evidentiary privilege under Rule 501 of the Federal Rules of Evidence. The Court's rationale for recognizing such a privilege was expressed as follows:

> Effective psychotherapy ...depends upon an atmosphere of confidence and trust in which the patient is willing to make a frank and complete disclosure of facts, emotions, memories, and fears. Because of the sensitive nature of the problems for which individuals consult psycho therapists, disclosure of confidential communications made during counseling sessions may cause embarrassment or disgrace. For this reason, the mere possibility of disclosure may impede development of the confidential relationship necessary for successful treatment.

Jaffee, 518 U.S. at 10.

2. C.R.S. § 13-90-107(1)(g) provides that a testimonial and evidentiary privilege exists involving communications between psychotherapist and client. This statute provides that "it is the policy of the law to encourage confidence and to preserve it inviolate." This privilege provides that a mental health professional shall not be examined as a witness in the following cases:

    > (g) A licensed psychologist, professional counselor, marriage and family therapist, social worker, or addiction counselor, an unlicensed psychotherapist, a certified addiction counselor, a psychologist candidate registered pursuant to section 12-245-304(3), C.R.S., a marriage and family therapist candidate registered pursuant to section 12-245-504(4), C.R.S., a licensed professional counselor candidate registered pursuant to section 12-245-604(4), C.R.S., or a person described in section 12-245-217, C.R.S., shall not be examined without the consent of the licensee's, certificate holder's, registrant's, candidate's, or person's client as to any communication made by the client to

> the licensee, certificate holder, registrant, candidate, or person or the licensee's, certificate holder's, registrant's, candidate's, or person's advice given in the course of professional employment.

See C.R.S. § 13-90-107(1)(g).

3. Because of the sensitive, personal, and private nature of mental health records, a Protective Order should be entered, protecting against production or disclosure of any documents or records in Movant's possession concerning any of his or her clients.
4. In *Dill v. People*, 927 P.2d 1315 (Colo. 1996), the Colorado Supreme Court discussed issues that are not directly related to this action; however, the court in dicta discussed the confidentiality of psychotherapy records. Citing the decision of the U.S. Supreme Court in *Pennsylvania v. Ritchie*, 480 U.S. 39 (1987), the Colorado Supreme Court observed that there is a strong public interest in protecting the type of sensitive information found in psychotherapy records of the type maintained by the Mental Health Center. In view of the magnitude of this public interest, the Colorado Supreme Court in *Dill* held that no need existed for the court to conduct an *in camera* inspection of notes and records of therapy sessions, requested by a defendant.
5. In *People v. Sisneros*, 55 P.3d 797 (Colo. 2002), the Colorado Supreme Court considered a criminal case in which charges of sexual assault on a minor had been filed and in which the defendant's attorney had issued a subpoena *duces tecum* to the victim's psychologist, demanding that the victim's treatment records be turned over. In its decision, the Colorado Supreme Court discussed the therapist-client privilege set forth in C.R.S. § 13-90-107(1)(g) and ruled that the trial court judge did not have the discretion to order the victim's records to be disclosed, even for the judge's *in camera* review.
6. No client of Movant's has consented to any testimony or disclosure of treatment information. Thus, the provisions of the privilege statute should be enforced, and the Motion for Protective Order submitted by Movant should be granted pursuant to the legal authority discussed above.

Respectfully submitted,

____

CERTIFICATE OF SERVICE

I hereby certify that on this _______ day of _______, 20 _____, a true and correct copy of the above and foregoing was deposited in the United States mail, postage prepaid, addressed to:

____

Form 2. Client Disclosure

DISCLOSURE STATEMENT

1. **INFORMATION**

   Name/Address/Telephone:

2. **CREDENTIALS**

   Licensure: ____________________

   Degrees: ____________________

   Professional Experience: ____________________

   Certifications: ____________________

3. **REGULATION OF PSYCHOTHERAPISTS**

   The practice of licensed or registered persons in the field of psychotherapy is regulated by the Division of Professions and Occupations. The regulatory boards can be reached at 1560 Broadway, Suite 1350, Denver, CO 80202, (303) 894-7800. The regulatory requirements for mental health professionals provide that a Licensed Clinical Social Worker, a Licensed Marriage and Family Therapist, and a Licensed Professional Counselor must hold a master's degree in their profession and have two years of post-masters supervision. A Licensed Psychologist must hold a doctorate degree in psychology and have one year of post-doctoral supervision. A Licensed Social Worker must hold a master's degree in social work. A Psychologist Candidate, a Marriage and Family Therapist Candidate, and a Licensed Professional Counselor Candidate must hold the necessary licensing degree and be in the process of completing the required supervision for licensure. A Certified Addiction Counselor I (CAC I) must be a high school graduate, and complete required training hours and 1,000 hours of supervised experience. A CAC II must complete additional required training hours and 2,000 hours of supervised experience. A CAC III must have a bachelor's degree in behavioral health, and complete additional required training hours and 2,000 hours of supervised experience. A Licensed Addiction Counselor must have a clinical master's degree and meet the CAC III requirements. A Registered Psychotherapist is listed in the State's Database and is authorized by law to practice psychotherapy in Colorado, but is not licensed by the state and is not required to satisfy any standardized educational or testing requirements to obtain a registration from the state.

4. **CLIENT RIGHTS AND IMPORTANT INFORMATION**

a. You are entitled to receive information from me about my methods of therapy, the techniques I use, the duration of your therapy, and my fee. Please ask if you would like to receive this information.

b. You can seek a second opinion from another therapist or terminate therapy at any time.

c. In a professional relationship (such as ours), sexual intimacy between a therapist and a client is never appropriate. If sexual intimacy occurs, it should be reported to the Board that licenses, certifies, or registers the therapist.

d. Generally speaking, information provided by and to a client in a professional relationship with a psychotherapist is legally confidential, and the therapist cannot disclose the information without the client's consent. There are several exceptions to confidentiality, which include: (1) I am required to report any suspected incident of child abuse or neglect to law enforcement; (2) I am required to report any threat of imminent physical harm by a client to law enforcement and to the person(s) threatened; (3) I am required to initiate a mental health evaluation of a client who is imminently dangerous to self or to others, or who is gravely disabled, as a result of a mental disorder; (4) I am required to report any suspected threat to national security to federal officials; (5) I am required to report abuse that I believe has probably occurred to an elder who is 70 years of age or older, or to an at-risk adult with an Intellectual or Developmental Disability (IDD), including institutional neglect, physical injury, financial exploitation, or unreasonable restraint; and (6) I may be required by court order to disclose treatment information.

e. When I am concerned about a client's safety, it is my policy to request a Welfare Check through local law enforcement. In doing so, I may disclose to law enforcement officers information concerning my concerns. By signing this Disclosure Statement and agreeing to treat with me, you consent to this practice, if it should become necessary.

f. Under Colorado law, C.R.S. § 14-10-123.8, parents have the right to access mental health treatment information concerning their minor children, unless the court has restricted access to such information. If you request treatment information from me, I may provide you with a treatment summary, in compliance with Colorado law and HIPAA Standards.

g. I agree not to record our sessions without your written consent; and you agree not to record a session or a conversation with me without my written consent.

5. **DISCLOSURE REGARDING DIVORCE AND CUSTODY LITIGATION**

   If you are involved in divorce or custody litigation, my role as a therapist is not to make recommendations to the court concerning custody or parenting issues. By signing this Disclosure Statement, you agree not to subpoena me to court for testimony or for disclosure of treatment information in such litigation; and you agree not to request that I write any reports to the court or to your attorney, making recommendations concerning custody. The court can appoint professionals, who have no prior relationship with family members, to conduct an investigation or evaluation and to make recommendations to the court concerning parental responsibilities or parenting time in the best interests of the family's children.

6. **CLIENT RECORD RETENTION POLICY**

   My records regarding the treatment of adults will be kept for seven (7) years after treatment ends or following our last session, but I may not retain them after seven years. My records for treatment of minors will be kept for seven (7) years, commencing on the last date of treatment or for seven years from the date when the minor reaches 18 years of age, whichever comes later. In no event am I required to keep these records for longer than 12 years.

7. **INFORMED CONSENT FOR TREATMENT**

   I have read this Disclosure Statement, understand the disclosures that have been made, and acknowledge that a copy of it has been provided to me. I hereby provide consent for treatment of the following client(s): ____________

I have read the preceding information, and it has been presented to me verbally. I understand the disclosures that have been made to me. I also acknowledge that I have received a copy of this Disclosure Statement.

______________________________		______________________________	
Client Signature or Responsible Party	Date	Client Signature or Responsible Party	Date

Form 2a. Surprise Billing Disclosure Form

SURPRISE/BALANCE BILLING DISCLOSURE FORM

Surprise Billing—Know Your Rights

Beginning January 1, 2020, Colorado state law protects you from "surprise billing" also known as "balance billing." These protections apply when:

- You receive covered emergency services, other than ambulance services, from an out-of-network provider in Colorado, and/or
- You unintentionally receive covered services from an out-of-network provider at an in-network facility in Colorado.

What is surprise/balance billing, and when does it happen?

If you are seen by a health care provider or use services in a facility or agency that is not in your health insurance plan's provider network, sometimes referred to as "out-of-network," you may receive a bill for additional costs associated with that care. Out-of-network health care providers often bill you for the difference between what your insurer decides is the eligible charge and what the out-of-network provider bills as the total charge. This is called "surprise" or "balance" billing.

When you CANNOT be balance billed:

Emergency Services

If you are receiving emergency services, the most you can be billed for is your plan's In-network cost-sharing amounts, which are copayments, deductibles, and/or coinsurance. You cannot be balance-billed for any other amount. This includes both the emergency facility where you receive emergency services and any providers that see you for emergency care.

Nonemergency Services at an In-Network or Out-of-Network Health Care Provider

The health care provider must tell you if you are at an out-of-network location or at an in-network location that is using out-of-network providers. They must also tell you what types of services that you will be using may be provided by any out-of-network provider.

You have the right to request that in-network providers perform all covered medical services. However, you may have to receive medical services from an out-of-network provider if an in-network provider is not available. In this case, the most you can be billed for covered services is your in-network cost-sharing amount, which is copayments, deductibles, and/or coinsurance. These providers cannot balance bill you for additional costs.

Additional Protections

- Your insurer will pay out-of-network providers and facilities directly.
- Your insurer must count any amount you pay for emergency services or certain out-of-network services (described above) toward your in-network deductible and out-of-pocket limit.
- Your provider, facility, hospital, or agency must refund any amount you overpay within sixty days of being notified.
- No one, including a provider, hospital, or insurer can ask you to limit or give up these rights.

If you receive services from an out-of-network provider or facility or agency OTHER situation, you may still be balance billed, or you may be responsible for the entire bill. If you intentionally receive nonemergency service from an out-of-network provider or facility, you may also be balance billed.

If you want to file a complaint against your health care provider, you can submit an online complaint by visiting this website: www.colorado.gov/pacific/dora/DPO File Complaint.

If you think you have received a bill for amounts other than your copayments, deductible, and/or coinsurance, please contact the billing department, or the Colorado Division of Insurance at 303-894-7490 or 1-800-930-3745.

*This law does NOT apply to ALL Colorado health plans. It only applies if you have a "CO-DOI" on your health insurance ID card.

Please contact your health insurance plan at the number on your health insurance ID card or the Colorado Division of Insurance with questions.

____________________________ ________________________

Signature of Client Date

Form 3-1. HIPAA Privacy Statement

NAME OF COMPANY

HIPAA DISCLOSURES RE CONFIDENTIAL INFORMATION

THIS NOTICE CONTAINS INFORMATION CONCERNING HOW CONFIDENTIAL MENTAL HEALTH TREATMENT INFORMATION CONCERNING YOU MAY BE USED AND DISCLOSED AND HOW YOU CAN OBTAIN ACCESS TO THIS INFORMATION. PLEASE REVIEW IT CAREFULLY AND LET US KNOW ANY QUESTIONS THAT YOU MAY HAVE CONCERNING THIS NOTICE. During the process of providing services to you, **[NAME OF COMPANY]** will obtain and use mental health and medical information concerning you that is both confidential and privileged. Ordinarily this confidential information will be used in the manner that is described in this statement, and will not be disclosed without your consent, except for the circumstances described in this Notice.

I. USES AND DISCLOSURES OF PROTECTED INFORMATION

A. General Uses and Disclosures Not Requiring the Client's Consent. **[NAME & ADDRESS OF COMPANY]** will use and disclose protected health information in the following ways.

1. *Treatment.* Treatment refers to the provision, coordination, or management of mental health care and related services by one or more health care providers. For example, **[NAME OF COMPANY]** therapists and staff involved with your care may use your information to plan your course of treatment and consult with other health care professionals or their staff concerning services needed or provided to you.

2. *Payment.* Payment refers to the activities undertaken by a health care provider to obtain or provide reimbursement for the provision of health care. For example, **[NAME OF COMPANY]** and other health care professionals will use information that identifies you, including information concerning your diagnosis, services provided to you, dates of services, and services needed by you, and may disclose such information to insurance companies and to businesses that review bills for health care services and handle claims for payment of health care benefits in order to obtain payment for services. If you are covered by Medicaid, information may be provided to the State of Colorado's Medicaid program, including but not limited to your treatment, condition, diagnosis, and services received.

3. *Health Care Operations.* Health Care Operations means activities undertaken by health insurance companies, businesses that administer health plans, and companies that review bills for health care services in order to process claims for health care benefits. These functions include management and administrative activities. For example, such companies may use your health information in monitoring of service quality, staff training and evaluation, medical reviews, legal services, auditing functions, compliance programs, business planning and accreditation, certification, and licensing and credentialing activities.

4. *Contacting the Client.* **[NAME OF COMPANY]** may contact you to remind you of appointments and to tell you about treatments or other services that might be of benefit to you.

5. *Required by Law.* **[NAME OF COMPANY]** will disclose protected health information when required by law. This includes, but is not limited to: (a) reporting child abuse or neglect to the Department of Human Services or to law enforcement; (b) when court ordered to release information; (c) when there is a legal duty to warn of a threat that a client has made of imminent physical violence, health care professionals are required to notify the potential victim of such a threat, and report it to law enforcement; (d) when a client is imminently dangerous to herself/himself or to others, or is gravely disabled, health care professionals may have a duty to hospitalize the client in order to obtain a 72-hour evaluation of the client; and (e) when required to report a threat to the national security of the United States.

6. *Health Oversight Activities.* Your confidential, protected health information may be disclosed to health oversight agencies for oversight activities authorized by law and necessary for the oversight of the health care system, government health care benefit programs, regulatory programs or determining compliance with program standards.

7. *Crimes on the premises or observed by* **[NAME OF COMPANY]** *personnel.* Crimes that are observed by **[NAME OF COMPANY]** staff, that are directed toward staff, or occur on **[NAME OF COMPANY]** premises will be reported to law enforcement.

8. *Business Associates.* Confidential health care information concerning you provided to insurers or to plans for purposes of payment for services that you receive may be disclosed to business associates. For example, some administrative, clinical, quality assurance, billing, legal, auditing and practice management services may be provided by contracting with outside entities to perform those services. In those situations, protected health information will be provided to those

contractors as is needed to perform their contracted tasks. Business associates are required to enter into an agreement maintaining the privacy of the protected health information released to them.

9. *Research.* Protected health information concerning you may be used with your permission for research purposes if the relevant provisions of the Federal HIPAA Privacy Regulations are followed.

10. *Involuntary Clients.* Information regarding clients who are being treated involuntarily, pursuant to law, will be shared with other treatment providers, legal entities, third-party payers and others, as necessary to provide the care and management coordination needed in compliance with Colorado law.

11. *Family Members.* Except for certain minors, incompetent clients, or involuntary clients, protected health information cannot be provided to family members without the client's consent. In situations where family members are present during a discussion with the client, and it can be reasonably inferred from the circumstances that the client does not object, information may be disclosed in the course of that discussion. However, if the client objects, protected health information will not be disclosed.

12. *Emergencies.* In life threatening emergencies **[NAME OF COMPANY]** staff will disclose information necessary to avoid serious harm or death.

B. Client Release of Information or Authorization. **[NAME OF COMPANY]** and other health care professionals may not use or disclose protected health information in any way without a signed release of information or authorization. When you sign a release of information or an authorization, it may later be revoked, provided that the revocation is in writing. The revocation will apply, except to the extent **[NAME OF COMPANY]** has already taken action in reliance thereon.

II. YOUR RIGHTS AS A CLIENT

A. Access to Protected Health Information. You have the right to receive a summary of confidential health information concerning you concerning mental health services needed or provided to you. There are some limitations to this right, which will be provided to you at the time of your request, if any such limitation applies. To make a request, ask **[NAME OF COMPANY]** staff for the appropriate request form.

B. Amendment of Your Record. You have the right to request that **[NAME OF COMPANY]** or your health care professionals amend your protected health information. **[NAME OF COMPANY]** is not required to amend the record if it is determined that the record is accurate and complete. There are other exceptions, which will be provided to you at the time of your request, if relevant, along with the appeal process available to you. To make a request, ask **[NAME OF COMPANY]** staff for the appropriate request form.

C. Accounting of Disclosures. You have the right to receive an accounting of certain disclosures **[NAME OF COMPANY]** has made regarding your protected health information. However, that accounting does not include disclosures that were made for the purpose of treatment, payment, or health care operations. In addition, the accounting does not include disclosures made to you, disclosures made pursuant to a signed Authorization, or disclosures made prior to April 14, 2003. There are other exceptions that will be provided to you, should you request an accounting. To make a request, ask **[NAME OF COMPANY]** staff for the appropriate request form.

D. Additional Restrictions. You have the right to request additional restrictions on the use or disclosure of your health information. **[NAME OF COMPANY]** does not have to agree to that request, and there are certain limits to any restriction, which will be provided to you at the time of your request. To make a request, ask **[NAME OF COMPANY]** staff for the appropriate request form.

E. Alternative Means of Receiving Confidential Communications. You have the right to request that you receive communications of protected health information from **[NAME OF COMPANY]** by alternative means or at alternative locations. For example, if you do not want **[NAME OF COMPANY]** to mail bills or other materials to your home, you can request that this information be sent to another address. There are limitations to the granting of such requests, which will be provided to you at the time of the request process. To make a request, ask **[NAME OF COMPANY]** staff for the appropriate request form.

F. Copy of this Notice. You have a right to obtain another copy of this Notice upon request.

III. NOTICE REGARDING USE OF TECHNOLOGY

1. *E-mail Communications.* Unencrypted e-mail may not be confidential, and any information regarding protected health information sent by e-mail may not be confidential.

2. *Skype, Facetime, or Other Similar Videoconferencing Technology.* Communication through Skype or Facetime may not be confidential.

3. *Internet Communications.* Counseling or communication through the Internet may not be confidential.

4. *Storage of Health Care Information.* Health care records and information maintained on the cloud may not be confidential, depending on the number of servers involved.

5. *Voicemail.* Telephone messages left through voicemail may not be confidential, if they may be accessed by individuals other than the client. Please let me know if you do **not** want me to use voicemail in contacting you.

6. *Facsimile Communication.* The submission of health care information or records by fax may not be confidential, and may lead to a disclosure of confidential information to third parties if the wrong fax number is used to send the information.

7. *Communication by U.S. Mail.* Communication of information by U.S. mail may lead to disclosure of private information to third parties, depending on who may open the mail. Please let me know if you do **not** want me to send you correspondence, billing invoices, or other information through the U.S. mail.

IV. ADDITIONAL INFORMATION

A. Privacy Laws. **[NAME OF COMPANY]** is required by State and Federal law to maintain the privacy of protected health information. In addition, **[NAME OF COMPANY]** is required by law to provide clients with notice of its legal duties and privacy practices with respect to protected health information. That is the purpose of this Notice.

B. Terms of the Notice and Changes to the Notice. **[NAME OF COMPANY]** is required to abide by the terms of this Notice, or any amended Notice that may follow. **[NAME OF COMPANY]** reserves the right to change the terms of its Notice and to make the new Notice provisions effective for all protected health information that it maintains. When the Notice is revised, the revised Notice will be posted in **[NAME OF COMPANY]**'s service delivery sites and will be available upon request.

C. Complaints Regarding Privacy Rights. If you believe **[NAME OF COMPANY]** has violated your privacy rights, you have the right to complain to **[NAME OF COMPANY]** management. Please submit a statement, in writing, addressed to **[NAME & ADDRESS OF COMPANY]**, concerning your complaint and the basis for it. You also have the right to complain to the United States Secretary of Health and Human Services by sending your complaint to the Office of Civil Rights, U.S. Department of Health and Human Services, 200 Independence Avenue, S.W., Room 515F, HHH Bldg., Washington, D.C. 20201. It is the policy of **[NAME OF COMPANY]** that there will be no retaliation for your filing of such complaints.

D. Additional Information. If you desire additional information about your privacy rights at **[NAME OF COMPANY]**, please ask us any questions that you may have.

V. CONFIDENTIALITY OF ALCOHOL AND DRUG ABUSE PATIENT RECORDS

A. The confidentiality of alcohol and drug abuse patient records maintained by **[NAME OF COMPANY]** is protected by federal law and regulations. Generally, the program may not say to a person outside the program that a patient attends the program, or disclose any information identifying a patient as an alcohol or drug abuser unless:

1. The patient consents in writing;
2. The disclosure is allowed by a court order; or
3. The disclosure is made to medical personnel in a medical emergency or to qualified personnel for research, audit, or program evaluation.

B. Violation of the federal law and regulations by a program is a crime. Suspected violations may be reported to appropriate authorities in accordance with federal regulations.

C. Federal law and regulations do not protect any information about a crime committed by a patient either at the program or against any person who works for the program or about any threat to commit such a crime. Disclosure may be made concerning any threat made by a client to commit imminent physical violence against another person to the potential victim who has been threatened and to law enforcement.

D. Federal law and regulations do not protect any information about suspected child abuse or neglect from being reported under state law to appropriate state or local authorities.

VI. EFFECTIVE DATE, THIS NOTICE IS EFFECTIVE ______________, 2____.

I understand these disclosures. I have received a copy of this Disclosure Statement and Notice of Privacy Rights.

____

Client Signature

Form 3-2. HIPAA Business Associate Contract

[letterhead]

HIPAA BUSINESS ASSOCIATE CONTRACT

This agreement serves as a binding, legal contract between ______________ (Health Care Professional) and ______________________ (Business Associate).

1. Business Associate agrees not to use or disclose protected health information, other than as permitted by this agreement or as required by law.

2. Business Associate agrees to use appropriate safeguards to maintain the security of confidential treatment information, communicated to Associate by Professional.

3. Business Associate agrees to use confidential health information only for the specific purpose for which such information is communicated to Associate by Professional.

4. Business Associate agrees to establish internal practices and procedures to safeguard the confidentiality of protected health information. Associate acknowledges that mental health treatment information is confidential, and is privileged information. Associate understands that even the identity of the client in a therapist-client relationship is confidential.

5. Business Associate agrees not to use confidential treatment information for any purpose other than the purpose authorized by the client whom the information concerns.

6. Business Associate agrees to request specific instructions from Professional if any questions exist concerning the proper use of confidential treatment information, which is transmitted from Professional to Associate.

7. Business Associate agrees to hold harmless and indemnify Professional for any damages incurred by the client, in the event that Business Associate discloses confidential treatment information in an unauthorized manner.

8. This agreement shall be effective, beginning on the _______ day of ________, 20__, and shall terminate when all of the protected health information provided by Professional to Associate has been destroyed or returned to the Professional.

9. In the event that Professional receives information concerning a breach of this agreement by the Associate, Professional shall either provide an opportunity for Associate to cure the breach, or Professional shall terminate this agreement and any business relationship between the parties to this agreement. In the event of termination of the business relationship between these parties, Associate agrees to the immediate return of all confidential health information in its possession to Professional.

____
Authorized Representative, Business Associate

____
Health Care Professional

Form 3-3. Accounting of Disclosures

ACCOUNTING OF DISCLOSURES

Keep the original of this form in the client record and update it each time information about the client is shared with someone outside this office/agency. When the client asks for an accounting of disclosures, copy this form and give the client the copy.

Client Name: ____

Last First Middle Initial

Client Date of Birth: ________________

Month/Day/Year

Disclosures of Protected Health Information about this Client:

Date of Disclosure	Name of Recipient	Address of Recipient	Information Disclosed	Purpose of Disclosure

Form 3-4. Request for Confidential Treatment Information

REQUEST FOR CONFIDENTIAL TREATMENT INFORMATION

Client Name: ______________________________ Date of Birth: __________
Client Number: ____
Client Address: ____
____

Information requested:

____
____
____

Date requested: ________________

Signature: ________________________

For Health Care Organization Use Only:

Date received ________________ Request has been Accepted Denied

If denied, check reason for denial:

☐ Confidential treatment information was not created by this organization.

☐ Confidential treatment information is not a part of patient's designated record set.

☐ Confidential treatment information is not available to the patient for inspection as required by federal law.

☐ Confidential treatment information may be obtained from:

____

____

____

Signature: ________________________

Form 3-5. Authorization to Disclose Protected Mental Health Information

AUTHORIZATION TO DISCLOSE PROTECTED MENTAL HEALTH INFORMATION

Patient Name:	SSN:
Address:	Birth Date:
Telephone:	Identity Code:

Health Care Information From:	Release to:

I authorize the above-named health care provider to disclose the privileged information specified below to the organization, agency, or individual named on this request:

INFORMATION REQUESTED:

Place/Dates of Service

Kind and amount of information to be disclosed

Purpose of disclosure/why information required

I understand that the information to be disclosed may include any or all information involving communicable or venereal disease, psychological or psychiatric conditions, and drug or alcohol abuse and/or alcoholism. It may also include, but is not limited to, diseases such as hepatitis, syphilis, gonorrhea, and human immunodeficiency viruses (HIV), also known as acquired immune deficiency syndrome (AIDS).

AUTHORIZATION: I certify that this request is made voluntarily and that the information given above is accurate to the best of my knowledge. I understand that I may revoke this authorization at any time in writing by sending a letter to the facility privacy officer or their designee and that it will expire at the end of litigation involving me. I understand my revocation will not be effective to the extent that action has already been taken in reliance on it. **This authorization expires six months from date of patient's or representative's signature below, unless otherwise specified:** ________________________. If I have authorized disclosure of my health information to someone who is not legally required to keep it private, it may be re-disclosed and may no longer be protected. A copy or fax of this authorization will be valid as the original.

I understand that authorization of disclosure of health information is voluntary. I understand that I may refuse to sign this authorization and that my refusal to sign will not affect my ability to obtain treatment, payment, or eligibility to obtain benefits. I understand that I may inspect or obtain a copy of the information to be disclosed. I understand a fee will be charged for any copy of my health record. I understand the facility will provide me a copy of the signed authorization form. If I have questions about disclosure of my health information, I can contact the facility privacy officer or their designee.

Signature: ______________________________________ Date: ____________

Patient (Parent or Guardian if patient is a minor)

Minor's signature is required for release of any records for treatment that the minor may have authorized.

RELATIONSHIP (if other than patient): ______________________________

IDENTIFICATION OF PATIENT OR DESIGNATED REPRESENTATIVE

☐ Drivers License # ____________________ ☐ Passport # __________________

☐ State ID # __________________________ ☐ Other ID # __________________

Form 4. Form M-1

FORM M-1
EMERGENCY MENTAL ILLNESS REPORT AND APPLICATION

Date ______________________ Time ____________

NAME ________________________________, hereafter referred to as Respondent.
Address ____
Date of Birth __________________

Place of Contact ____, Colorado.
Previous Psychiatric Care ____
Where When

Who brought respondent's condition to the attention of the undersigned?

Nearest relative ____
Name Address Phone

APPEARANCE AND GENERAL BEHAVIOR (Circle Items That Apply):

DRESS—Neat, Untidy, Dirty, Eccentric

POSTURE—Erect, Tense, Relaxed, Lying down

FACIAL EXPRESSION—Fixed, Changing, Angry, Perplexed, Sad, Happy, Suspicious

PHYSICAL ACTIVITY—Normal, Underactive, Overactive

EMOTIONAL REACTION (Circle Items That Apply):

ATTITUDE—Composed, Polite, Cooperative, Reserved, Indifferent, Silent, Scared, Sad, Happy, Carefree, Cocky, Hilarious, Excited, Angry, Sarcastic, Antagonistic, Suspicious, Insulting, Profane, Combative, Sleepy

TALK (Circle Items That Apply):

FORM—Logical, Conversational, Illogical, Rambling, Nonsensical

RATE—Normal, Over-talkative, Under-talkative

QUALITY—Controlled, Humorous, Dramatic, Forceful, Shouting, Screaming, Mumbling

EXPRESSIONS (Circle Items That Apply):

Ideas of Being Persecuted, Feels People Are Watching Him/Talking About Him, Ideas of Grandeur, Strange or Bizarre Physical Complaints, Very Self-Critical, Hearing Voices, Seeing Things, Homicidal Thoughts, Suicidal Thoughts, Unusual Sexual Ideas

DOES PATIENT KNOW (Circle Items That Apply):

Who he is? (Yes No), Where he is? (Yes No), Date? (Yes No),

How he feels? (Yes No)

Counting from 20 to 1 Backwards—Result: Good Fair Poor

GENERAL KNOWLEDGE (Circle Items That Apply):

President? (Yes No), Governor? (Yes No), Mayor? (Yes No)

Pursuant to the provisions of C.R.S. § 27-65-105, as amended, the respondent was taken into custody by the undersigned and detained for 72-hour treatment and evaluation at ______ (designated or approved facility).

The respondent appears to be mentally ill and, as a result of such mental illness, appears to be *an imminent danger to others or to himself or herself* gravely disabled*. The circumstances under which the undersigned believes there is probable cause leading to the above action are as follows:

____

____

* Strike between asterisks if inapplicable.

List any property owned by subject that may be jeopardized by his or her detention:

Location: ______________________

____

Location: ______________________

____

____

Signature

Ser./Colo. License No. ________________

____

Officer/Professional Person

____

Signature

Ser./Colo. License No. ________________

____

Officer/Professional Person

NOTICE TO RESPONDENT

C.R.S. § 27-65-105(3), provides that if the evaluation and treatment facility to which you are admitted does not have evaluation and treatment services available on Saturdays, Sundays, or holidays, then the facility may exclude those days in calculating the 72-hour detention period.

Original to facility

Copy to respondent

Copy to records

Form 5. Disclosures for Forensic Evaluation

DISCLOSURES FOR FORENSIC EVALUATION

A. EVALUATOR

Name ____________________

Address ____________________

Telephone ____________________

Fax ____________________

E-mail ____________________

B. EVALUATOR'S CREDENTIALS

1. Professional Education ____________________
2. Licensure ____________________
3. Degrees ____________________

   Professional Experience ____________________

   Professional Associations ____________________

C. ROLE OF THE EVALUATOR

I have been requested to conduct an evaluation of you and to prepare a report concerning my evaluation. All information that you provide to me including sensitive, personal information will not be confidential, because it will be shared with others, including the court. This evaluation has been requested by __________ (Requesting Authority).

Although I am a healthcare provider by training and experience, the purpose of my evaluation will not be to provide treatment for you. We do not have, and will not have, a professional relationship with one another. I want to make it clear that I will not be providing treatment for you, and I will have no duty to make referrals for you to healthcare providers, just as I will not have a duty to make treatment recommendations for you.

D. PROCESS

The evaluation that I will be conducting will probably include a review of records concerning you and an interview of you, and may include testing. I will then prepare a report, which will be submitted to the Requesting Authority. My report will be used by the court to make any necessary determinations. Any fees for my professional services will be paid by _____. If you have specific questions concerning how the information that I obtain will be used or concerning who may receive a copy of my report, please let me know, and I will try to answer your questions. You are not entitled to a copy of my report unless the court orders that it be provided to you.

E. REPORTING REQUIREMENTS

I am required to report any suspected child abuse or neglect to the local county Department of Social Services or to law enforcement, unless the suspected abuse or neglect has already been reported. If you make a threat to harm any person, I am required to notify the person threatened and also to report the threat to law enforcement.

By signing this document, you are acknowledging that you understand the disclosures that have been made in it, that you understand my role as an evaluator, and that you understand how this evaluation or my report will be used.

_______________________ _______________________________

DATE **SIGNATURE**

Health Insurance Claim Form

PLEASE DO NOT STAPLE IN THIS AREA

[redacted]

APPROVED OMB-0938-0008

CARRIER

PICA **HEALTH INSURANCE CLAIM FORM** PICA

1. MEDICARE (Medicare #) MEDICAID (Medicaid #) CHAMPUS (Sponsor's SSN) CHAMPVA (VA File #) GROUP HEALTH PLAN (SSN or ID) FECA BLK LUNG (SSN) OTHER (ID)

1a. INSURED'S I.D. NUMBER (FOR PROGRAM IN ITEM 1)

2. PATIENT'S NAME (Last Name, First Name, Middle Initial)

3. PATIENT'S BIRTH DATE MM DD YY SEX M F

4. INSURED'S NAME (Last Name, First Name, Middle Initial)

5. PATIENT'S ADDRESS (No., Street)

6. PATIENT RELATIONSHIP TO INSURED Self Spouse Child Other

7. INSURED'S ADDRESS (No., Street)

CITY STATE

8. PATIENT STATUS Single Married Other

CITY STATE

ZIP CODE TELEPHONE (Include Area Code) ( )

Employed Full-Time Student Part-Time Student

ZIP CODE TELEPHONE (INCLUDE AREA CODE) ( )

9. OTHER INSURED'S NAME (Last Name, First Name, Middle Initial)

10. IS PATIENT'S CONDITION RELATED TO:

11. INSURED'S POLICY GROUP OR FECA NUMBER

a. OTHER INSURED'S POLICY OR GROUP NUMBER

a. EMPLOYMENT? (CURRENT OR PREVIOUS) YES NO

a. INSURED'S DATE OF BIRTH MM DD YY SEX M F

b. OTHER INSURED'S DATE OF BIRTH MM DD YY SEX M F

b. AUTO ACCIDENT? YES NO PLACE (State)

b. EMPLOYER'S NAME OR SCHOOL NAME

c. EMPLOYER'S NAME OR SCHOOL NAME

c. OTHER ACCIDENT? YES NO

c. INSURANCE PLAN NAME OR PROGRAM NAME

d. INSURANCE PLAN NAME OR PROGRAM NAME

10d. RESERVED FOR LOCAL USE

d. IS THERE ANOTHER HEALTH BENEFIT PLAN? YES NO *If yes, return to and complete item 9 a-d.*

READ BACK OF FORM BEFORE COMPLETING & SIGNING THIS FORM.

12. PATIENT'S OR AUTHORIZED PERSON'S SIGNATURE I authorize the release of any medical or other information necessary to process this claim. I also request payment of government benefits either to myself or to the party who accepts assignment below.

SIGNED DATE

13. INSURED'S OR AUTHORIZED PERSON'S SIGNATURE I authorize payment of medical benefits to the undersigned physician or supplier for services described below.

SIGNED

PATIENT AND INSURED INFORMATION

14. DATE OF CURRENT: MM DD YY ILLNESS (First symptom) OR INJURY (Accident) OR PREGNANCY(LMP)

15. IF PATIENT HAS HAD SAME OR SIMILAR ILLNESS. GIVE FIRST DATE MM DD YY

16. DATES PATIENT UNABLE TO WORK IN CURRENT OCCUPATION FROM MM DD YY TO MM DD YY

17. NAME OF REFERRING PHYSICIAN OR OTHER SOURCE

17a. I.D. NUMBER OF REFERRING PHYSICIAN

18. HOSPITALIZATION DATES RELATED TO CURRENT SERVICES FROM MM DD YY TO MM DD YY

19. RESERVED FOR LOCAL USE

20. OUTSIDE LAB? YES NO $ CHARGES

21. DIAGNOSIS OR NATURE OF ILLNESS OR INJURY. (RELATE ITEMS 1,2,3 OR 4 TO ITEM 24E BY LINE)

1. ___ . ___ 3. ___ . ___

2. ___ . ___ 4. ___ . ___

22. MEDICAID RESUBMISSION CODE ORIGINAL REF. NO.

23. PRIOR AUTHORIZATION NUMBER

24. A DATE(S) OF SERVICE From MM DD YY	To MM DD YY	B Place of Service	C Type of Service	D PROCEDURES, SERVICES, OR SUPPLIES (Explain Unusual Circumstances) CPT/HCPCS MODIFIER	E DIAGNOSIS CODE	F $ CHARGES	G DAYS OR UNITS	H EPSDT Family Plan	I EMG	J COB	K RESERVED FOR LOCAL USE
1											
2											
3											
4											
5											
6											

25. FEDERAL TAX I.D. NUMBER SSN EIN

26. PATIENT'S ACCOUNT NO.

27. ACCEPT ASSIGNMENT? (For govt. claims, see back) YES NO

28. TOTAL CHARGE $

29. AMOUNT PAID $

30. BALANCE DUE $

31. SIGNATURE OF PHYSICIAN OR SUPPLIER INCLUDING DEGREES OR CREDENTIALS (I certify that the statements on the reverse apply to this bill and are made a part thereof.)

SIGNED DATE

32. NAME AND ADDRESS OF FACILITY WHERE SERVICES WERE RENDERED (If other than home or office)

33. PHYSICIAN'S, SUPPLIER'S BILLING NAME, ADDRESS, ZIP CODE & PHONE #

PIN# GRP#

PHYSICIAN OR SUPPLIER INFORMATION

(APPROVED BY AMA COUNCIL ON MEDICAL SERVICE 8/88) *PLEASE PRINT OR TYPE* FORM HCFA-1500 (12-90), FORM RRB-1500, FORM OWCP-1500

BECAUSE THIS FORM IS USED BY VARIOUS GOVERNMENT AND PRIVATE HEALTH PROGRAMS, SEE SEPARATE INSTRUCTIONS ISSUED BY APPLICABLE PROGRAMS.

NOTICE: Any person who knowingly files a statement of claim containing any misrepresentation or any false, incomplete or misleading information may be guilty of a criminal act punishable under law and may be subject to civil penalties.

REFERS TO GOVERNMENT PROGRAMS ONLY

MEDICARE AND CHAMPUS PAYMENTS: A patient's signature requests that payment be made and authorizes release of any information necessary to process the claim and certifies that the information provided in Blocks 1 through 12 is true, accurate and complete. In the case of a Medicare claim, the patient's signature authorizes any entity to release to Medicare medical and nonmedical information, including employment status, and whether the person has employer group health insurance, liability, no-fault, worker's compensation or other insurance which is responsible to pay for the services for which the Medicare claim is made. See 42 CFR 411.24(a). If item 9 is completed, the patient's signature authorizes release of the information to the health plan or agency shown. In Medicare assigned or CHAMPUS participation cases, the physician agrees to accept the charge determination of the Medicare carrier or CHAMPUS fiscal intermediary as the full charge, and the patient is responsible only for the deductible, coinsurance and noncovered services. Coinsurance and the deductible are based upon the charge determination of the Medicare carrier or CHAMPUS fiscal intermediary if this is less than the charge submitted. CHAMPUS is not a health insurance program but makes payment for health benefits provided through certain affiliations with the Uniformed Services. Information on the patient's sponsor should be provided in those items captioned in "Insured"; i.e., items 1a, 4, 6, 7, 9, and 11.

BLACK LUNG AND FECA CLAIMS

The provider agrees to accept the amount paid by the Government as payment in full. See Black Lung and FECA instructions regarding required procedure and diagnosis coding systems.

SIGNATURE OF PHYSICIAN OR SUPPLIER (MEDICARE, CHAMPUS, FECA AND BLACK LUNG)

I certify that the services shown on this form were medically indicated and necessary for the health of the patient and were personally furnished by me or were furnished incident to my professional service by my employee under my immediate personal supervision, except as otherwise expressly permitted by Medicare or CHAMPUS regulations.

For services to be considered as "incident" to a physician's professional service, 1) they must be rendered under the physician's immediate personal supervision by his/her employee, 2) they must be an integral, although incidental part of a covered physician's service, 3) they must be of kinds commonly furnished in physician's offices, and 4) the services of nonphysicians must be included on the physician's bills.

For CHAMPUS claims, I further certify that I (or any employee) who rendered services am not an active duty member of the Uniformed Services or a civilian employee of the United States Government or a contract employee of the United States Government, either civilian or military (refer to 5 USC 5536). For Black-Lung claims, I further certify that the services performed were for a Black Lung-related disorder.

No Part B Medicare benefits may be paid unless this form is received as required by existing law and regulations (42 CFR 424.32).

NOTICE: Any one who misrepresents or falsifies essential information to receive payment from Federal funds requested by this form may upon conviction be subject to fine and imprisonment under applicable Federal laws.

NOTICE TO PATIENT ABOUT THE COLLECTION AND USE OF MEDICARE, CHAMPUS, FECA, AND BLACK LUNG INFORMATION (PRIVACY ACT STATEMENT)

We are authorized by HCFA, CHAMPUS and OWCP to ask you for information needed in the administration of the Medicare, CHAMPUS, FECA, and Black Lung programs. Authority to collect information is in section 205(a), 1862, 1872 and 1874 of the Social Security Act as amended, 42 CFR 411.24(a) and 424.5(a) (6), and 44 USC 3101;41 CFR 101 et seq and 10 USC 1079 and 1086; 5 USC 8101 et seq; and 30 USC 901 et seq; 38 USC 613; E.O. 9397.

The information we obtain to complete claims under these programs is used to identify you and to determine your eligibility. It is also used to decide if the services and supplies you received are covered by these programs and to insure that proper payment is made.

The information may also be given to other providers of services, carriers, intermediaries, medical review boards, health plans, and other organizations or Federal agencies, for the effective administration of Federal provisions that require other third parties payers to pay primary to Federal program, and as otherwise necessary to administer these programs. For example, it may be necessary to disclose information about the benefits you have used to a hospital or doctor. Additional disclosures are made through routine uses for information contained in systems of records.

FOR MEDICARE CLAIMS: See the notice modifying system No. 09-70-0501, titled, 'Carrier Medicare Claims Record,' published in the Federal Register, Vol. 55 No. 177, page 37549, Wed. Sept. 12, 1990, or as updated and republished.

FOR OWCP CLAIMS: Department of Labor, Privacy Act of 1974, "Republication of Notice of Systems of Records," Federal Register Vol. 55 No. 40, Wed Feb. 28, 1990, See ESA-5, ESA-6, ESA-12, ESA-13, ESA-30, or as updated and republished.

FOR CHAMPUS CLAIMS: PRINCIPLE PURPOSE(S): To evaluate eligibility for medical care provided by civilian sources and to issue payment upon establishment of eligibility and determination that the services/supplies received are authorized by law.

ROUTINE USE(S): Information from claims and related documents may be given to the Dept. of Veterans Affairs, the Dept. of Health and Human Services and/or the Dept. of Transportation consistent with their statutory administrative responsibilities under CHAMPUS/CHAMPVA; to the Dept. of Justice for representation of the Secretary of Defense in civil actions; to the Internal Revenue Service, private collection agencies, and consumer reporting agencies in connection with recoupment claims; and to Congressional Offices in response to inquiries made at the request of the person to whom a record pertains. Appropriate disclosures may be made to other federal, state, local, foreign government agencies, private business entities, and individual providers of care, on matters relating to entitlement, claims adjudication, fraud, program abuse, utilization review, quality assurance, peer review, program integrity, third-party liability, coordination of benefits, and civil and criminal litigation related to the operation of CHAMPUS.

DISCLOSURES: Voluntary; however, failure to provide information will result in delay in payment or may result in denial of claim. With the one exception discussed below, there are no penalties under these programs for refusing to supply information. However, failure to furnish information regarding the medical services rendered or the amount charged would prevent payment of claims under these programs. Failure to furnish any other information, such as name or claim number, would delay payment of the claim. Failure to provide medical information under FECA could be deemed an obstruction.

It is mandatory that you tell us if you know that another party is responsible for paying for your treatment. Section 1128B of the Social Security Act and 31 USC 3801-3812 provide penalties for withholding this information.

You should be aware that P.L. 100-503, the "Computer Matching and Privacy Protection Act of 1988", permits the government to verify information by way of computer matches.

MEDICAID PAYMENTS (PROVIDER CERTIFICATION)

I hereby agree to keep such records as are necessary to disclose fully the extent of services provided to individuals under the State's Title XIX plan and to furnish information regarding any payments claimed for providing such services as the State Agency or Dept. of Health and Humans Services may request.

I further agree to accept, as payment in full, the amount paid by the Medicaid program for those claims submitted for payment under that program, with the exception of authorized deductible, coinsurance, co-payment or similar cost-sharing charge.

SIGNATURE OF PHYSICIAN (OR SUPPLIER): I certify that the services listed above were medically indicated and necessary to the health of this patient and were personally furnished by me or my employee under my personal direction.

NOTICE: This is to certify that the foregoing information is true, accurate and complete. I understand that payment and satisfaction of this claim will be from Federal and State funds, and that any false claims, statements, or documents, or concealment of a material fact, may be prosecuted under applicable Federal or State laws.

Public reporting burden for this collection of information is estimated to average 15 minutes per response, including time for reviewing instructions, searching existing date sources, gathering and maintaining data needed, and completing and reviewing the collection of information. Send comments regarding this burden estimate or any other aspect of this collection of information, including suggestions for reducing the burden, to HCFA, Office of Financial Management, P.O. Box 26684, Baltimore, MD 21207; and to the Office of Management and Budget, Paperwork Reduction Project (OMB-0938-0008), Washington, D.C. 20503.

Form 6. Professional Will

PROFESSIONAL WILL

I, ______________________________, a resident of the County of ______________, State of ______________, being of sound and disposing mind and memory, declare this to be my Professional Will. This supersedes all prior Professional Wills, if there are any. **This is not a substitute for a Personal Last Will and Testament.** It is intended to give authority and instructions to my Professional Executor regarding my counseling practice in the event of my incapacitation or death.

FIRST

I am a therapist in independent practice. My __________ License # is ________.
My office address is ____.
I also maintain an office at ____.

SECOND

In the event of my death or incapacitation, I appoint ____________________, whose phone number is ____________________ and whose office is located at ________________________________ as my Professional Executor.

In the event that ____________________ is unavailable or unable to perform this function, I appoint ___________ whose phone number is ____ and whose office is located at ________________________ as a backup Professional Executor.

I grant my Professional Executors full authority to:

a. Act on my behalf in making decisions about storing, releasing, and disposing of my professional records.

b. Carry out any activities deemed necessary to properly administer this Professional Will.

c. Delegate and authorize other persons to assist and carry out any activities deemed necessary to properly administer this Professional Will.

THIRD

My attorney for my Professional Will is ______________________, whose phone number is __________________ and whose office is located at ___________.

FOURTH

The executor of my current personal will is ______________________, whose phone number is __________________, and who resides at ________________.

FIFTH

A. My current client records are located at ______________________.

B. My past client records are located at ______________________.

C. Billing and financial records related to my psychology practice are located at ______________________.

D. Some or all of my client, billing, and financial records are on a computer, located at ______________________.

E. My appointment book and client phone numbers are located at ______________________.

F. My e-mail address is ______________ and the password is ________.

G. My office phone number is ________ and the voice mail access code is _____.

H. Any necessary keys you will need for access to my office, filing cabinets, storage facilities, etc. are located at ______________________.

I. For assistance in locating and accessing my records you may contact ________, whose phone number is ____________ and whose address is ____________. In addition, the following person(s) may be helpful in locating/accessing my records ______________________.

SIXTH

My specific instructions for my Professional Executor are:

A. First of all, I would like to express my deep appreciation for your willingness to serve as the Professional Executor for this will.

B. There are four copies of this Professional Will. They are located as follows:

1. One is in your possession.
2. One is in the possession of my attorney.
3. One is with my personal will.
4. One is with my professional liability insurance policy.

C. A list of current and selected past clients and their phone numbers who are to be notified about my death and any planned memorial services is located with the copy of my Professional Will in my professional liability insurance file.

This file is located at ______________________.

1. Please use your clinical judgment and discretion in deciding how you want to notify current and past clients and whether to publish a notice in the newspaper notifying clients of my death and who to contact for further information.

2. Please use your clinical judgment and discretion in deciding whether to arrange a special memorial service for clients only. In that eventuality you may wish to request that one or more therapists actively participate in the service.
3. If clinically indicated, you may wish to offer a face-to-face meeting with some clients. You may also wish to provide three referral sources, which can, of course, include yourself.

D. My professional liability insurance is currently provided by ________________, whose phone number is ____________, and whose address is ________________. My policy # is ____________________________.

Please notify my professional liability carrier in writing of my death as expeditiously as possible and arrange for any additional coverage that may be appropriate.

Please also notify the state Licensing Board.

E. Please arrange for copies of referred clients' records to go to their new therapists.

All remaining records should be maintained according to the Record Keeping regulations of the State Licensing Board.

When disposing of outdated records, please ensure it is done in a manner that destroys all materials that could identify the client, *e.g.*, burning or shredding.

F. You may bill my estate for your time and any other expenses that you may incur in executing these instructions. Unless otherwise ordered by the court, the hourly rate of $75.00 per hour is acknowledged to be reasonable.

I declare under penalty of perjury and under the laws of the State of ____________ that the foregoing is true and correct.

Executed at ______________________________________, on ________________.
(location) (date)

____
Signature

WITNESSES:

Printed Name: ______________________ Signature: ______________________
Residing at: ____

Printed Name: ______________________ Signature: ______________________
Residing at: ____

Form 7. Contract for Clinical Supervision

CLINICAL SUPERVISION CONTRACT

The parties to this contract are ______________________, supervisor, and ______________, supervisee. The fee for clinical supervision will be $_________ per hour for an individual session and $_________ per hour for group supervision sessions. Both supervisor and supervisee agree to keep accurate records concerning the dates and times on which supervision occurs, and information concerning whether the supervision was individual or group.

Supervisor and supervisee also agree as follows:

1. Supervisee will maintain a policy of professional liability insurance during the clinical supervision process, and will provide a copy of her Certificate of Insurance to supervisor.
2. Supervisee agrees to comply with the Code of Ethics adopted by:

   ___ The American Counseling Association, and hereby acknowledges receipt of a copy of the ACA Code of Ethics;

   ___ The National Association of Social Workers, and hereby acknowledges receipt of a copy of the NASW Code of Ethics;

   ___ The American Association for Marriage & Family Therapy, and hereby acknowledges receipt of a copy of the AAMFT Code of Ethics.
3. In addition, supervisee agrees to comply with the rules adopted by the Colorado Board of Licensed Professional Counselor Examiners, and acknowledges receipt of a copy of the current Rules. These Rules are posted on the Board's website.
4. Supervisee agrees to comply with the Prohibited Activities Statutes, C.R.S. § 12-245-224, and the other mental health statutes posted on the DORA website for the Mental Health Boards. Specifically, supervisee agrees to provide each counseling client of his/hers with his/her client disclosure statement in compliance with C.R.S. § 12-245-216, and agrees to name _________ as his/her clinical supervisor in his/her disclosure statement. Supervisee also agrees not to engage in any dual relationship with a counseling client in violation of C.R.S. §§ 12-245-224(1)(i) and (j).
5. Supervisor and supervisee agree in compliance with C.R.S. § 12-245-220, HIPAA Standards, and Ethical Provisions that clinical supervision is a confidential process. The limitations on confidentiality for this confidential

process include: (1) waiver of the confidentiality by the counseling client; (2) reporting of suspected child abuse or neglect; (3) the duty to warn and protect (*see* C.R.S. § 13-21-117); (4) the duty to initiate a 72-hour hold pursuant to C.R.S. § 27-65-105; and (5) compliance with any court order for disclosure of treatment records.

6. Supervisee agrees to obtain informed consent in writing from any counseling clients whose treatment session is to be videotaped, recorded, or observed through 1-way glass.
7. Frequency of clinical supervision sessions: One hour of clinical supervision will occur for every twenty hours of client counseling.
8. In compliance with Colorado Statutes and Ethical Provisions, the duty of the clinical supervisor will be to direct the therapy process and to assist the supervisee in complying with all legal and ethical standards.
9. The supervisee agrees to submit bills for her counseling services that accurately reflect the amount of time spent in counseling sessions.
10. As part of the supervision process, supervisee agrees to provide treatment records and billing statements to the clinical supervisor upon request. Supervisee agrees to maintain treatment records in compliance with the LPC Board's record-keeping rule.
11. Clinical supervisor agrees to keep notes concerning case consultations, issues discussed in clinical supervision, and training provided in supervision.

Dated: ______________________ ______________________________

Clinical Supervisor

Dated: ______________________ ______________________________

Supervisee

Form 8. Collateral Disclosure Form

COLLATERAL DISCLOSURE FORM

1. As you know, I am providing services to a client, ______________, who has authorized me to share information with you and to obtain information from you. You are a "collateral" in the treatment process.
2. You are **not** my client, and you will not be receiving treatment or services from me.
3. If you would like to receive counseling from a mental health professional, please let me know, and I will refer you to a therapist.
4. Any treatment information that I share with you is confidential. You may **not** share that information with anyone else.
5. Any information that you share with me will be confidential, as part of my client's treatment record, and I may share that information with my client.

I understand these disclosures and agree to comply with them.

______________________________________ Date: ____________________

Collateral

Form 9. Fee Policy

[THERAPIST'S LETTERHEAD]

FEE POLICY

My fees for subpoenas to a deposition or to testify in court are as follows:

1. My fee is $________ **per hour**, portal to portal, from office to court and back.
2. **Payment in advance:** Payment of an expert fee for testimony is required at least 48 hours in advance of the hearing.
3. **Minimum fee:** My minimum fee for testifying at a deposition or in court as an expert witness is $________ for a 2-hour minimum.
4. **Acknowledgement of the fee policy:** If you have issued a Subpoena *duces tecum* or a Subpoena to me to testify in court, you need to sign this fee policy at the bottom, stating that you understand and will comply with these policies.
5. **Consent for disclosure of treatment information:** I must receive written consent from my client(s) before I can testify in court.

ACKNOWLEDGEMENT OF FEE POLICY

I understand the fee policies stated above, and agree to comply with them.

____

Client or Attorney

Form 10. Policies for CFIs

Policies for CFIs re Communication with Counsel and the Handling of Sensitive Information

COMMUNICATON WITH COUNSEL

In communicating with counsel for the parties or with *pro se* parties, my policy is to have counsel arrange a conference call, so that I can communicate with both attorneys or *pro se* parties at the same time. This prevents allegations of bias or a claim that I spent more time talking to one party's attorney than I spent in communication with other counsel or pro se parties. Whenever a conference call with all counsel cannot be arranged or is not possible, then it will be the obligation of the attorney who speaks with me to inform other counsel of the nature of our communications for the sake of ultimate fairness. While this policy is not mandated by CJD 04-08, Standard 17, it is a best practice, which has been successful for years in eliminating the appearance of any bias or lack of fairness to the parties.

In order to contact my office to schedule the time for a conference call, please contact me by phone or email in order to schedule the time for a conference call. As stated above, it is my policy not to have non-disclosed conversations with the attorney for one party. Information with one attorney may be shared with the attorney for the other party or with any pro se party. If circumstances do not allow for conference calls with all counsel, or joint meetings with counsel, the attorneys and I may agree in writing to a different procedure. Counsel must send a copy of any correspondence or documents sent to me to all other counsel or unrepresented parties in order to assure fairness in this process.

POLICIES REGARDING THE HANDLING OF SENSITIVE INFORMATION

I am required pursuant to CJD 04-08 to report suspected child abuse or neglect, based upon information that is provided to me or based upon conduct that I have observed. Any such report will be made directly to the County Department of Human Services or to the appropriate law enforcement agency and to the court.

As a mental health professional, I have a duty to warn and protect pursuant to Section 13-21-117, C.R.S., if a party or other individual makes a serious threat of imminent physical violence against a specific person or location.

I may seek protective orders from the court for information I learn from the children that I believe is sensitive, or the disclosure of which would be detrimental to the children. My file, in addition, may contain information that is sensitive to the people involved in my investigation.

During the pendency of my appointment, a party, or their counsel, may request a copy of underlying data or reports in my file, after paying for the copying charges. If I believe that the release of any particular information or test data would endanger any person's welfare, or would be sensitive or detrimental to the best interests of the parties' child or children, or where the confidentiality of the materials is in dispute, I will inform the court of my concerns, and await a court order regarding the release of the information. To expedite the matter, I may file the particular information under seal with the court. Psychological test instruments may not be released in compliance with ethical standards for psychologists and mental health professionals.

The parties shall not show to or disclose either directly or indirectly to their children my report or the contents of my file. If either party believes that the children need to be aware of some aspect of my report or file, their counsel must make a request in writing to the court, and obtain a court order for disclosure of such information.

________________ (insert name of CFI here)

Date

Form 11. Teletherapy Consent Form

INFORMED CONSENT FOR TELETHERAPY

This Informed Consent for Teletherapy contains important information concerning engaging in electronic psychotherapy or teletherapy. Please read this consent carefully.

Benefits and Risks of Teletherapy

Teletherapy refers to the remote provision of psychotherapy services using telecommunications technologies such as video conferencing or telephone therapy. One of the benefits of teletherapy is that the client and therapist can engage in services without being in the same physical location. This can be helpful in ensuring continuity of care if the client or therapist are in a situation where they are unable to continue to meet in person due to extenuating circumstances. It can also increase the convenience and time efficiency of both parties.

There are benefits of teletherapy, as well as some inherent risks of teletherapy. There are some differences between in-person psychotherapy and teletherapy.

Risks to confidentiality: Because teletherapy sessions take place outside of the typical office setting, there is potential for third parties to overhear sessions if they are not conducted in a secure environment. We will take reasonable steps to ensure the privacy and security of your information, and it is important for you to review your own security measures and ensure that they are adequate to protect information on your end. You should participate in therapy only while in a room or area where other people are not present and cannot overhear the conversation.

Issues related to technology: There are risks inherent in the use of technology for therapy that are important to understand, such as: potential for technology to fail during a session, potential that transmission of confidential information could be interrupted by unauthorized parties, or potential for electronically stored information to be accessed by unauthorized parties.

Crisis management and intervention: As a general rule we will not engage in teletherapy with patients who are in a crisis situation. Before engaging in teletherapy, we will develop an emergency response plan or safety plan to address potential crisis situations that may arise during the course of our teletherapy work. It is urgent that you share with your therapist any thought that you may have of harming yourself; and any history that you may have of suicide attempts or hospital treatment which you received for suicidal thoughts.

Efficacy: While most research has failed to demonstrate that teletherapy is less effective than in person psychotherapy, some experienced mental health professionals believe that something is lost by not being in the same room. For example, there is debate about one's ability when doing remote work to fully process non-verbal information. If you ever have concerns about misunderstandings between you and your therapist related to the use of technology, please bring up such concerns immediately and your therapist will address the potential misunderstanding together.

Electronic Communications

We will discuss which is the most appropriate platform to use for teletherapy services. You may be required to have certain system requirements to access electronic psychotherapy via the method chosen. You are solely responsible for any cost to you to obtain any additional/necessary system requirements, accessories, or software to use electronic psychotherapy.

For communication between sessions, that email exchanges and text messages with the office should be limited to matters such as setting and changing appointments, and other related issues. You should be aware that no therapist can guarantee the confidentiality of any information communicated by email or text. Therefore, we will not include any clinical material by email and request that you do not as well.

Treatment is most effective when clinical discussions occur at your regularly scheduled sessions, however if an urgent issue arises, you should feel free to attempt to reach us by phone. We will make every effort to return your call on the same day you make it. If you are unable to reach us and feel that you cannot wait for us to return your call, please contact our on-call therapist or 911 in the case of an emergency.

Confidentiality:

Counselors have a legal and ethical responsibility to make our best efforts to protect all communications, electric and otherwise, that are a part of our teletherapy. However, the nature of electronic communications technologies is such that we cannot guarantee that our communications will be kept confidential and/or that a third party may not gain access to our communications. Even though we may utilize state of the art encryption methods, firewalls, and back-up systems to help secure our communication, there is a risk that our electronic communications may be compromised, unsecured, and/or accessed by a third party.

The extent of confidentiality and the exceptions to confidentiality that are outlined in our Disclosure Statement still apply in teletherapy. Please let us know if you have any questions about exceptions to confidentiality.

Emergencies and Technology

Assessing and evaluating threats and other emergencies can be more difficult when conducting teletherapy than in traditional in-person therapy. In order to address some of these difficulties, we will ask you where you are located at the beginning of each session and we will ask that you identify emergency resources that are near your location that we may contact in the event of a crisis or emergency to assist in addressing the situation. We may also ask that you sign a separate authorization form allowing us to contact your emergency contact person as needed during such a crisis or emergency.

If the session cuts out, meaning the technological connection fails, and you are having an emergency do not call us back, but call 911, the Colorado Crisis Hotline at 844-493-TALK (8255), or go to your nearest emergency room. Call us after you have called or obtained emergency services.

If the session cuts out and you are not having an emergency, disconnect from the session and we will wait five (5) minutes and then re-contact you via the teletherapy platform on which we agreed to conduct therapy. If you do not receive a call back within five (5) minutes, then call us on the phone number we provided you.

If there is a technological failure and we are unable to resume the connection, you will only be charged the prorated amount of actual session time.

Fees:

The same fee rates shall apply for teletherapy as apply for in-person psychotherapy.

Consent:

This agreement is intended as a supplement to the general informed consent that we may have agreed to at the outset of treatment. Your signature below indicates agreement with its terms and conditions. This agreement is supplemental to the consent for treatment that is given when you sign a Client Disclosure Statement and does not amend any of the terms of that agreement.

I, ______________________________, the client, having been fully informed of the risks and benefits of teletherapy; the security measures in place, which include procedures for emergency situations; the fees associated with teletherapy; the technological requirements needed to engage in teletherapy; and all other information provided in this informed consent, agree to and understand the procedures and policies set forth in this consent.

______________________________ ______________________________

Signature of Client Date

Tables of Authorities

Table of Statutes

Table of Cases

Index

References are to section numbers